Stewart Brothers

Sonderho Press, Ottawa K2P 0V4
Copyright © 2019 Graham Stewart Ford.
All rights reserved. Published 2019.

Designed and published by Sonderho Press.
Edited by Maria Ford.

ISBN # 978-0-9917484-8-8

This book is printed on acid-free paper.

Front-cover oil paintings of Norman and Tom Stewart by Esther Freeman (commissioned by Stewart and Eileen Ford).

Back-cover silk screen painting of John Hay Stewart by Dennis Moffat (commissioned by Stewart Ford).

Stewart Brothers

An Alberta Family Business History

Stewart Ford

SONDERHO PRESS

Contents

Acknowledgements

I am blessed to have grown up in a family filled with natural storytellers, writers, and historians; people who knew the present would soon become the past and believed that the past was worth saving. Thanks to their memories and artefacts, this book is richer and more complete. I am grateful to:

Norman Stewart, for his foresight in writing a history of his family, *Children of the Pioneers*, which I have relied on for quotations, excerpts, facts, and photographs.

Tom Stewart, for his anecdotes pertaining to this story, his part in bringing me up, and his help when I started full-time in the family business.

Jack Stewart, **Gwen Calverley**, **Svend and Patsy Storm**, and **Pat Schmidt** for the stories they contributed, as well as **Nellie Watson** for providing the letter from her father, Les Jarvis.

The **Western Retail Lumber Association**, which prompted me to write an initial business history for inclusion in its hundredth anniversary publication issued in 1990.

Stewart Brothers, the business itself, for its wealth of preserved information, including Business Ledgers and Journals from 1902-1910; General Ledgers from 1929-1980; business year-end financial records from the 1930s; contract ledgers from the 1960s; advertising flyers and catalogues.

Michael Dawe, who, during his time as the Red Deer City Archivist, was invaluable in uncovering documents, historical information, and helping put it all into context. Also, the **Red Deer & District Archives** and the **Innisfail & District Historical Society** for their assistance in locating and obtaining photographs and clippings from their collections.

Scott Hoyland, for his invaluable technical support in developing the searchable archives that contain much of the information this book is based on, and which made the research for this book much simpler.

My parents, **Graham** and **Muriel Ford**, as well as customers of the business and their offspring, whose oral stories and memories have enriched my life, my appreciation for my ancestors, and this book.

Maria Ford, my daughter, for her input into storytelling, her substantive editing, and her zeal in keeping me focused and on track.

My wife, **Eileen**, for our life together and for her patience and eagle-eye for copy editing.

Our son, **Tom**, whose unique talents as a welder have helped build critical infrastructure, and a good life for his wife Rhonda and daughters, Laurel and Jordan.

"*History will be kind to me for I intend to write it.*"

Preface

This history of the Stewart Brothers business began with a pet project in which I set out to catalogue the memories of my youth, intending to expand them into a story of my life. Not long into that project, I realized that most of my life *is* the business story.

The author in 2017

My childhood memories are intertwined with the business. Only children of small-business owners are likely to understand how the rhythms of business shape a life. Every family member was in some way tied to the business. We personally witnessed parents, grandparents, aunts, uncles, and cousins engaged in work every day – and often at night and on weekends as well. Customers or travelling salespeople joined us at the family dinner table and we would frequently be accorded the same hospitality when we travelled to meet with customers and suppliers.

The store, the wood shop, the truss shop, the lumberyard – these were our playgrounds. We loaded trucks, rode on forklifts, and drove machines long before we had driver's licenses. We learned how money worked – how to ask for it, save it, invest it, make it grow, and turn it into other things. We learned to pitch for loans and barter for the materials we needed for our youthful projects. I inherited (or learned) a tireless work ethic, a "customer first" disposition, and a deeply empathetic value system from my ancestors.

Today, they would be called entrepreneurs, yet when the Stewart brothers began in business, they were simply the sons of struggling pioneers looking to improve their lot. Where others failed, they prospered and grew by searching out opportunities and seizing upon

chances that came their way. They ventured beyond the safety of their local community, extended credit to worthy individuals, and gave a "hand- up" to other pioneering families. They dealt with First Nations, settlers, and new immigrants alike, without prejudice. They complemented each other's skills and worked respectfully side by side for a lifetime.

Stewart Brothers[i] was one of numerous businesses in Alberta upon which communities relied for products, services, and credit – particularly during tough times, like the war years and depressions. From an early partnership in a hay baling venture and a threshing outfit, Stewart Brothers evolved and continuously broadened its product lines, eventually becoming a full-service provider of farm machinery, hardware, and building supplies.

Stewart Brothers remained an active family business for more than one-hundred years even as others closed their doors or were absorbed through acquisition and consolidation. Stewart Brothers began and ended as a family business. It passed from the original Stewart Brothers, Norman and Tom; to their descendants; and finally to me, Tom's grandson, and my wife. I've always enjoyed the cyclical rhythms of history and business, and I am honoured to have the privilege of closing the circle of the Stewart Brothers family enterprise.

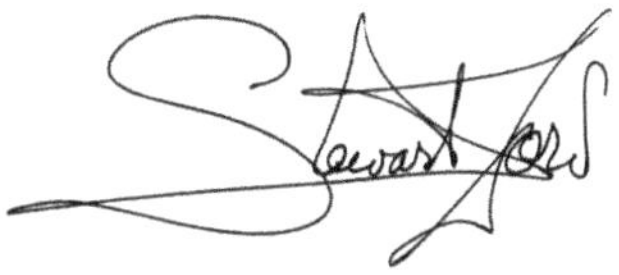

Stewart Ford

---

i Unless otherwise specified, throughout this book I use "Stewart Brothers" to include the various related legal entities that would evolve from it.

John Hay Stewart Family on their original Alberta homestead, about 1905. Standing, L to R: Norman and Tom. Seated: Mabel (with cat), Edna (with dog), Irene.

1884

Norman and Tom Stewart arrive in Alberta with their parents and siblings; the family begins farming in the Fairlands district.

1896

Norman begins work for Columbia River Lumber Co. in Beavermouth, British Columbia.

1898

HH3 cattle brand is registered to John Hay, Tom, and Norman Stewart.

1901

Tom, twenty, is hospitalized for six months due to an accidental gunshot wound, followed by typhoid fever.

Chapter 1:
Go West, Young Man!

The Stewart Brothers' Canadian legacy began with Colquhoun Stewart[1] (p.189), a whaling captain from Dundee, Scotland, who immigrated to Canada in 1840, settling his family on land he had purchased sight-unseen near Goderich, Ontario.

His son, John Hay Stewart[2] (p.190), would spend time in eastern Canada and the U.S.A. before coming to western Canada. In 1884, the year considered the benchmark for white settlement in central Alberta, John Hay and his wife, Irene[3] (p.190), settled their young family, including two sons – Norman and Tom – in the Fairlands District of what would become Alberta. The homestead was located on SW S14-T37-R28-4, some of which is now part of the Red Deer Regional Airport. Norman and Tom would become the enterprising young men who would found Stewart Brothers, a central Alberta business that would serve the area's rural and urban community for more than one-hundred years.

Pioneering was a family affair, and both sons began work early to contribute to the family's meagre fortunes. In 1896, Norman, aged twenty, the eldest brother, headed to British Columbia for his first job. He worked in a saw mill, taking and piling the sawn boards off the live rollers – a job called "tailing".[4] (p.191) When the mill closed for the winter, Norman

1902	1904	1905	1906
Stewart Brothers opens in November.	Hardware added to line of merchandise.	Alberta becomes a Province.	New bridge construction begins west of Penhold.
	CPR opens a station house in Penhold.		
	Penhold incorporated as a Village.		

stayed to work in the bush camps, felling trees to be milled the following season. In 1894, fourteen-year-old Tom headed West, working as a gardener's helper at the Canadian Pacific Railway (CPR) hotel in North Bend, B.C., and returning home in the fall.

Learning the ropes

During Norman's time in B.C., there was a large amount of construction in the Crow's Nest Pass. Recognizing the need of feed for the horses that were invaluable to the heavy work, the Stewart family partnered with Bill Douglas to acquire a horse-powered hay press. Irene was a great help. She wrote to Uncle Tom Stevens in Ontario, who had married their father's sister and owned a company that manufactured various items of machinery. He sent them a horse-powered hay press, including a couple of extra heavy cast parts which were subject to breakage. It was a half-sweep press, meaning the horse walked around a half circle, turned and walked back, repeating the process until a bale was formed. It pressed hay into 18"x22"x48" bales weighing one hundred and forty to one hundred and eighty pounds and these were loaded by hand onto railcars for shipment. A day's baling of twelve tons was all that could be squeezed into the small railcars of the day. This was the start of the Stewart and Douglas threshing business, and their success eventually led to the purchase of their own threshing outfit. The combination of the pressing and threshing was an excellent source of cash for the partners.[5 (p.191)]

The threshing business provided Norman with skills in managing groups of men, dealing with customers, collecting accounts, and keeping records – adding to his already well-developed skills in bartering. He became acquainted with the farmers in the surrounding districts, most of whom would become future customers of Stewart Brothers. This, combined with Tom's natural mechanical skills, made taking on a machine agency a natural progression. In 1902, twenty-six-year-old Norman approached Mr. Manning at the Merchant's Bank in Red Deer for a business loan. Manning judged the brothers an excellent risk and granted the loan. In later years, Mr. Manning would take up farming and become a customer of the business he had helped get off the ground.

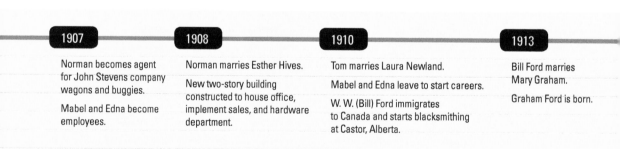

1907

Norman becomes agent for John Stevens company wagons and buggies.

Mabel and Edna become employees.

1908

Norman marries Esther Hives.

New two-story building constructed to house office, implement sales, and hardware department.

1910

Tom marries Laura Newland.

Mabel and Edna leave to start careers.

W. W. (Bill) Ford immigrates to Canada and starts blacksmithing at Castor, Alberta.

1913

Bill Ford marries Mary Graham.

Graham Ford is born.

The Douglas-Stewart Threshing Outfit. Top row, L to R: Unidentified, Unidentified, Bill Douglas, Dave Van Ambers. Bottom row, L to R: Unidentified, Unidentified, Jim Reeves, Martin Thorsen, Bill Beckley, Norman Stewart, Joseph Cole.

A threshing outfit was an expensive enterprise that involved an array of equipment. Few farmers owned one; more often, there was one threshing outfit to service the farmers in a district. The required assets included a threshing machine, steam tractor, water wagon, straw wagon, and hay racks. Depending on the weather, once a crop had been cut with a binder and sheaves placed into stooks, a threshing crew of a dozen or so men, recruited from the district, would make its rounds of the local farms.

With the threshing machine and steam tractor hooked up, crews with racks would go out into fields, pitching the sheaves up onto racks then hauling these to the threshing machine. At the thresher, the sheaves were pitched onto the feeder chute head-first, where they were carried forward by the feeder raddle through twine-cutter knives to the separator cylinder, and onto the straw walkers where the kernels and chaff were separated. The grain kernels were carried away to a bucket elevator to be put in sacks or directed into the farmer's wagon and hauled to a grain bin. The chaff went on to the end of the separator, falling into a fan, then blown out into a straw stack, which would frequently house families of hogs.

1914

The Great War begins. Stewart Brothers sells IHC Mogul 10-12 tractor to James Bower of Red Deer.

1916

Stewart Brothers takes on Ford car agency, John Deere plows, De Laval cream separators, B-H paints, windmills, and gasoline engines.

1918

Great War ends.

1920

Stewart Brothers dealership sets records for tractor sales during the decade.

In 2006, Eldon Kaun invited me to look at a horse mower that was on his property. Eldon had purchased the Dixon homestead from Robin Dixon, who had inherited the farm from his parents. According to Robin, the five-foot McCormick horse mower was the first machine sale Stewart Brothers made, likely in 1903. I took the photograph of the mower seen here.

1921

Stewart Brothers purchases a Delco electric plant.

Ford dealership is relinquished.

1926

Family summer cottage built at Sylvan Lake.

1928

Calgary Power comes to Penhold, Stewart Brothers sells electrical plant.

Another event played a role in the brothers' decision to start in business together. A year earlier in 1901, Tom was critically wounded in a hunting accident and spent his twenty-first birthday in the Calgary Hospital. During his hospitalization, he contracted typhoid fever; only the strength of youth saved him. Upon his return home three months later, it was apparent that Tom would not be able to sustain the heavy workload of a turn-of-the-century farm. Other opportunities had to be found.

The following is Norman's telling of their start in business, excerpted from his book, *Children of the Pioneers*.

"We Venture Into Business

"About the turn of the century both Tom and I began to feel that we would like to try something other than farming. By this time, we had been farmers for almost twenty years. One of the things we had naturally picked up was a little knowledge of the Agricultural Machines then in use. We both felt the Farm Implement Business was one line we would like to try our hand at.

"Our opportunity came about 1902. We heard that Mr. Harrison, who owned a little Lumber and Implement business down in Penhold, was wanting to sell out. As soon as I could I went down to see him and got an idea of what he had to sell and about how much. It wasn't much. His lumber stock was very small. The Implement side of the business was only a little larger.

"The word soon spread that Mr. Harrison was going to sell. That evidently gave his opposition in the lumber business (Mr. Griffin) the same idea and he came after us to buy him out as well.

"I went to see the manager of the Merchant's Bank in Red Deer, Mr. M. J. Manning. He now farms at Delburne. He asked what I intended to do with the money and I told him. It didn't take him long to fix me up with the six-hundred-dollar loan I had came after. This enabled us to pay off in cash, both Mr. Harrison and Mr. Griffin. We were in business!

"For some time, things moved very slowly. We could not afford to leave the farm for more than a short time. My youngest sister, Alma (Allie), was a real help to us at the time. She used to ride down each day on horseback, look after the office for the day and then ride home. She was just the person for the job, and little by little the business began to grow.

"To get into the farm implement business, we first of all became 'sub-agents' under Lattimer and Botterill of Red Deer. Theirs was the 'McCormick Line'. They put in several machines for us on straight 'consignment'. We didn't have to invest a cent until a machine was sold.

"About this time a third Penhold businessman, Mr. Morley McCall, came to us wanting to sell his Hardware Store. We didn't wish to borrow more money just then to buy him out, but I had a quarter section of good land which I had 'homesteaded' when I came of age. We made a trade with Mr. McCall and added hardware to our lines.

"I often wonder how we managed in those early years. It was a mystery that we didn't go under. We were completely without experience. More than that, we were extremely cautious and were afraid to take a chance on anything, but our years on the farm stood us in good stead. We were well used to trading and bartering. It was the only way business was done in those early years. We have never completely departed from it in all the dealing we have done since.

"Mother was a great help to us in our book work. In fact, she could handle almost any job that the rest of us were afraid to tackle.

"It is a truth, and should be mentioned here, that the early settlers, especially the heads of families, put up with great hardships. Roughing it as they had to do, no doubt shortened their days considerably. On cold winter days, I can still remember some of the trips dad had to make to Red Deer or Innisfail. He never did have a fur coat but wore only a cloth coat and not a very heavy one at that. He remained in the sleigh box and drove the team all the while. They seldom went faster than a walk, and he would never tie up the lines or frolic along behind the sleigh to keep warm as most of us did. Indeed, it seems to me now that on some of those trips he must have almost perished with the cold. My father died in 1900 and Mother passed on some ten years later. Neither of them reached more than sixty-three years of age".[ii]

In the early pioneering years, enterprising young men and families like the Stewarts were attracted to the Canadian prairies by government initiatives to encourage settlement with offers of inexpensive farmland. Central Alberta offered particularly rich soil for farming.

Norman and Tom always owned some farmland. When they were able, each filed on land for his homestead; Norman on NE S26-T37-R28-4 in 1897, and Tom on NE S12-T37-R28-4 in 1901. Having decided to file on a homestead, Tom left Penhold in a buggy for a trip to the Land Title Office in Red Deer. Along the way, he came across Bill Henderson walking into Red Deer and offered him a ride. Bill had Tom drop him off at the outskirts. In town, Tom filed on NE ¼-S12-T37-R28-4. On the way home, he once again encountered Bill Henderson on foot and offered him a ride. Tom asked if Bill had got his business done. Bill replied that he had gone in to file on the north east quarter of section 12, only to discover that Tom had beat him to it!

Tom's homestead was sold to Bill Douglas in the 1920s, Norman having traded his earlier for Mr. McCall's hardware business.

---

ii   Stewart, Norman. *Children of the Pioneers*, Chapter XXVI, page 120. Self-published in 1964.

A hand-up

Those early years were the start of a business practice that became an unwritten policy of reaching out to the community with the proverbial "hand-up". The brothers knew what it was to start out with few resources, and the importance of people who were willing to take a risk on you. Their parents had been helped by their uncle, Tom Stevens, who gave them a deal on a wagon to haul their settler's effects and later provided a hay press.

Tom Stewart, canvassing in a cutter.

When and where they could, the brothers reached out to help those in need. Once those people became established they did not forget the help, and Stewart Brothers became the supplier of choice for their needs. That loyalty carried on for decades, in some cases into the second and third generation of families. A letter written by Les Jarvis in 1956, and recently brought to me by his daughter, Nellie Watson, offers a poignant example:

> "I will never forget the occasion in the year 1928 when you called at my farm at a time when I was completely without funds and severely handicapped in carrying on my farming operations because I did not have the necessary farm equipment. You asked me what item I considered I needed the most and I told you of the great difficulty I was having in watering my livestock because I did not have a pump engine or water tank. You immediately delivered to me a new pump engine and water tank and told me that I could pay for it at such time in the future as I felt able to. I am mentioning this pump engine and tank because to me it is symbolic of many, many ways in which Stewart Brothers have assisted me in the course of the last 27 years."[6 (p.192)]

Despite the brothers' generosity, business records indicate that the early years were lean ones. An entry on page 170 in the 1902 ledger shows that Tom drew $25, only half of his first wages, on January 1, 1903.[7 (p.193)]

To drum up business, the brothers would call on settlers in the surrounding countryside. This "canvassing", as it was referred to, was undertaken on horseback, buggy, or sleigh over two or three days. Thanks to pioneer hospitality, the brothers and horse were always sheltered and fed on their overnight journeys.

Implements were sold with little or no money down. Rather, the dealer would take a promissory note in favour of International Harvester Co. (IHC). The notes were usually due in the fall, at which time an agent for IHC would come to the dealership with a list of note holders, get directions from the dealership, and call on the customers to collect. If full payment could not be made, IHC would endorse the note for the amount due and extend it for another year.[8 (p.193)]

When opportunity knocks…

Another source of income was the Stewart Brothers' hay press, used to press their own hay to sell for cash, as well as to barter with interior British Columbia lumber mills. One account shows the sale of fifteen carloads shipped to Vancouver, as well as one car sent to the Columbia River Lumber Co.,[9 (p.193)] where Norman had previously worked. Part of the payment was taken in lumber to be resold. Stewart Brothers also baled and shipped hay for local farmers, earning income from the work and a commission of $3 on the sale of a twenty-four-thousand-pound carload.

Penhold got a boost in 1904 when the CPR built a station. This brought with it a passenger, freight, and express shed. Penhold was now on the map, literally, and the village was incorporated later that same year. Alberta and Saskatchewan became provinces the following year. Importantly for Penhold, a bridge was built across the Red Deer River directly west of the village in 1906-07, providing quick, direct access to the west country.[iii] Stewart Brothers even weighed some of the steel for the construction of the bridge, using its big beam scale. The business also sold lumber for the form work of the concrete piers, and drayed material from Penhold to the bridge site.[10 (p.194)]

During this time, Norman was an agent for John Stevens Company of Ontario (no relation). He represented its line of buggies, wagons, plows, and discs. Entries in the 1907 ledger indicate that Norman was active in setting up a John Stevens Company dealer network between Edmonton and Calgary. Stewart Brothers acted as distributor and agent, transferring items to the dealers as necessary. The 1907- '08 ledger contains a

---

iii By "west country", I am referring to land west of Innisfail, Penhold, Red Deer and out as far as Rocky Mountain House.

half-page of sales entries to customers for democrat buggies and wagons[iv]. Interestingly, one of the buggies was known as the Alberta Model.

Family affairs

Three of Norman and Tom's four sisters each worked for the business at one point or another. They were paid $18 per month and kept most of the earnings in the business, the money bearing interest at 6%. Their employment established a practice of hiring women as equals – their voices, intelligence, and opinions were valued. It also provided each of the sisters with earnings that enabled them to obtain higher education and pursue independent lives. By the end of 1910, the women had all moved on and started their own careers:

Eva Elizabeth Stewart (b. 1883)[11 (p.195)] started her education in Regina as a nurse, thanks to the help of Norman, who would send her a portion of his earnings from his job at the lumbermill. Eva was a gold-medal graduate. She married Jack Biggs, later dying in childbirth in 1912.

Mabel Alberta Stewart (b. 1885)[12 (p.195)] was possibly the first white child born in Calgary. After schooling, she became a medical receptionist in Calgary.

Alma (Allie) Jane Stewart (b. 1886)[13 (p.195)] was the youngest of the sisters, and in *Children of the Pioneers*, Norman credits her for helping them when they first started into business. She would ride the three miles from the family homestead to open the door and "man" the store when her brothers were unable to be there. She later found employment at the Land Titles Office in Red Deer.

The eldest sister, Edna Margaret Stewart[14 (p.195)] (b. 1878), worked at the store during the same period as Mabel, keeping the books and working at the sales counter. She obtained a teaching diploma from Regina.

Norman and Esther's home (left) and Tom and Laura's home (right), were side by side in Penhold. Both homes would be extensively renovated over the years, but still exist as residences.

---

iv These entries continue into the 1910 ledger, after which there are no surviving business records until 1930.

During this time, Norman and Tom started families of their own. Norman married Esther Hives on June 17, 1908. Her family had emigrated from England to the Penhold district in 1904, settling on land adjacent to the Stewart homestead. Norman and Esther's new home stood on two lots on Fleming Avenue, north of the Stewart Brothers store. There, they raised a family of six, including John (Jack) (b. August 6, 1909); Irene (b. December 21, 1910); Norman Stevens (b. September 21, 1916); Mary (Betty) (b. August 6, 1918); Kathleen (Kaye) (b. December 15, 1919); and Gwendolyn (Gwen) (b. March 9, 1923). Esther was a life-long member of the Penhold Women's Institute (W.I.) and a stalwart supporter of St. George's Anglican Church.[v]

About two years later, on July 16, 1910, Tom married Laura May Newland. Her parents had come west to the Three Hills district before her father, Frank C. Newland, established himself in the grocery business in Penhold in 1906. Tom and Laura met at a dance held upstairs in the Stewart Brothers store. Their new home was built on two lots bordering on the north side of Norman and Esther's residence. They adopted a daughter, my mother, Ella Muriel. Like Esther, Laura was a life member of the Penhold W.I. She was also a member of the congregation of

v Refer to family trees on pages 184-185

The Stewart Brothers store in 1916. Norman can be seen standing on the left; the man on the right is unidentified.

In 1907, the Stewart Brothers Penhold properties included a 30'x70' warehouse and hall, as well as one hundred and fifty chairs! That's because the hall was used for dances, social events, and meetings. When a new store was constructed in 1908, its upper level was used for dances. It was at one of these that Tom and Laura met.

Chalmers Presbyterian Church, where she taught in the Sunday school. The Roman Catholic priest in Red Deer allowed the children of the Hamill family, new immigrants from Ireland, to attend her Presbyterian Sunday school – a mark of the respect in which she was held.

In the story of the business, the importance of the brothers' wives in providing a stable home environment cannot be over-stated. Norman's wife, Esther, was mother to six children, while Tom's wife, Laura, made a home for their adopted daughter, Muriel. Among their contributions were the meals both women often provided on short notice for various business visitors. They lived next to each other for over fifty years without a harsh word. They were formidable women in their own rights and in their own gentle ways. Their deportment set an example for their neighbours.

Within the first decade of the business, the brothers' fortunes increased both personally, with their marriages, and financially. Ledgers from the period indicate that the business grew steadily:

1902: 121 customers
1905: 230 customers, $27,635.35 net worth
1907: 257 customers, $31,094.12 net worth
1909: 276 customers, $33,243.32 net worth

The company's hay business continued shipping into Vancouver and Victoria, enjoying sizeable, brisk sales.

Norman also stumbled into municipal leadership during this time. It was difficult to find candidates to run for office, and those who did often feuded with their fellow councillors. When things came to a head in 1907, the Provincial government stepped in and appointed Norman as Village Constable, Overseer and Secretary-Treasurer – a position he held until 1913.

Fueling up

As their family obligations and the business grew, some time after 1910 the brothers wound down the Stewart-Douglas partnership, becoming sole owners of the assets. There is no definitive date in the available company records as to when they stopped custom threshing, but it was likely close to this time. With increases in their product lines, staff, and families, the brothers would have needed to spend more time in Penhold. Organizing and staffing a threshing crew likely proved a burden they could do without.

Canvassing remained an important activity, often undertaken with a salesman from one of the product lines. Traveling far and wide through the countryside, the brothers garnered new clients and cemented their reputation as fair dealers who were willing to help customers get started by providing the equipment required and granting the credit needed. This became more important as the machine companies stopped providing financing.

STEWART BROS.

Lumber, Farm Implements and Hardware

This is without doubt one of Penhold's most important commercial enterprises. The lines handled by this firm include farm implements of all kinds and for all purposes, lumber and building materials, hardware, harness and feed. They also have the agencies for several of the most responsible life and fire insurance companies. In farm implements they are agents for Deering machinery; De Laval separators; J. I. Case threshers and engines; McLaughlin and Greer carriages; Rock Island and John Deere plows. They are also the owners of the Pine Lake stage and mail line, and are the local representatives for the Alberta Pacific Elevator Company.

Their place of business is located at the corner of Fleming and Lucina streets and occupies a half block of ground.

Messrs. Norman Stewart and Thomas Stephens Stewart comprise the firm. They came originally from London, Ontario, and have been residents of this section for the past twenty-six years. They established their present business six years ago and, owing to their up to date, square deal business methods, have prospered from the beginning.

In addition to their other interests they are extensively engaged in farming and own a section of land. They are also one-third owners of a large threshing outfit.

By virtue of their many business interests, Stewart Bros. are entitled to rank with the most enterprising residents of the Red Deer district.

This clipping is from a publication produced to encourage investment in property throughout the Penhold area. Other businesses featured were E.P. Morris, general merchant and Post Master; Brown Brothers, general merchant; Imperial Hotel; Standard Bank; W.H. Eyre, hardware; Smith's Barber Shop and Pool Room; Lee Brothers Meat Market and Feed Mill. By 1920, only Stewart Brothers, Lee Brothers, and the Bank of Montreal remained.

By 1910, Penhold's business district on Fleming Avenue was a block long, anchored at the north end by Stewart Brothers on Lucina Street, and at the south end by Wilson Brothers grocery and mercantile store on Minto Street. Other merchants included a Chinese restaurant, shoe maker, butcher, pool hall, hotel, and bank.

Stewart Brothers began to add new lines of equipment to supplement the IHC line, such as John Deere,[15] (p.196) reputed for its plow. They were still agents for John Stevens wagons and buggies and took on De Laval[16] (p.197) cream separators. The cream separator quickly became a bread-and-butter item for the business, as every farmer needed one. The cream was sold to creameries and used to make butter on the farm.

Just before the Great War, the first fuel-powered tractors began to appear. Smaller, lighter, easier to run and maintain than large steam machines, the new tractors could be used as stationary engines to power threshing machines, feed grinders, and saw mills. Initially, kerosene was the common fuel; later, gasoline models were introduced. Stewart Brothers was ideally positioned to handle the new technology. Norman had the sales skills and Tom had the mechanical talent which, in the early years of the internal combustion engine, would be put to the test.

The first IHC tractor model Stewart Brothers dealt in was a 10-20 Mogul. Produced from 1912 to 1919 (11,430 were produced between 1916 and 1919 alone), the first one they sold went to James Bower, who farmed near Red Deer.

The first Mogul the brothers sold was still on the Bower farm in 1955, at which time it was brought in pieces to the Stewart Brothers implement shop in Red Deer to be rebuilt, painted, and put back into working order for the province's fiftieth anniversary celebrations. I was in the shop when the mechanics started up the old engine. It had a governor that would fire, miss a rotation or two, then fire again. Suddenly, it started to fire on every cycle. I've never seen anyone move as fast as those mechanics did to shut the engine down before it blew itself apart! This photo shows the tractor in the Stewart Brothers' display at the Red Deer Exhibition grounds. Later, the tractor was displayed at Heritage Park in Calgary for several years before being reclaimed by a member of the Bower family and sold.

The Titan three-plow tractor came out in late 1915 and eventually replaced the Mogul. The Titan was very successful for IHC and its dealers. The machines shipped by rail on flat cars to Penhold and were unloaded at the CPR loading dock. The Titan tractor seen in the photo on the following page was built in 1920. Its serial number, 49325, is just seven hundred and ten tractors shy of the end of the product's run.

Tom was a natural mechanic who liked the old steam tractors. He said they were slow to get going, as they had to be fired up at least a half hour before they generated enough steam to move, but once online, they offered awesome power. No clutches or gearshifts, just a valve which let the steam into the cylinder that drove the fly-wheel and axle from a dead stop. And, nearly any combustible material could be used to keep them running.

The store in 1921 with Titan tractor in foreground.

Norman recalled the role of tractors in the 1920s:

"Tractors began to take over as the main source of farm power after the end of World War 1. The old Titan was the tractor that first gained popularity. About the mid 1920s the Titan was superseded by the McCormick-Deering 15-30. This new tractor, the forerunner of today's tractors, marked the first real breakthrough into complete tractor farming. It replaced horses in large numbers. Dealers everywhere were almost forced to trade in horses on many of their tractor deals. We were no exception. Luckily, we had always kept a piece or two of farm land. At least we had a place to put our four-legged trade-ins. Many a time we had over a hundred head on hand."

In addition to tractors, Stewart Brothers sold two other essential pieces of IHC farm equipment during this era. Norman explains:

In 1916, Stewart Brothers took on the Ford car agency. It wasn't one of their better business decisions. Some fifty years later, Tom told me, "We're still waiting to be paid for some of them." He liked to tell the story of one of his most memorable test drives. In 1916, he took an elderly prospect out to try a Model T. They came to a fork in what passed for a road at the time. The prospect froze at the wheel, yelled, "Whoa!" and drove straight into the bush. There was no sale that day.

"In the days of the old Titan, the farmer was a greenhorn indeed if he could not and did not pull off the head and grind the valves a couple of times a year. He also put in a new set of rings and from time to time, a new connecting rod bearing whenever the engine hammered out.

"Along with these older tractors we often sold International wood, and later 'all steel', threshers. Having spent a good many of our earlier years on and around threshing rigs, we liked to sell these machines. The International was always a smooth, easy-running thresher, and a good grain saver.

"Of all the machines we sold, none ever received the genuine affection which we had for the binder. To us it was a wonderful piece of engineering, and the tying mechanism, or knotter, was the perfect invention.

"Even though threshing was the final operation, it always seemed that binding was the one that counted most. To see four good horses going down the field with an eight-foot binder behind them, the binder whip sticking high in the air, and the discharge arms kicking out a bundle a couple of times a minute, gave one  the feeling which could not be equaled by any other machine.

"Parts service was good on these machines. We took pride in being able to fill all parts orders, and Harvester certainly backed us up. Seldom did a farmer have to go home without at least a good second-hand piece if we happened to be out of what he wanted. They came from miles around to get repairs. It was a wonderful way to get people into the store. While there, they also bought many other items. Binder whips, nose nets, axle grease, machine oil, pots and pans and even a new cook stove on occasion." [vi]

The second-hand parts Norman refers to were one of Tom's initiatives. Used equipment that was not worth repairing was stripped for its useful parts, especially the expensive cast ones, and kept upstairs in the store. Tom saved many customers the expense of buying a new part while keeping farm operations going.

vi International Harvester. "An Enviable Record – 60 years of continuous service". *The Harvester,* 1962 Christmas Edition.

The Penhold W.I. Memorial Hall exterior, and its stage curtain, which has been restored and now resides at the War Museum in Ottawa.

Despite new technologies, coal remained an important fuel, and Stewart Brothers sold it from a shed on the CPR siding. Norman's son, Jack, wrote this description of the coal business:

> "Coal used to be an important part of the lumber business. Each yard had its coal shed on the railway. The train crews spotted the carloads beside the shed. Unloading one of those cars with just a scoop shovel was a long job. It seemed that the men could never get the car empty, carrying the coal, as they did, one shovel full at a time, and throwing it into the bin.[17 (p.198)]

"There were worthwhile savings if the customer took it right off the car. Many farmers would ask us to phone them when a carload was due. Often, there would be a line of three or four rigs waiting to pull up to the car door for a load. This pleased the men doing the unloading because usually the farmer came with his scoop shovel to help."

Stewart Brothers had its own electrical plant since before the Great War. In 1921, the business purchased a larger Delco 115-volt gas-powered unit. Mounted on a concrete pad in Norman's garage, it powered lights in the company store, the machine shop, lumber shed, and their two homes. It also powered a dozen or so other properties in the village. Tom told me of an occasion when a customer wasn't paying his electricity bill. Tom literally cut the power off with a wire cutter. With the arrival of Calgary Power in 1928, they sold the electrical plant for $1,800.

Great war memorial

With the end of the Great War on November 11, 1918, local communities across Canada began to plan memorials for those who had made the supreme sacrifice, and to honour those who had returned. Penhold must surely have been among the first. Within six months, in the spring of 1919, the local head of the W.I., Mrs. H.R. McDougall, organized the community around the construction of the Penhold W.I. Memorial Hall, a 32' x 80' structure. Funds were raised by canvassing the district, holding box socials, card parties, and selling individual $25 shares. The hall was constructed during the summer and fall, opening on October 31 with a grand costume ball and banquet, which saw some two hundred twenty-five celebrants fed at banquet tables. Admission was 75 cents for Gentlemen, 50 cents for Ladies, supper an extra 50 cents; Returned Soldiers were free.

Stewart Brothers was the principal supplier of the building materials, extending credit at 6% interest, and purchasing some of the $25 shares sold to raise the final funds for completion of the Hall. The brothers forgave the interest on the account. Their shares were redeemed in 1925, when the last of the hall debt was paid off.

Other than a record of the net worth in 1914 and some General Ledger entries, no business records survive between 1910 to 1929, making it difficult to know with certainty how the war impacted the business and the community. The war boosted prices for grain and livestock, and with high demand for both overseas, I believe the farm population did well during that time. The growth in the shareholders' accounts available for the year 1930 would indicate that the business did very well over the previous decade. The immediate post-war period was a different story.

A late-1930s aerial photograph of Penhold. In the foreground between the two elevators on the left are Stewart Brothers' bulk fuel tanks. The store is the white building behind the third elevator on the left. The buildings shown in this photograph can be identified by matching them to their location on The Western Canadian Fire Insurance Underwriters Association 1924 map of Penhold on pages 186 & 187.

1930

Stewart Brothers takes over Ball & Van Slyke IHC dealership in Red Deer and Norman's eldest son, Jack, manages the agency.

Garage for cars and delivery trucks built in Penhold.

Start of the Great Depression.

1934

Stewart Brothers begins a period of expansion with the purchase of section 26-T36-R28-4 next to Penhold, construction of a two-story home in Penhold for a farm manager, a 32'x60' barn for milk cows and horses, and the first deep-water well in Penhold.

Business restructures as Norman's son, Jack, comes on as a partner.

1935

Jack Stewart becomes a junior partner.

New implement office and repair shop constructed in Red Deer.

Chapter 2:
Hardship and Success

1919 got off to an inauspicious start. The Spanish flu epidemic was rampant and there was a short, sharp depression caused primarily by the collapse of prices for agricultural products at the end of the war. This resulted in numerous business bankruptcies in Red Deer. Well capitalized and diversified, however, Stewart Brothers weathered the storm.

To accommodate the increase in business, the store was reconfigured to allow for more efficient use of floor space and display cabinets, as well as greater product accessibility. One of the additions was a rolling ladder that provided easy access to a new bank of drawers along the north wall. Each drawer displayed the item contained fastened to its front face. The ladder was a favourite of the farm children

> When Eileen and I built our home in 1980, I recovered the ladder and we cleaned it up. It is a centrepiece in our library, used as a rolling staircase to give access to the bookshelves.

who came in with their parents. I certainly had fun rolling it back and forth myself, and when I started work at the store it was still used to access hardware items in the higher bin drawers.

The storefront got large new display windows. A single-story addition at the rear held drums for non-bulk oil sales. Customers would bring in their pails and the oil would

1936
Central Lumber Yard in Red Deer purchased.

1937
New building supply store and lumber shed built in Red Deer.

Orie & Nina Thorne are hired to manage the new facility.

1938
Department of Transport purchases land on section 26 for radio beacon towers.

be metered out with a gallon measure. There was also a square fifty-gallon tank and pump for kerosene. The balance of the space was used for larger implement parts and the receiving and shipping of orders. Staff also used the new back door as a quick way to get behind the counter.

My mother, Muriel, got to travel with her dad on some of his canvassing trips and service calls. On one such trip in the Markerville area, the customer bent down and picked up a beautiful, undamaged white-flint Indian arrowhead. He gave it to Muriel as a souvenir. She treasured it, but in relating the story to me, mentioned that she wondered if he had it in his pocket and "palmed it".

Tom with Muriel at three years old and their Overland car, circa 1915. In her hand, she holds freshly picked flowers.

Jack Stewart has eloquently recorded some of his recollections of how things were done during the 1920s and '30s:

> "From the earliest days in Western Canada, even the smallest village had its grain elevator, general store, post office (often in the store), livery barn, and of course, lumberyard. Our village was just a wide spot on the road, but we laid claim to at least one of each of these businesses.
>
> "I learned to crawl by going over and under 'dry piles' in my dad and uncle's (Stewart Brothers) lumberyard. It was right behind our house and as we kids became more mobile we found it a great place to play hide-and-seek. The centre of most of the activity was the lumber shed. Like all the rest, ours was a long building with a driveway down the centre and a big sliding door on each end. On either side of the driveway were dozens of bins to store the different sizes and kinds of lumber. The horse-drawn rigs drove in one end (if the horses weren't too skittish), put on their load and left.
>
> "Each spring, several farmers would decide to do some building. Fifteen hundred feet of lumber was a good load for a team, so to get all the material on site for a house or barn meant many trips to the lumberyard. Unlike the modern barn or home, lumber in the form of dimension stock and boards, for framing, wall and roof sheathing, and siding made up a large volume of the material required for the construction.

1921, L. to R. Sandy Huston, Vera Johnson, Norman Stewart and Mr. Sorensen (IHC).

Well into the 1950s, the store's large glass showcases displayed household items and chinaware. The store was a maze of clutter filled with wonderful smells: linseed-oiled floors, hemp ropes, leather harness, coal oil, and paint powder all combined to make shopping as much a joy for the nose as the eye. For the horse: sweat pads, harness, rope, horseshoes and nosebags. For the farm shop: a swede saw, centrifugal pump, tow rope, binder canvas, nails and bins and boxes full of shelf hardware. For the household: garden seeds, plates, a variety of pails, pots and pans, cutlery, bed frames, sideboard, kitchen range and even a bright brass cuspidor!

For the farm: a line of International Harvester equipment, as shown in an outdoor display at the Red Deer Fair in the 1920s. From left to right: a 15-30 tractor hitched to an eight-foot binder. A one-way tiller in the centre (of the two men leaning against the tiller, Norman is the one on the left). A cream separator supports the wooden sign. To the right of it is a 1 ½ horsepower McCormick-Deering stationary engine. In the background: an IHC truck and threshing machine, with two men sitting on it, watching activities on the fairgrounds beyond the fence.

The story of the barn in this photograph illustrates how Norman and Tom helped neighbours get ahead. Don McEachern farmed four miles north of Penhold. A regular customer of Stewart Brothers, he had purchased a new 15-30 tractor from them in 1925. In 1929, Don came to see Norman. With a promissory note due in the order of $2,500, he told Norman he had the money to pay off the note, but he also needed a barn. Norman said: "You build the barn, I'll find the money." Stewart Brothers sold the material, with the new barn protecting Don's livestock and winter feed. The promissory note was extended and paid off in due course.

Don's son, Ernie, told me that story many years later, in the 1970s, when he and his wife had me draw plans and supply materials to build one of our Lu-Re-Co component homes. I also drew the plans for their second home and for a hog barn. They remained loyal customers because of Norman's decision to help a neighbour get ahead in the early years.

"You could always tell when a farmer was on his way to town for a load of lumber. He had his team hitched to a wagon gear only. A good logging chain would be wrapped around the rear bolsters and a sack of oats for the horses' noon meal, tied on somewhere. I often wonder how those men managed to ride all the way to town with only 'the reach' (about the size of a 2x4) to sit on. It didn't seem to bother them.

"At the yard they built their loads by putting timbers and two-inch stuff on the bottom. Above it they piled shiplap, boards, siding and flooring. Most even managed to perch a few bundles of cedar shingles, a keg or two of nails, and several rolls of paper on top.

"It was interesting to watch what came next. That was the binding down of the load to be sure it stayed there until it reached home. They usually drove out into the yard for this job. First, the chain was wrapped around the reach, under the centre of the load. An end of the chain came up each side of the load and was fastened on top. Just the right amount of slack had to be left for the final tightening. A 'roller', which could be a short piece of 4x4, or an old fence post, was put across the load right behind the chain. A few pieces of shiplap had been set aside when loading. They were now handed up to the man on the load. He stood them upright, poked the lower end between the roller and the chain then swung them through an ark towards the back of the waggon. As they lowered they tightened the chain, bound the load and held it solid on the wagon. As it jolted along on the way home, the load settled into place, the tightener boards dropped lower and kept the chain tight. It must have been a good system because they always got home with their loads intact.

"Some used to joke about the chap who came to town for a load but forgot his chain. According to the story, this poor fellow had to pull off every few miles, and back his load against a telephone pole to push it forward again. No one ever explained why the loads always shifted to the back of the wagon." [vii]

vii A reminiscence by Jack Stewart written for Stewart Ford's 1990 history of the business.

In 1930, the former Windsor Livery building on 49th Street became the Stewart Brothers Red Deer office until late 1935, when a new Implement Office and Machine Shop were opened a block south on 48th Street and Gaetz Avenue.

During the 1920s, more farmland would be purchased, acquired on machine deals, or taken in settlement for debts. The land would usually be sold, and the cycle repeated. The brothers also purchased a water-front property in Sylvan Lake, where they built a holiday cottage for their families to use during the summers.

The business' land holdings within Penhold grew as well. A garage was built to house the company cars and half-ton trucks, while one of its buildings on Fleming Avenue was leased out as a restaurant. A "visible" gas pump and underground tank were installed in front of the store.

In 1929, the sale of material for the Wright Jersey Dairy, located west of Penhold, boosted profits. The farm brought many economic benefits to the community. In addition to the large dairy, there were two smaller barns for horses and calves, as well as a large implement shed and two houses, one for the Wrights and the other for the farm manager. A tennis court was a unique feature of the property.[18 (p.198)]

Norman's eldest son, Jack, joined the business full-time in 1929 after taking a business course in Calgary. The timing was perfect, as the IHC dealer in Red Deer wanted to sell. It was an ideal opportunity for expansion into Red Deer and Jack was available to manage the new location.[19 (p.199-200)]

Weathering the great depression

The 1930s would test all businesses. Stewart Brothers entered the "Dirty '30s" in a strong financial position. The business enjoyed the highest credit rating for implement dealerships west of Winnipeg, had a loyal customer base, and was able to maintain excellent inventories across a broad line of products. Its parts service was second to none, with used equipment serviced and ready to sell.

Among the numerous vehicles the company owned were cars for sales and repair visits, as well as trucks for delivering building supplies and implements. Some of the vehicles were trade-ins, used until they could be sold. During the 1930s the fleet included a Whippet coupe, Ford V8 coach, Nash four-door car, Dodge truck, Ford truck, and an IHC truck.[20 (p.201)] Trucks were needed to deliver or pick-up much of the machinery sold at the time because it was transported in a knocked-down state and set-up on the farm, either by the customer or by a crew sent from Penhold. Assembled machines were simply too large for the small trucks of the day. Steel wheels and poor roads often precluded pulling them home.

The store's safe was blown in 1931, but the would-be robbers weren't too bright. Norman had left the safe door unlocked and taken the money home. The pointless explosion made a mess of the office, with the safe, typewriter, desk, and chair all having to be replaced.

In difficult times, when people are put to the test, their true natures emerge. Throughout the depression years, the brothers' empathy was evident. It is a value system that can be traced back to their family's earliest days, when their mother helped an aboriginal woman with her sick infant, or fed passing strangers who would just drop in. No one was turned away from the home or from the business.

Norman's daughter, Gwen, recalls:

> "Because of the hardships encountered in their youth, both Tom and Norman demonstrated their empathy in many ways during their business years. To 'give a leg up' to others seemed to be their motto, as it was with many folks in those days. No one came to Stewart Brothers needing help who was turned away. Someone once questioned Norman about extending credit to a penniless farmer. Norman replied, 'that man is gilt-edged: he is just down on his luck at the moment, but with a little help he will prosper and pay back his debits.' Literally hundreds of customers got help when they needed it.

> "During the '30s a large number of families from dried areas of Saskatchewan were relocated in Central Alberta. Except for a bit of government assistance to buy food, they were without a cent. Stewart Brothers supplied many of them with building materials, tractor fuel, and implements to get them started, and while there were a few who fell between the cracks, most of them prospered and paid their debts whenever they were able to do so. The farm that Stewart Brothers purchased on the outskirts of Penhold was acquired to enable them to take horses and other livestock, grain and hay in exchange for lumber and building materials, as well as farm implements. Money was certainly not the reason the two brothers were in business as much as to feel they were helping others in this harsh land." [viii]

In 1931, Norman's share in the business was valued at $125,471.87 and Tom's at $126,941.27 – a total of just over a quarter million dollars. In the Proprietor's account from that year[21 (p.202)], an unusual item is present: $20 monthly remittances by each of the brothers to Mrs. C. E. Sturtzel in Los Angeles, California, U.S.A. Carrie Eugenia Sturtzel was born a Purkiss and was related to Norman and Tom through their mother, Irene Purkiss. Likely, she was a widow who needed help. The last remittance was sent in 1940.

As a young boy, I recall seeing members of the local farm community setting up farm machinery, their wages being applied to their book account or promissory note. During my tenure, some of our pre-builts were assembled by customers, with their wages being applied to an account. It wasn't usually intended that a bill would be paid that way, but when it was possible to collect through "work-in-kind", both parties would benefit.

---

viii A reminiscence by Gwen Calverley prepared for Stewart Ford's 1990 history of the business

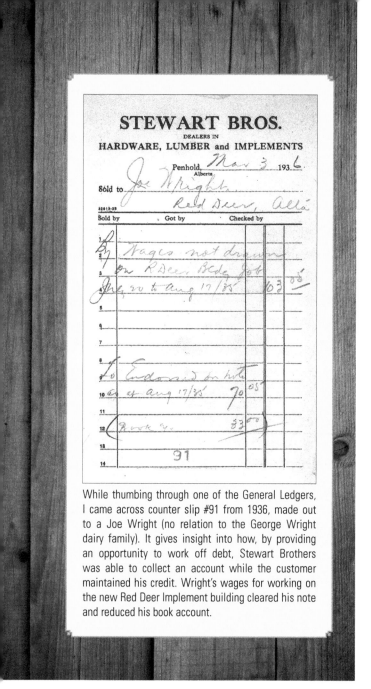

STEWART BROS.

DEALERS IN

HARDWARE, LUMBER and IMPLEMENTS

Penhold, *Mar 3* 193 *6*.
Alberta

Sold to *Joe Wright*

Red Deer, Alta

Sold by	Got by	Checked by		
1				
2	*Wages not drawn*			
3	*on R Deer Bldg Job*			
4	*June 20 to Aug 17/35*		63	05
5				
6				
7				
8				
9	*To Endorsed for note*			
10	*of aug 17/35*		70	05
11				
12	*Book a/c*		53	00
13				
14	91			

While thumbing through one of the General Ledgers, I came across counter slip #91 from 1936, made out to a Joe Wright (no relation to the George Wright dairy family). It gives insight into how, by providing an opportunity to work off debt, Stewart Brothers was able to collect an account while the customer maintained his credit. Wright's wages for working on the new Red Deer Implement building cleared his note and reduced his book account.

It wasn't just about giving a hand-up. Norman and Tom believed in going the extra mile to help a customer in any circumstance. Jack remembers: [ix]

"About the middle of the dirty '30s, Frank Cobbald of Pine Lake built a fine new home. The next year he decided to add a barn. One morning after a couple of loads of lumber for the barn had been delivered and the carpenters were on the job, word came in that the municipal grader was going to rip up and rebuild several miles of the only road to Frank's place. We had two trucks of our own and were able to hire two more. Everyone spent a busy few hours getting all four trucks loaded. When all was ready, the convoy left for Pine Lake. They were there before the graders began their work. By the time the carpenters had used up all the material, the road was fit to carry loads again. Customers don't forget such things." [22 (p.202)]

Expansion

At the beginning of 1934, Norman and Tom made the decision to expand operations. Over the years, they continued to invest the cash not needed for day-to-day operations in stocks and bonds.[23 (p.203)] By selling some of these investments, they had the money to purchase S26-T36-R28-4 next to Penhold. Meanwhile, a dwelling for a farm manager and a barn for milk cows and horses were built on the farmland in Penhold. Corrals and fences

ix A reminiscence by Jack Stewart prepared for Stewart Ford's 1900 history of the business

The manager's house and the barn on Stewart Brothers' farm. Note the windmill between the house and barn – the farm had Penhold's first deep-water well.

Farm manager Phil Tweten had an interesting history. Born in Minnesota, his Norwegian parents both died of diphtheria when Phil was eleven. His younger siblings were adopted by neighbours, while Phil put a saddle on his father's horse, a blanket behind the cantle, and took off for the west country of newly established Alberta. He had heard there was lots of work for people who knew cows and horses.

Phil spent most of his youth working as a cow-hand on many of the ranches of the south-west country – including Cochrane Ranches, the Bar U, Waldron Ranches, and others – before being hired by Stewart Brothers. In later years, Phil's three sons, Terrence, Buddy, and Vernon, also found employment with Stewart Brothers.

were constructed to hold more livestock, which would be taken on trade for machines and building supplies. The farm also had the first deep-water well in Penhold. Equipped with a windmill, it provided water for the house and livestock.

Phil Tweten was hired as farm manager, and the company's cattle brand, HH3 (first registered in 1900 by Norman, Tom, and their father but since let lapse), was taken up again in 1934. For the horse brand, they used Phil Tweten's T-connected-T.[24] (p.204)

Canvassing for business continued throughout the '30s, particularly during the busy spring and fall seasons. Often, Norman would take Phil along on these trips. It was common that they'd see a farmer harrowing with a bunch of branches dragged by horses over a plowed field. Norman would stop and wait for the farmer to come to the end of the field by the road, where he'd call him by name and say: "I could have a set of harrows delivered here in a couple of days." If the farmer replied that he couldn't afford it, Norman might say, "Well, you pay for them whenever you can," or, "I saw some nice cattle in the next field. Do you need to cull some of them?" Then he and Phil would have a look at the cattle (or horses) and strike a deal.

Restructuring for growth

By the end of 1934, Norman and Tom realized the need to restructure the partnership. Norman's eldest son, Jack, had been managing the Red Deer operation since 1929 and was now brought in as a third partner. Norman Sr. held 7/12 of the partnership; Jack was given 1/12; Tom's holdings were reduced from 6/12 to 4/12. The reduction of Tom's holdings signifies an understanding that, of the two brothers, Norman was the "face" of the business; Norman also had the larger family to support.[25] (p.204)

The Penhold business took a loss of over $9,600 in 1933. The Alberta economy was still agriculture-based, and the rural farm population held the votes that elected the provincial government. The depression had hit the farm population hard. Wheat prices collapsed and poor weather in many regions meant reduced crop yields or total crop failure. It was tough going for all businesses. Most of the 1933 losses can be attributed to $4,000 in higher expenses; sales were lower and the gross margin percentage was lower, creating a $2,000 loss; and lastly, loss on the sale of bonds was $1,800. In 1934, the business had 676 customer accounts on the books. This did not include any cash customers. Outstanding promissory notes amounted to $105,407.69. The balance sheet for the businesses in Penhold and Red Deer was $265,718.52, and Norman and Tom's capital accounts were $224,048.44. The net profit for the 1934 was $1,075.48. The effect of the Depression is highlighted by the difference in the price of a bushel of oats in the 1931 farm inventory at 41 cents, compared to 27 cents in the 1934 inventory.[26] (p.205)

For the new Red Deer implement show room, sales office, and machine shop, Norman bartered the City's $3,000 asking price down with an offer of $2,000 – one third less than the asking price, with only half the amount paid up front. The Stewart Brothers property fronted on Gaetz Avenue with 48th Street on the north side. A CPR siding at the rear of the new building allowed for carloads of machinery to be unloaded directly onto a railcar-height loading dock. The new building opened on December 2, 1935, a full month before the deadline stipulated by Red Deer City Council. It was arguably the finest sales and repair facility in the province, if not in all western Canada, at the time.[27] (p.206-207)

The following year, Stewart Brothers continued its acquisition spree in Red Deer with the purchase of Central Lumberyard from Mr. Peterson in April 1936. In 1937, they began construction of a new builders' store.[28 (p.208)]

In 1940, IHC's dealer magazine, *The Harvester*, ran a full-page article about the Stewart Brothers business: "Thirty-Eight Years of 'Doing What It Took to Get Started' Brings Success to Stewart Bros."[29 (p.209)] The article puts the combined Penhold-Red Deer staff at twenty-three individuals and suggests another element of the business's success: "No sale is too large or too small."

Location, location, location

Both Stewart Brothers businesses in Penhold and Red Deer were located at crossroads of north-south and east-west traffic through the centres, thanks to bridges across the Red Deer River and to the main CPR railway. In Red Deer, the W. E. Lord department store was kitty-corner from the new implement shop and the lumberyard was a block south. Together, the three businesses were a shopping district all on their own.

Penhold also had a geographical advantage. Situated in a bowl, with land rising to the east and to the west, Penhold was a downhill trip for farmers delivering grain, making it easier on horses in the early years and saving on fuel in later years. With five elevator companies, Penhold offered a competitive marketplace. Stewart Brothers, the area's largest implement

Stewart Brothers' new Red Deer Builders Store, circa 1937.

dealer, also offered lumber and an extensive line of hardware and household items, helping make Penhold a sell-and-shop destination.

To manage the new Red Deer lumberyard, Stewart Brothers hired Ora and Nita Thorne. Jack, in addition to running the Red Deer implement office, also oversaw the lumberyard operation just a block to the south. His recollections follow:

> "The Lumberyard in Red Deer was run by a very loyal and capable couple, Ora and Nita Thorne. Not young when they began working for Stewart Brothers, they were certainly experienced, having operated at least one lumberyard previously. Mr. and Mrs. Thorne were like characters out of a Hollywood movie. Ma and Pa Kettle

My father told me of an incident when he was working with Orie at the Red Deer lumberyard. A customer with a heavy accent came in for a material quote and had a bill of material already priced from a competitor. He proceeded to read off the items to Orie. Orie seemed to have difficulty understanding what the fellow was saying, repeatedly asking questions, getting mixed up and muddled. Finally, in frustration, the fellow handed Orie the material list, which of course Orie was hoping to get all along. With full knowledge of what he was up against, he proceeded to price out the bill of materials, making the sale.

doesn't quite describe them, because they were infinitely more educated and cultured. Nita Thorne was a plump lady with a hearty laugh. She also had one of the loudest voices projected over a phone. The rule was if Nita was calling— hold the receiver at least six inches away from your ear. The Thornes were very musical. Nita played the piano and Orie (as she called him) played the saxophone. In their slightly younger days they had a dance band and played dances all over the country. In Red Deer they were active in the United Church, she playing the organ and he in the choir. These and other community activities meant that they were very well known, and folks liked to do business with them. Nita had a very 'green thumb'. Customers used to wonder if they were entering a lumberyard or a florist shop. She was generous with plant cuttings and advice to go along with them. Orie and Nita worked as a team, with Nita giving most of the signals and always the last word. A jolly couple, who had no family of their own, they tended to treat their customers like they were 'family' and went the extra mile to prove it. Their congeniality was what the customers seemed to like, and the resulting public relations was good for business. If a customer wanted to build a barn or house, the Thornes would spend no end of time and fuss to give them what they wanted.

The Nazarene Church chose Red Deer as the place to build the Nazarene College in Western Canada. Looking about for people with integrity with whom to deal they favoured the Thornes and gave them most of their business. While not a big institution by today's standard, it grew to quite a size. Materials for many contracts resulted from the amiable association with Wayne Wiley, their contractor. Students from the College earned pocket money by working after classes and on Saturdays at the yard piling lumber, unloading cars of plywood, helping out at the planer mill, etc.

The Thornes treated the yard as if it was their own, and both thoroughly enjoyed their work. Orie had a few eccentricities. He didn't believe in a cash register; the help might have sticky fingers if they got into it. Likewise, he kept the price list and his job quotes locked up. His theory was pure 19th-century capitalism. If the help got trained to do the boss's job they would have to be paid more for fear they would go down the street and get hired by Atlas or Beaver!"

Lumber mills

Stewart Brothers had developed good relationships with the small lumber mills operating in the west country. Most were family affairs owned by farmers who would harvest spruce, pine, poplar, and tamarack during the winter, then saw the lumber in the spring and summer. Typically, the lumber was sold rough-cut and needed to be dressed out. The company had two planers – one on the Penhold farm by Fleming Slough, and later, a second one in Red Deer's new planer shed. S4S Douglas fir lumber and split-cedar fence posts came in by rail from British Columbia.

These relationships were possible because the brothers were able to support the family-run mills with outright cash purchases, and by accepting lumber on trade for machinery and household items. Farm animals could be taken in trade, with horses, cattle, hogs, and sheep being fed out and sold. Most importantly, the machine shop in the Red Deer Implement Store could repair the mill machinery, vital during the Second World War when new parts were scarce or unavailable. It was a unique service that other local lumberyards and implement dealers couldn't match.

The coastal British Columbia mills supplied clear-finish lumber, mouldings, and cedar shingles. At Christmas, they would send a box filled with grapefruit, mistletoe and holly on the CPR express car. It was their way of saying, "Thank-you for the business." The treats were divided up among, and much enjoyed by, all staff

Graham and Muriel Ford on their wedding day in 1936, outside Tom and Laura's home.

1935	1936	1938	1939	1940
Muriel Stewart graduates from Normal School; begins teaching east of Penhold. Muriel meets Graham Ford.	Tom's daughter Muriel, marries Graham Ford of Castor, Alberta.	Stewart Ford born, October 27.	Second World War begins. Graham Ford starts work at the business full-time.	Kaye and Gwen manage Red Deer business.

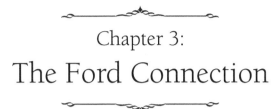

Chapter 3:
The Ford Connection

The Normal School – now Rosehaven Care Centre in Camrose, Alberta – was built by the province in 1915 to educate teachers, doing so until 1945. In 1935, Tom's daughter, Muriel, graduated with a professional second-class certification. She began teaching in the Edwell and Willowdale districts east of Penhold.

Graham Ford, the son of Bill Ford, a blacksmith and businessman from Castor, Alberta, was also a teacher. He had trained at the University of Alberta and, during summers, would take further upgrading courses at the Camrose Normal School, where he and Muriel met.

Graham and Muriel were married in July 1936 and moved to a teacherage just east of Graham's hometown of Castor. Graham taught at the rural Beaverdale school for the 1936-1937 and 1937-1938 school years. They would spend summers in Penhold with Muriel's parents, when Graham would work for Stewart Brothers before returning to teach in September.

I was born in Castor on October 27, 1938. At the end of the school year in 1939, my parents returned to Penhold and my father again joined Stewart Brothers for the summer. But this time, as the 1939-1940 school term approached, it was obvious that war was about to break out in Europe, so Graham stayed on in Penhold.

1941	1942	1945	1946
Twelve members of staff enter active service with the Canadian forces.	Norman's daughters, Gwen and Kaye, become employees in the Red Deer machine agency.	Second World War ends.	All thirteen employees who had enlisted return from the war.
	Business grows to ten partners as Norman's children, Tom's daughter and son-in-law enter the business.		
	Stewart Brothers granted status as "essential to the war effort".		
	New carpentry, saw, and planer shed constructed in Penhold.		

Graham's father, William (Bill) Walter Ford, immigrated to Canada in the fall of 1910, arriving in Halifax. After an eleven-day train trip, he settled in Castor, Alberta — at that time the end of the rail line being constructed east to Saskatchewan. He came to join Mr. Hird, who had been his employer in Wales before emigrating and opening a blacksmith shop in Castor.

Within a few years, Bill and his fellow employee, Sam Colwill, took over the business. Bill married a Scottish lass, Mary Graham, and started a family. They had two sons, Graham and Percy, and two daughters, Betty and Doreen. In 1929, Bill and Sam switched from blacksmithing to constructing and owning a service station and business block they rented to other merchants.

Look closely at the photo and you'll see that Bill had only three fingers on his right hand. He lost his pinky finger to a pig bite when he was three years old.

Members of Staff
on
Active Service
Red Deer · Penhold
Stewart Brothers

Vernon Sweten
Jack Stewart
Norman Stewart
Earl McAllister
Robert Lee
Biddy Sweten
Bruce Lee
Tom Curtis
Leonard Sweten
Keith Sim
Vernon Leonard
Jim Downey
Keith Mayse

This poster was created around 1942 by Norman, in honour of the men of the business who went into service. All thirteen of the men returned safely.

Most of the men in the business would soon enlist. Graham was disqualified from service due to his poor eyesight. He was needed in the business, and from that time, my parents lived permanently in Penhold, first in a small cottage on 1109 Windsor Avenue owned by Mrs. H. R. McDougall and later in a company-owned house on 1219 Windsor Avenue, closer to the business. Little did anyone realize at that time that my father would have a momentous impact on the future of the business.

Norman's eldest son, Jack, was a reservist and was called up to serve overseas in London. Norman's younger son, Norman Jr., joined the Royal Canadian Air Force (RCAF) and served in British Columbia. Another eleven men of the business enlisted. Other than Norman and Tom, my father was the only male family member left working at the Penhold store during the Second World War.

Graham already had a good knowledge of the business and of the area. He would become a jack-of-all-trades during those years. Primarily, he was a truck driver, delivering machines and building supplies to customers, picking up lumber from the local mills, and making trips to Calgary to pick up supplies from various wholesalers.

Essential to the war effort

The war presented challenges to all businesses. Stewart Brothers had a lot going for it that many others did not. Norman and Tom were at the top of their game, and the business had come through the depression largely unscathed. The building supply in Red Deer was predominant, with the experienced Orie and Nita Thorne managing it. In the Red Deer implement office, Ralph Robertson operated the machine shop, which would become indispensable in repairing and rebuilding older machines that could not be replaced. Norman's daughters, Kathleen and Gwen, would prove capable in the parts department and on the sales floor.

During the war, the Red Deer implement store was a Victory Loan headquarters. This photo shows the store displaying the Victory Loan flag.

In Penhold, alongside Norman, Tom, and Graham, were hardware man Tom Suffern, bookkeeper Gar Minaker, and carpenter Bill Hoyle. This team kept things running smoothly.

Gar started with the firm in the early 1930s, after a previous bookkeeper had appropriated $5,000 of the company's money. Gar became a key employee, keeping an excellent set of books. In writing this history, I've been able to pinpoint dates and costs thanks to information that Gar entered in the company records. There was no company pension plan, but upon the deaths of those three men, the business provided each of their widows a monthly pension of $50. I signed the last of those cheques in 1984, upon the death of Bill Hoyle's wife, twenty-five years after her husband's passing.

> My father, Graham, liked to tell the story of a trip he made to Rocky Mountain House, delivering and picking up lumber for the drive home. When he parked on the street he was surrounded by a crowd of men agog at seeing a "new" truck. They all wanted to know how Stewart Brothers had managed to get it, and one fellow offered $4,000 cash on the spot to buy it.

When Jack enlisted, Gwen and her sister, Kaye, were left in charge in Red Deer. They took over bookkeeping and other clerical duties and handled sales for the few of the machines available on their quota. Both women took their duties seriously. Overtime work in the evenings, particularly during the busy season, was the norm. The staff in the shop, although depleted, was a loyal group of men who did their jobs with few problems for Kaye or Gwen.[30 (p.210)]

One of the disruptions caused by the war was that international trade had dried up, making it harder to move grain. The solution was to build more storage facilities, including annexes next to existing grain elevators and more grain bins on farms. Because both Penhold and Red Deer had workshops with their lumberyards and machine dealerships, Stewart Brothers was designated "essential to the War Effort." This enabled the business to obtain a restricted supply of equipment during the war – with

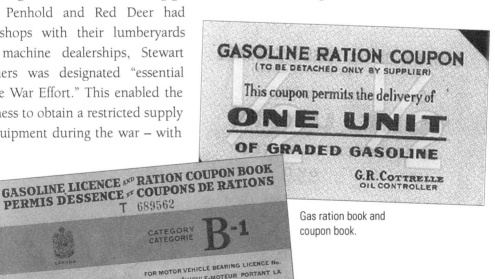

Gas ration book and coupon book.

permits from Ottawa and Washington, D.C. – which included a $1,435.38 IHC K5 three-ton truck in 1940, and a $900 De Walt Woodworker sixteen-inch radial-arm saw in 1942.

1942 saw another adjustment to the partnership structure of the business. With Norman's daughters, Tom's daughter, Muriel; and son-in-law, Graham, all involved in the business, all second-generation family members were brought into the partnership. The new arrangement was: Norman Sr. 20/48, Tom 10/48, Jack 5/48, Norman Jr. 5/48, Kaye 1/48, Gwen 1/48, Betty 1/48, Irene 1/48, Muriel 2/48, Graham 2/48. In 1948, Norman Sr. would further distribute 10/48 of his shares to the members of his family.

Many items were restricted during the war because of lack of availability or because they were required for the war effort. Price controls were established, and rationing was used to distribute limited resources such as gasoline, sugar, and vehicle tires. It was a fortunate coincidence that Tom's 1939 Nash had the same tire size as the small delivery truck. Essential to the war effort or not, Stewart Brothers was treated like anyone else, with ration books for business and farm fuel.

Bill Hoyle, a veteran of the Great War, joined the business in 1939 as carpenter and worked for the company until his death in 1959. His work included milling drop siding on the sticker planer, precutting framing on the saw, and assembling windows for homes and buildings.

Clear fir window jamb and sill lumber stock was assembled with the window stop, parting stop, and outside casing lumber into which the glazed sash was placed. Exterior and interior doors were also fitted and hung in rabbited fir jamb. 1x6 drop siding – the staple exterior finish for farm buildings – was planed out during the winter from boards selected from the regular stock of shiplap. Templates were kept on hand for several wagon and sleigh components, which would be traced onto a 2" or a 2-½" Douglas fir plank and cut out. These included runners, bolsters, and reaches. Sweep teeth were made by angle-cutting a fir 2x6 or 2x8 lengthways, usually in 8' or 9' lengths. The machine workshop had a forge, which proved very useful, providing some of the metal parts for the sleighs, particularly steel feet for the runners.

The business' reputation helped immensely during lean times. The small lumber suppliers in the west country made sure Stewart Brothers had first chance at their lumber. This was critical, as war-related construction depleted the supply from British Columbia's large interior and coastal mills.

My understanding about the allocation of new farm machinery in wartime comes from my father. It seems that the different manufacturers, either by choice or agreement, allocated their resources to different equipment. This was particularly true of steel. Massey-Harris allocated most of its steel to combines, while IHC gave priority to tractors. Stewart Brothers held the Cockshutt and Oliver agencies as well as IHC, which helped them get a few more machines. But there was never enough new equipment to be had.

Gwen recalled the business during the war years:

"In early 1940, Stewart Brothers saw many of their men enlist in the Armed Services. Norman Stewart Jr. joined the RCAF. Replacements were hard to find. Kathleen (Kaye Stewart), who was completing her high school in Red Deer, came to work the Red Deer office full time in the repair parts department. Because new machines were almost non-existent, due to the war effort, it was extremely important to keep the old ones going. The Parts Department was therefore a busy place, as was the shop where tractors and trucks were repaired, and the machine shop which made many unavailable parts. Kaye took over the Parts Department and amazed the men folk with her ability to remember parts numbers and provide customers with efficient service. A perpetual inventory, by means of a card system, recorded what was running low, so each evening a large order was sent to the Calgary Branch House, and the next day a shipment arrived to be entered on the cards and put away. Farmers still talk about Kaye and her keen perception in the Parts Department.

"The machine shop did a roaring business on such things as building up tracks and replacing pins and bushings on machines needed for working in the bush and lumber mills west of town. Ralph Robertson, the wizard of the machine shop, had a great sense of humour but also a quick temper and unsavoury vocabulary if things didn't go right. Kaye often had to go into his very noisy shop to relay a phone message. Ralph found it embarrassing if he was in the midst of a

One day, a customer came by, distraught with the wet weather. His hay, he said, had been turned and was dry enough to bale. But as the ground was still wet, his baler wheels got so clogged up with mud that they would not turn. Gwen took him out to the machinery lot and showed him that the wheels were reversible. He could remove them and turn them around, curving out instead of in, giving more clearance. Problem solved!

colourful dissertation just as Kaye entered. The shop men thoughtfully bought a large whistle on a cord and instructed Kaye to wear it around her neck and blow it loudly as she approached. That did the trick and gave everyone a good laugh."[x]

Kaye and Gwen continued to manage both Red Deer facilities until the men returned after the war. Kaye was with the business for 10 years and Gwen for seven.

Indeed, well into the '70s, customers would inquire about Kaye or Gwen, recalling their abilities and especially Kaye's memory for part numbers.

In the late 1930s, the Department of Transport began construction of a radio beacon station on a twenty-acre legal subdivision (LSD) at the north-east corner of the company's newly purchased section 26. Land was also purchased two miles to the north for the support buildings and a future airport. A portion of the property included part of the original Stewart family homestead. Shortly after the war started and the British Commonwealth Air Training Plan (BCATP) was created, the site became a hub of activity with the construction of runways, barracks, and hangars. The base was operated by the Royal Air Force (RAF) until 1944. In Red Deer, new barracks and drill halls were constructed for an army induction and training centre. These projects boosted the local economies.

In Penhold, housing was needed for civilian staff working at the air base. To help with the demand, Stewart Brothers constructed three 20'x24' cabins on Lucina Street, across from the business. They were intended as temporary housing, which would later be sold and moved off the property. They were nicknamed "chicken houses", as that was a possible

---

x A reminiscence by Gwen Calverley written for Stewart Ford's brief 1990 history of the business.

Royal Air Force servicemen arriving at the Penhold train station.

use for them after the war. Only one was sold off, however. The other two, with updates, remained until the late 1970s.

In 1942, a new 30'x60' saw shop was built in Penhold to house the De Walt saw and sticker planer. The saw sped up the pre-cutting of material for 12'x16' material packages and the planer enabled stock 1x6 shiplap lumber to be milled into 6" drop siding. The shop's 2x6 tongue-and-groove wood floor allowed jig blocking to be set up for the construction of truss rafters and gothic-arch barn rafters. About sixteen feet of the front (south) end of the building was partitioned off as a heated carpenter shop. Initially, it was heated with an oil-burning heater, later converted to natural gas.

The Red Deer yard kept busy with the same trade as Penhold, as well as supplying materials for the construction of wartime housing near the army training grounds.

A couple of years after I started full-time in the business, my "office" was in the heated portion of the saw shop. My drafting board, a simple parallel arm type, was set up in a small area in the south-east corner. A high wall, bowstring-truss roof machine shop was built at the south end for servicing combines and other large equipment. The space was used to spray paint machines. I had to be sure my plans were covered, otherwise they would end up a shade of pink thanks to a fine dusting of the IHC red overspray paint.[31 (p.211)]

In an article published in The Harvester in 1939, Noman mentioned that when the business first introduced the combine to the area in 1928, people were very slow to catch on. Many felt the parkland area wasn't "combine country". With the shortage of manpower during the war, however, the combine became popular. Threshing crews required a dozen or more men, while a combine needed only about three. If you could find a combine, it was likely a Massey-Harris.

The men return

With the end of the war, all thirteen staff members who had enlisted returned, many of them to the firm. Jack Stewart took up where he had left off, managing the Red Deer operation. Norman Stewart Jr. returned to Penhold, as did Bruce Lee and Jimmy Domoney. Others spent a short time with the business while sorting out their futures. Kaye stayed on in Red Deer for a few more years before taking up a position in Calgary, where she met her future husband, Jack Gallagher. Gwen travelled to Ontario to take further schooling in Guelph, where she met her future husband, returned soldier Mike Calverley. She brought him back to Alberta where they purchased land from the company. Here, they would farm and raise a family.

Combining on section 26 in 1942. Kaye, Gwen, and Tom can be seen on and beside the D2 truck as a grain tank is emptied from the combine into the truck box.

The harvesting taking place in these photos is on section 26, purchased by Stewart Brothers in 1935. The four radio beacons mentioned earlier can be seen behind the combine in one of the photos. The grain tank on the combine was no larger than the box on the IHC D2 truck also pictured. The grain would be taken to one of several small 12'x16' granaries in the field and would be augered up into the bin.

Shortly after the end of the war, Nance Co., owned by Ted Nance, enlarged its footprint with a new building at the corner of Ross Street and 47th Avenue, on the site now occupied by the Jackpot Casino. There was also a branch operation in Innisfail. Nance soon made it known that he was going to put Stewart Brothers out of business!

One of his first actions was to attempt to corner the local supply of lumber from the west country. He offered the producers an extra $5 per thousand board feet above the asking price to exclusively secure their production. It didn't work, because many of the producers remembered the assistance Stewart Brothers had provided them during tough times and during the wartime shortages. They weren't about to turn their backs now. At the retail end, Nance also came up against Orie and Nita Thorne, who had a loyal group of contractors and regular customers.

In the implement business, Nance did not have a mainline dealership – IHC, Massey-Harris, John Deere, Case, Cockshutt, and Oliver already had established dealers. Nance had some initial success with a British import, the Field Marshall tractor. It was a single-cylinder 30+ HP two-stroke diesel and very different from the tractors in the marketplace at that time. Once the domestic production of familiar brands caught up, however, demand for the Field Marshall alternative waned. Nance failed in his intended goal and was out of business by the late 1950s.

It is an adage that you don't go into business to put someone else out of business. Rather, you seek to grow wealthy with your competitors. Norman and Tom were successful because they believed in providing outstanding service combined with integrity. They succeeded, and in doing so provided their families and employees with a good living. Keen competitors, they kept the opposition on their toes and the consumer reaped the benefits.

In 1947, Imperial struck oil near Leduc and forever changed Alberta's future.

1947

Imperial strikes oil in Leduc, Alberta.

Business supplies Nazarene College building in Red Deer.

Supplies new Pine Hill Hutterite Colony.

1948

Graham and Muriel build new home.

1950

Stewart Ford, not yet twelve, begins work in the business during summer holidays.

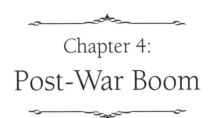

Chapter 4:

Post-War Boom

Shortly after the end of World War II, a group of citizens in Innisfail formed a committee to work towards the construction of a memorial arena and swimming pool. The pool was built first, completed in 1947. The arena, the more expensive part of the project, was started in 1951. Construction was delayed during 1952 until the roof trusses were brought up to a higher standard, and the arena was officially opened in February 1953. Despite there being two local lumberyards, Stewart Brothers Penhold was chosen as the supplier. The dollar value for about 68,000 board feet of lumber was $15,520.90.

Gradually, rationing ended, industry returned to peace-time production, and products restricted during the war became available. New farm machinery, trucks, automobiles, window glass, plywood, cement, and finish materials could again be had. There was money to purchase goods and labour to use them. With its outlets in Red Deer and Penhold, Stewart Brothers was once again ideally positioned to meet the needs of the community.

Not all products made possible by the new peace-time economy were successes. There was a surplus of aluminum after the war. Corrugated aluminum sheets for roofing and siding, and aluminum nails for framing and sheathing, entered the market. The corrugated aluminum was prone to tearing off roofs in high winds, while the nails were prone to bending.

1951	1952	1954
Obtains Hume Reel agency for Alberta, Saskatchewan, and western B.C.	Supplies new Penhold curling rink. Supplies Innisfail arena.	Red Deer Building Supply store fire.
	Independent Order of Odd Fellows (IOOF) hall and property along highway 2A purchased; hall moved and leased to Post Office.	New building constructed.

Alberta strikes it rich

No story of Alberta would be complete without mention of Imperial striking oil near Leduc in 1947. It was the beginning of a new era that brought high-paying jobs, new citizens, new roads, and a change in demographics to the province. Increased government revenues funded expansion of the education system, healthcare, highways, and social services.

In 1947, the southern Alberta Hutterite colony of Lakeside, split. Half the colony moved onto ten sections of land they had purchased from Einer Stephenson in the Pine Hill district, eight miles west of Penhold. There was considerable resistance to the newcomers, who practiced communal living, schooled their children on the colony, and were pacifists. With the war fresh in everyone's minds, the community wasn't feeling very welcoming.[32 (p.212)]

I remember hanging out with the carpenter, Bill Hoyle, while he was building a floor for a grain bin. He was nailing the 2x6 tongue-and-groove floor with four-inch aluminum nails. The soft nails were no match for the hard Douglas fir skids, and the bend rate was close to fifty percent. I would straighten the bent nails and hand them back to Bill. However, the bend rate on my refurbished nails was close to one hundred percent. In disgust, Bill told me to find something else to do with my time. He had to use up the rest of the stock though, because we couldn't sell it.

A delegation of three local farmers came to see Norman, seeking his support to oppose the coming of the colony settling in the district. His opinion carried a lot of weight. He met the three farmers at the front counter of the Penhold office and heard them out. Norman had a way of gazing past the person he was talking to – not ignoring them, but giving the conversation enough space that, when he did speak, you knew it was the last word. He told them simply: "Well the Indians didn't stop us from coming."

A large community meeting was convened in the Ridgewood Hall to discuss the matter. The colony brought an MLA, a veteran of the war, to speak. He said that he had not spent his time fighting for freedom from tyranny to see tyranny raised in Canada, and by a group

1958	1959	1960
Becomes a limited company on July 9, 1958, renamed Stewart Supplies (Penhold) Ltd. Red Deer Building Supply leased to Monarch Lumber.	Red Deer implement office leased to Sears Canada.	New machine shop built for Bob Parker.
Stewart Ford joins full time.	Jack Stewart moves to Penhold to manage the farm.	Peggy "Smitty" Smith joins the firm in Penhold.
	Obtains Interprovincial Component Homes franchise and ventures into component home sales.	

STEWART BROTHERS
PENHOLD - ALBERTA
PHONE 17

FARM EQUIPMENT

MOTOR TRUCKS

LUMBER • HARDWARE

COPYRIGHT 1948, AIRVIEW PHOTOS

"Serving the Penhold District over many"

With cameras, pilots, and planes available after the war, it became popular and affordable to have aerial photos taken of farmsteads, industrial sites, villages, towns, and cities. In 1948 my father had this photo taken of Penhold, showing all five elevators. The inset features the Stewart Brothers business properties. Just visible on the street to the right of the store is my father with a board on his shoulder. The photos were printed and handed out to customers at Christmas.

1961

IOOF building Post Office burns; Stewart draws plans for new building constructed on same site.

Stewart draws plans for new Royal Bank building that company leases to bank.

Bunker silo constructed on Penhold farm.

Norman's wife, Esther, dies.

1962

Stewart Brothers celebrates sixtieth anniversary.

Stewart leaves for eighteen months to gain experience working for Monarch Lumber.

IHC honours company for sixty years as dealers.

of Canadians. The message must have got across, as the colony's carpenter told me years later that most of those at the meeting made a point to visit and personally apologize.

Stewart Brothers was the new Pine Hill Colony's supplier of choice for building materials and some of its machinery. Later, in the 1960s, Revelstoke, a large building supply chain with yards in Alberta and Saskatchewan, aggressively sought and won the colony business across both provinces. In the 1980s, I was able to win it back.

A first for Penhold

Started in 1947, Penhold's water and sanitary sewer system was completed in 1948.[33 (p.213)] Of particular interest, the article says, "Penhold is thought to be the smallest community in Canada to have established its own water and sewer system. The population is around 160." In the aerial photograph preceding, eight-inch vitreous clay sewer tile from the project can be seen piled on a vacant lot along the edge of Minto Street, to the left of the Memorial Hall.

We young fellows had a ball playing on the pile of excavated soil alongside the open trench. I don't recall anyone admonishing us for playing close to the open trenches or of any of us falling in. 1948 was a fun summer with the excavated streets being our gigantic playground.

Make yourself at home

The Veterans Land Act (VLA) was created to help veterans obtain low-interest mortgages. In 1948, Norman was approached by a couple of veterans who asked if he would sell them land along the township road at the north end of the north-west quarter of section 36. Norman agreed and had a strip of land surveyed into lots. In April 1948, C. G. (Red) Johnson paid $155 for a 3.10 acre lot and C. R. Pendergast paid $118.50 for 2.37 acres. Stewart Brothers sold the materials that the men used to build their homes. In that same year, Stewart Brothers sold an adjoining quarter-section in the county to E. G. (Ted) Knight for $9,600. (In 1934 Stewart Brothers had purchased section 26 for $9,700. Quite a change in land values over twelve years!) Sixty years later in 1996, the same quarter section sold for $190,000.

By 1948, the peacetime economy was getting a foothold, and 1948 to 1953 were good years. Business profits averaged a bit over $76,000 per year, after returning significant dividends to the shareholders. Those prosperous years kickstarted the lives of the second generation. As with their aunts previously, Gwen and Kaye had the means to begin independent lives of their choosing. Irene had a comfortable living, not having to rely on her nurse's salary alone. To raise their growing families, Jack built a new home in Red Deer and Norman Jr. purchased my grandfather's home next to his dad's. In 1952, Tom and Laura tried retirement at Victoria, only to return to Alberta a year later. They built a new home at 4926-46th Street in Red Deer and lived there until Tom's death in 1973. He commuted to Penhold to work until he was eighty. My parents, Graham and Muriel, built a new home in Penhold, purchased their own car, and paid off their house account.

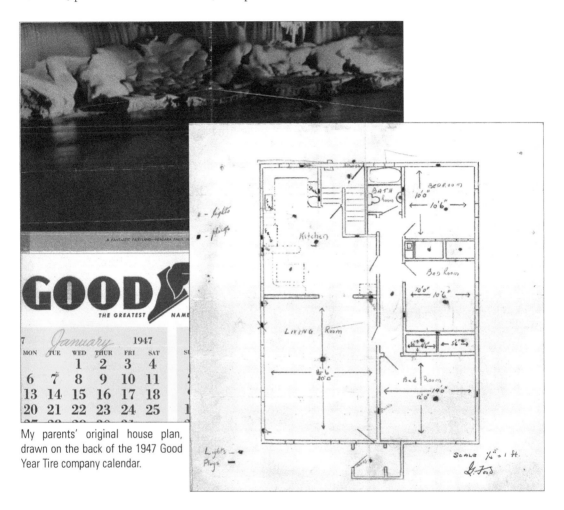

My parents' original house plan, drawn on the back of the 1947 Good Year Tire company calendar.

My parents and I had been living in a company-owned house at 1217 Windsor Avenue across the highway from the hotel. It was a great location for a young lad like me, who enjoyed watching the wartime traffic going past what was then Highway 2. On the odd Saturday evening, the events spilling out of the bar in the hotel also provided entertainment. Later, in 1947, my parents decided to build their own home on a 50-foot corner lot, one block south at 1102 Windsor Avenue. The lot was purchased from the business for $35. My mother had the floorplan in her mind since she had been a teenager. The plan, as my father drew it on the back of the first page of Good Year Tire company's 1947 calendar, is shown here. There were no permits, no inspections, no survey – just find the lot boundary pegs, measure, and dig!

When the house was built in 1948, there was still a shortage of some materials. The cement for the foundation came from the U.S.A. and the window glass came from some left over from a hospital in Montreal. The lumber was readily available but finding someone to plaster the interior walls was a challenge, and the quality of that workmanship was poor. Thankfully a local farmer, Ed Stickland, was the carpenter and he did a wonderful job. We moved in the fall, enjoying the brand-new town water and sanitary sewer.

In post-war years, the business helped many local farmers by providing money to purchase land. Gordon Stickland was able to get a $5,000 loan to purchase his first quarter-section. His dad wouldn't provide the funds, but Norman did, securing it with a mortgage.

When I was around ten or eleven years old, I remember seeing Gordon with some other local farmers setting up IHC swathers in the yard just north of the store. Just as Joe Wright had paid off his bill by working on the new implement office construction in 1935, Gordon's pay would likely have been credited to his mortgage.

The reason I remember seeing Gordon working on the swather is because I had been given a quarter by my grandmother to go to the grocery store for a quart of milk. The quarter was significant to me and I proudly showed it off to Gordon, who asked to see it. I gave it to him and he teased me by suggesting that I wasn't getting it back. I went back to my grandmother, who sorted Gordon out, and I proceeded to get the milk. All was soon forgotten and in later years I dealt with Gordon when he needed building material.

My halcyon days

The business is entwined with my childhood and all my memories. My family's activities, conversations, obligations, and even leisure time revolved around the business. My father would make trips to Calgary to pick up machinery, hardware, and building supplies from distributors. On many occasions before I started school in 1944, my mother and I would get to ride along with him. It was a great adventure. I was required to memorize the names of all the towns and railway sidings between Penhold and Calgary. Like Jack, I got to play in the lumber piles. Occasionally, I also had tractor rides with my dad or grandfather. The business properties were my playground and I made the most of it.

I had other business adventures with just my dad, accompanying him on deliveries to farms in surrounding districts. A couple of those trips stand out. When I was about four years old, we headed east on a trip that took us up Horn Hill. The truck was fully loaded with lumber, so we were geared down and travelling very slowly. My father told me to

Me and my father on a Cockshutt 70 tractor, about 1940.

hang onto the steering wheel to keep it steady. He opened the door, jumped out, and let the truck move past him while he checked to see that the chains binding the load were still tight. Then, he ran alongside and hopped back in.

On another occasion, we were in a little Chev half-ton pulling a four-wheel trailer loaded with lumber. It wasn't a big load, but a bit much for the Chev when going up a hill. We had made it up over Horn Hill, a straight run, but further on, we had to make a sharp turn before approaching another hill. The Chev wasn't up to the challenge, and my father had to stop to take a run at the hill. My job was to find a big rock and place it behind one of the front wheels of the trailer. I found a rock. However, a four-year-old's idea of a "big rock" wasn't quite what my father had in mind. He selected an adult-sized big rock and moved the truck ahead slightly while I shoved the rock behind the wheel. Then I jumped into the cab, my father revved up the engine, and away we went up the hill.

During my childhood, my grandfather Tom was my "banker". Before I started school, and later after school was out, I would hang around the shop and lumberyard to play. At some point I began to hit him up for spending money to buy candy at Dave Field's pool hall. Dave counted the large old George V pennies as two cents. Despite this, I quickly learned that pennies didn't have much purchasing power and informed my grandfather, "I don't want any 'red' money". From then on, I got a nickel, or if I had a friend along and we were making swords from wood lath but needed to buy some nails, we could get 10 cents. Tom Suffern, the hardware man, would meticulously weigh them out for us, dribbling them into the metal bucket on the scale platform, watching the weight arm crawl across the price scale above.

For all of us kids – at least the boys, and sometimes the girls – the lumberyard was a great place to play. The lumber shed was excellent for hide-and-seek, as was the large machine shed with its myriad bits and pieces of equipment. But the open lumber storage yard south of the store was where we had the best fun. That was where the fence posts and rails were stored. Up until my very early teens, a group of friends and I would use the posts to construct log towers. We'd pile the six- or seven-foot posts on top of each other, log-house style without the locking corner notches, forming a hollow square. Every four feet or so, we'd make a partial floor by piling the posts tight together. This gave us a standing platform to continue upward with the construction. The round posts tended to roll, so we would brace the towers with sixteen-foot fence rails angled up against the sides. I think the tallest one we built was around ten feet high, which I know because I was usually the fellow on the top placing the posts and I recall that I could see the top of the roof on Dave Field's pool hall, which was over ten feet above ground level. That was the same evening that my parents drove by. The tower was brought down very quickly, and I don't believe we built any after that. Looking back, it's a wonder none of us was injured.

When I got a bit older, I also got to use some of the hand tools in the carpenter shop. The draw knife was my favourite. In the spring, when there were lots of puddles and water in the ditches, I would carve out the hull of a boat from a 2x4, make masts from small scraps, and sail the boat.

My apprenticeship begins

I started work in the family business during summer school holidays in 1950. I was just short of twelve years old. Stewart Brothers had a planer on the farm on the west side of the railway, set up on the high ground at the east edge of Fleming Slough. Rough lumber purchased during the winter and hauled in from the west country would be dry piled, waiting to be milled during the summer. The planer was belt-driven by one of the firm's tractors, usually a W-6 or W-9. The shavings were blown out into a pile, just like the straw from a threshing machine. At the end of the planing run, there would be a heap of shavings. I have no idea what became of them.

My job was just like Norman's had been at the Columbia River Lumber Company, albeit on a much smaller scale. I was tailing the planer alongside a couple of men. The boards or dimension lumber, depending what was being planed that day, would spew out from the planer without stop. We would pull the lumber off the runway and place it into various piles according to width and length. The steady, unending line of lumber coming out of the planer kept me on my toes. For this, I was paid the princely sum of $1 a day. By the end of the holidays, I had accumulated something like $35. My heart's desire was to own a set of binoculars. The Japanese had started to market an affordable quality binocular with German lens technology. I blew my roll on a set of Karl Wetzlar 7x50 binoculars.

The July-August summer holiday period was when the harvest machinery would come in, most of which required setting up. I would usually be part of the crew assembling hay rakes and swathers. Any open space of company property was requisitioned for this effort. I remember setting up Cockshutt swathers in the lumberyard south of the office. I think that's when I began to think the lumber end of the business was a lot more to my liking. It was cleaner, there was no grease or oil, no prying reluctant parts to line up for the bolt, and lumber didn't bash your fingers when a wrench slipped.

My cousin, Patsy Storm (Jack Stewart's daughter), began working at the Red Deer implement office in 1952, also at twelve years old. She recalls her experience:

From a larger family reunion photo, there I am with the fruits of my labour hanging around my neck: Karl Wetzlar 7x50 binoculars. My mother is in front of me.

> "Back in 1952, at age 12, I began changing a child's idle summer for work: initially, time at Dad's business—Stewart Brothers International Harvester business in Red Deer. I took on various small roles—taking deposits to the bank; picking up pastry treats at the bakery on the way back for our coffee time; running the Gestetner copy machine and folding the pamphlets that it cranked out. I learned to put new parts on the shelves in the parts department, and sometimes to do odd jobs in the basement where parts were cut and fitted to repair an implement or tractor.

> "The front part of the building was a showroom for four or more tractors displayed in front of large windows facing Gaetz Avenue.

> "One day at lunch time, it seemed everyone had some errand to run and I was the only person in the office area, eating my lunch, when a couple of bearded Hutterites came in the front door. I put my sandwich down; went over to meet

them, and was going to suggest they come back later, but actually asked them if I could help them (thinking they might have come for a machine part they had on order).

"NO; they wanted to look at the Farmall Cub on display. I took them over to it and suggested they climb up on the seat to see how it felt, while I went to get a pamphlet that I'd run off on the Gestetner. They asked some questions, and I was looking up the details to show them. It seemed like they had been there a good half hour when one of the staff returned and could take over to help them, and I went back behind the desk.

"A deal was closed then and there. Later I was joshed about being the one to sell them the tractor. Apparently, they said I was helpful. Earlier in the month, I had been hiking with my mother, and a large group of Skyline Trail Hikers in the mountains, with no other children to talk to. I felt at ease speaking to adults, which gave me confidence, so maybe that helped."[i]

One of my early jobs was building archrafters. Barns built in the 1940s and '50s still had hay lofts above the first floor. Their gambrel (hip) roofs were built with dimension lumber, or gothic arch roofs constructed with laminated 1x4 lumber. Glue-laminated arches also became available from manufacturers in Alberta and Manitoba. We built the gothic arch-rafters on the shop floor.

First, my father would lay out the curve of the arch shape with a string line and pencil. We'd nail short pieces of 2x6 stacked two-high to the shop floor along the curve of the arch, forming the "jig". We would then set 1x4 boards on edge in front of the jig blocks. Typically, there would be six rows of varying lengths set so none of the joints lined up with the row on either side. With pipe clamps, the 1x4 was drawn up against the blocking. Joints were tightened by hitting the boards at the peak end, forcing them tight. Once the clamps were fully tightened, we'd drive four-inch coated nails through the 1x4 from each side of the arch, eight inches apart. With the arch fully formed in the jig, we'd then drive a six-inch eavestrough spike through the archrafter from the inside every twelve inches and clinch it over on the outside face. The top of the arch was trimmed, as the bottom was already finished, the 1x4s having been driven down onto a bottom base block during the setup. Finally, we'd stack the arches, ready to load onto a delivery truck. A pair of 32' arches sold for $18, later raised to $19.

It was uncomfortable work, as all the nailing was done bent over ninety degrees. After a season of arch building I found I could hit a nail properly only if I was bent over! In a normal year we'd build arches for three or four barns in Penhold. A similar number were done in Red Deer.

---

i A reminiscence of Patsy Storm, written for this publication.

In Red Deer, a new 50'x100' shed, known as the "planer shed" was constructed a block south of the lumberyard. Its bowstring trusses were built on site using the TECO ring connector system. The building housed a planer, industrial table saw, and radial arm saw. There was room to store building supplies and jig space to build archrafters and truss rafters. The building was heated by large overhead hot-water radiators with fans to force the heat downward.

The new building's boiler, which was housed in a concrete block building alongside, came from the Stewart Brothers Case steam tractor, part of the old threshing rig.[35 (p.214)] The steamer had sat for close to two decades on a back lot in Penhold. It was called into service during the construction of the Penhold air base in the early 1940s then returned to the back lot. It was Norman's idea that the boiler would be just the thing to provide the heat source for the new building.

In 1951, an organizing committee was formed in Innisfail to head up a fundraising drive for the construction of a Memorial Arena, originally envisioned when the Memorial outdoor swimming pool was built in 1947. Stewart Brothers supplied the lumber to the tune of $15,520.20, as reported in the Innisfail Province. The two local yards, Atlas and Crown, could not compete on price and, importantly, could not extend the credit necessary until the organizing committee had raised the money. Payment was delayed due to changes in the design required to strengthen the trusses. A new builder assumed the oversight of the project and the Town of Innisfail had to provide $20,000.00 to see it to completion. By February of 1953, Stewart Brothers was paid, and Innisfail had its Memorial Arena.[34 (p.213)]

To get the boiler to Red Deer, the steamer had to be driven there and dismantled. Mechanics from the Red Deer implement shop brought down a W-6 tractor engine power plant with a pulley on the drive shaft, which was hung under the steamer with a belt connecting the pulley on the engine to the large fly wheel above. The gas engine powered the "hybrid" into Red Deer. I remember seeing the mechanics fixing the engine under the steamer, but I did not see the drive to Red Deer.

Stewart Brothers was still selling coal in the '50s, and my experience with it wasn't much different than what Jack Stewart related earlier in this book. We used the same coal shed and the coal arrived in forty-ton carloads. It was either stoker or lump coal. Stoker was easiest to shovel because it came in small lumps designed to be fed into the furnace from a bin via an auger. Lump coal was miserable, large, and difficult to handle with a shovel.

Unloading coal cars was a "contract job": $15 dollars split three ways. I would get two of my friends – the National Elevator agent's son Keith Johnston, and the B-A garage owner's son Dennis Lunt – and we'd tackle the car, which had been spotted at one of the coal-shed doors. We'd bridge the gap between the car and coal using the door boards from the grain cars. Once we'd cleared the doorway by shovel, we'd use a large wheeled scoop, running it into the coal pile, scooping up the coal, then rolling it over the makeshift bridge, to dump the coal into the shed. As the pile filling the coal bin grew, we would extend the runway by laying more door boards across the coal. It wasn't pleasant work, but we could usually empty a coal car in a day or day-and-a-half. I never regretted the conversion to oil, and later, to natural gas. Unloading coal is one of the jobs from the "good old days" I didn't miss.

Coal was also available from mines close by at Ardley or Nevis, east of Penhold, on the aptly named "Coal Trail". Occasionally, as a back haul, we would truck a load from there. It was not the high quality coal produced by the mines at Drumheller, however.

Harvest time and the Hume reel

The early 1950s were "wet" years. This posed a heart-rending challenge when farmers tried to harvest crops lodged in a mess on the ground. The fixed flat-batt reel on the swathers and combines couldn't lift the tangled grain up to the cutter knives. Reels with fixed metal tines attached to the batts couldn't catch most of the downed grain. More importantly, they were not designed to draw the raised grain back into the cutter knives on the header table.

The Hume Pick-Up-Reel, manufactured in Mendota, Illinois by the H. D. Hume Co., solved these problems. My dad spotted an ad for it and immediately realized its potential in Central Alberta. As it turned out, H. D. Hume Co. needed an agent in western Canada. Stewart Brothers had the financial and physical resources to handle the product and soon became the key dealer in Saskatchewan, Alberta, and eastern British Columbia starting in 1951.[36 (p.214-215)]

What made the Hume Reel unique and able to out-perform any tined or fingered reel was the use of an offsetting polygon on the outside end. It literally made the grain stand up to be cut and harvested. Instead of the reel moving in a circle, on the down stroke the action was broken as the reel batts moved horizontally, drawing and lifting the grain back through the cutter knives and onto the header deck.

The biggest challenge as a Hume Reel dealer, and especially as a distributor, was having the correct size of reels available for the numerous models of swathers in the marketplace. Being able to supply the correct drive-end for the machine it was attached to was even more important. While a few reels were ordered for specific customers, most were for an unknown customer and machine. Uniquely, Stewart Brothers had the solution in its Red Deer machine shop. Hume provided the engineered drawings for various drive ends and Bob Parker, the machinist, manufactured them as required. He often put in extra hours, as the drive-ends were frequently needed for last-minute sales.

The reels would be picked up at Mendota, Illinois using our own truck, or Ed Elkin's, a trucker and service station owner in the Edwell district east of Penhold. Most of a load of reels would be sold before the truck arrived back in Penhold. Graham would have the shop

In this photo, taken for an H. D. Hume publication, Simon Hussar can be seen rescuing his flattened crop on his Hume Reel-equipped Massey-Harris combine. Simon wept when he saw his crop being picked up. It had been flattened by an early snow and he had lost hope of harvesting it.

make up the correct drive-ends for the sales and have them ready for the customer when the reels arrived, the trip taking about five days one-way.

Things got hectic at harvest time. Besides being busy with its regular farm customers, Stewart Brothers had to take care of a dealer network for Hume reels across western Canada. Most of the reels were shipped to dealers via CPR Express. It was a great business for the local CPR agent, Elmo Johnson, who got a five-percent commission on express shipments, but Elmo earned that commission! The reels weighed in at around three-hundred pounds and were unwieldy with prickly tines. They had to be lifted up six feet and placed on top of the baggage cart end-frames so the express car workers could reach them. It wasn't unusual for a single shipment to consist of twenty or more reels.

The Hume reel line was a very profitable part of the machine business. No trades were involved, and Stewart Brothers kept the dealer discount on direct sales.[37] (p.215)

Much of the credit for the success of the Hume dealership contract can be traced straight to the decision to expand in the mid '30s. The business was key to the survival of many farmers during the war, keeping machines in adequate repair. Now again in the '50s, the machine shop allowed the company to serve customers in three provinces, saving downed crops and many farms as well.

In the late 1940s and early '50s, many customers, whose promissory notes from the 1930s had been written off, settled them with Norman once they had the money to do so. It was a tribute to the integrity of the customers and to the respect they had for Stewart Brothers in helping them survive the difficult times.

About this time, Norman sold the last threshing machine. It was an old wood model, well past its prime. He had promised to have it ready for the fall harvest, but the customer came in a bit prior to needing it and was disappointed when Norman told him it hadn't yet been brought up to the shop and made ready. But, Norman hadn't lost his touch. Redeeming the situation, he informed the fellow that because of the wet weather, he had thought it best to keep it protected in the shed on the farm. The customer couldn't thank Norman enough for his thoughtfulness, and the machine was readied that same week.

A curling rink for Penhold

Curling was a popular winter sport and my father was a keen curler. In 1952, one hundred and nine townsfolk and district farmers raised $3,250 by purchasing shares towards the construction of a two-sheet curling rink in Penhold. It was built on vacant town lots directly north of the W.I. Memorial Hall. The rink was complete with washrooms, a kitchenette, and spectator seating on both floors. Stewart Brothers supplied the material and built the gothic archrafters.

The roof of the building was finished with cedar shingles, which I helped install by laying them along a 1x6 guide board ahead of the fellow doing the nailing. Care had to be taken to make sure that the shingles were properly spaced and that the spaces between the shingles did not overlap those in the previous row. It was a fun job for a thirteen-year-old, even more so as we rose close to the peak and it became a bit of a race to see which crew would be first to the top.[38] (p.216)

Fire destroys Red Deer lumberyard store

The Red Deer building supply store burned down in 1954. The fire insurance policy was through the Western Retail Lumbermen's Association (WRLA), with the co-insurance being carried by an American company. The loss was sizeable enough that the president of the company came to check on it.

I was going to high-school in Red Deer and our bus drove past the site each day. On the weekend after the fire, I went in and helped the staff clear the show room area, salvaging any saleable items. People would drop by to look for a bargain. It was great fun. I would price an item and make the sale. The Pine Hill Hutterite Colony bought all the plywood – the fire had scorched only about an inch of the edges, leaving the bulk of the sheets unharmed.

I took these photos of Norman and Tom – both in their 70s – setting up a dump rake, likely the last one they sold. These implements were being replaced by side-delivery rakes that speedily put mown hay into a swath ready to bail.

After the site was cleared, a new retail building supply store was constructed. In preparing the ground for the foundation, it was discovered that the previous building had been built over the original bed of Piper Creek, which had been diverted and filled in. The new building was the most brightly lit show room in Red Deer at the time.[39 (p.217)]

Other than the new building supply store, the business district in Red Deer was largely unchanged. Our IHC agency was still located a block north, Jenkins Grocery had located on the north side of 48th Street across from the lumberyard, while Eaton's (later W. E.Lord) and the garage were still across the street from the implement store.

The only employee who worked exclusively in the Penhold building supply was the carpenter, Bill Hoyle. Everyone else was in the machine shop, repairing, setting-up, or making service calls. When a boxcar load of finish lumber, cedar shingles, and plywood, was spotted on the railway siding, the machine shop crew would unload the car onto a trailer, moving the plywood and finish into the lumber shed and piling the cedar shingles outside. The trailer we used was a tilting platform model purchased on February 28, 1947 for $334.64. It had a single axle with dual tires. Sturdily built, the tilt deck was lowered with a hand winch, relying on the load being weighted to the rear, to tilt when the catch was released. We usually pulled it around with a W-4 IHC or #30 Cockshutt tractor. Its main use was to bring lumber from the piles to the saw shop for cutting or planing. It also served for in-town and nearby country deliveries.

1955 was the fiftieth anniversary of the founding of the Province of Alberta. Celebrations in Red Deer took place during the Red Deer Exhibition. A parade was to pass by the implement office on 48th Street before turning north on to Gaetz Avenue. Charlie Parker, a district farmer and service station owner, was also an antique car collector and he entered his 1902 Oldsmobile in the parade, inviting Norman to accompany him. Charlie decked out in period driving costume, Norman wore a top hat, and the two of them did the parade circuit in style. I took a photo of them as they rounded the corner toward Stewart Brothers implement store. Norman is the dapper passenger on the right.[40 (p.217)]

Stewart Supplies (Penhold) Ltd.

The partners in the business were advised to incorporate to avoid an important tax issue. Unfortunately, the new company was unable to retain its historic identity, as "Stewart Brothers" had already been registered by another corporation. So, on July 9, 1958, Stewart

The Red Deer store, circa 1955. L to R: Tom, Jack, Norman Jr., and Norman. Note the IHC household appliances, such as the washing machines, in the window.

Brothers became the limited company, Stewart Supplies (Penhold) Ltd. The partnership forty-eighths now became share units of the same value, as shown in the Appendix.[41 (p.218)]

At Jack Stewart's request, the Red Deer implement office was closed in 1959. The building was leased to Sears Canada and managed by Lorie Forgy. Jack moved into the Penhold farm house and took over the farm operations, which then consisted of a section and a half of arable land at Penhold, plus a quarter-section of grazing land near Pine Lake. With Jack at the helm, the feed lot expanded and in 1961 a 40'x184'-10' bunker silo was constructed at the north end of the feed lot pens to handle six-hundred head of feeder cattle. In 1959, the Red Deer lumberyard was leased to Monarch Lumber Company for five years.

I became a draftsman by accident and grew to take great satisfaction in doing it. Our custom plan service became central to the success of the building supply business.

1959

Red Deer implement office leased to Sears Canada.

Jack Stewart moves to Penhold to manage the farm.

Company obtains Interprovincial Component Homes franchise.

1960

New machine shop built for Bob Parker.

Red Deer lumberyard leased to Monarch Lumber Company for five years.

Peggy "Smitty" Smith joins the firm in Penhold.

1961

IOOF building Post Office burns down. St draws plans for new building constructe same site.

Stewart draws plans for new Royal Ban that company leases to bank.

Bunker silo constructed on Penhold farn Norman's wife, Esther, dies.

Chapter 5:
Becoming a Lumberman

Despite the company's name change, I do get to claim that I worked for Stewart Brothers full-time, as I started in March 1958, fresh out of Lindsay Thurber High School with my grade twelve Senior Matriculation.

As the new guy, I got the short-end of the stick when it came to the more unpleasant tasks, such as having to pile lumber in the winter when the green spruce and pine dimension lumber and boards were brought in from the Murray Brothers mill at Caroline. The lumber piles were very disorganized, stacked in a random order of mixed sizes. I recall the piles of 2x6-16 were twelve-feet wide because the spacer lumber, every second layer, was 2x6-12. Filling an order needing twelve foot lengths was quite a chore.

As a member of the WRLA,[42 (p.219)] Stewart Supplies had access to an industry training course. I took it during my first winter at the business, receiving a diploma and lapel pin in May 1959. Although the course was out of date, I did learn helpful things. Among them, the proper way to stack lumber in piles that sloped, so water would drain off the rear. I put my new knowledge to work. In the fall, when the lumber stock was at its lowest, I started at one end and worked my way to the other end of the yard, rebuilding the five rows of supports along Fleming Avenue. My grandfather Tom helped me. We leveled eight-inch concrete building

1962

Stewart Brothers celebrates sixtieth anniversary.

Stewart leaves the business to gain experience working for Monarch Lumber.

IHC honours company for sixty years as dealers.

1963

Stewart returns to manage the Penhold building supply.

Supports for the old lumber piles.

blocks, four feet apart, in five rows. On top of the blocks we placed a three-ply 2x8 beam, on which we stacked 2x4s, starting from four-high to none, front to back, thereby giving a slope to the piles. We then piled the lumber in lengths from eight feet to twenty feet in four-foot wide piles. As the lumber was green and needed to dry, it was cross-lathed every second row, in line with the support beds below. The front edges of each row were stepped forward the width of a finger, so the rain water would drip off rather than run back into the pile – another trick I had learned in the course. It took over a year to complete the project, but it was well worth it. Loads were made up faster and stock was easier to keep track of.

The price book from the 1950s when I started work full time makes for interesting reading:

1) 12'x14' Granary on five skids, 2x6 T&G floor 2x6 stud 24" o c #3 Cedar Shingles built for $315, material only $245.

2) 1100 bus Circular Plywood Bin with painted roof, $210.

3) 12'x20'-8' Garage, 2x4 studs, 5/16 fir plywood walls, 125 lb shingles over shiplap, split double door, side door & sash pre-cut material $300, built $100 extra.

3) Barn rafters (gothic arch built in our shop) price per pair 32' span $19.

4) Fir sleigh and wagon parts (these are some of the items mentioned in the earlier piece about Bill Hoyle) 2 ½" clear fir runner $3.50.

5) Select fir bench for wide sleigh $3.50; select fir roller for wide sleigh $1.15; select fir bolsters for wide sleigh $1.50; oak sleigh and wagon pole $10.00; material for a fir wide bench sleigh $110.

6) Custom millwork on the planer or saw $3.00 per hour.

7) Sweep rake teeth: 2x6 ripped diagonal 8' $1.00, 9' $1.15. 2x8-8' ripped diagonal $1.35. (At the time, a fir 2x6-8 was 62 cents; ripped diagonally it produced two teeth which were sold for $1.00 each. The teeth were cut out of clear fir dimension, selected out of the regular stock. Good luck trying to do that now!)

8) Custom millwork on the planer or saw $3.00 per hour.

9) 1x6 spruce shiplap $88 per MBF. Selected stock milled into drop siding $125 MBF. (As I piled the shiplap delivered from the Murray Brothers mill in Caroline, I recall selecting 10,000 MBF out of 40,000 MBF of shiplap to mill into 1x6 drop siding. The better boards were set aside onto a trailer deck to be taken to the saw shop for planing into drop siding.)

I was no whiz at math. In grade six, I worked forty-two pages ahead in the math textbook so I wouldn't be behind when I got back to school from a once-in-a-lifetime family holiday with my parents to see Old Faithful. (See it I did, thirteen times on the same day!) When I got back, I was only six pages behind the class, and as I've always said, that's where my math stayed for the rest of my life: six pages behind.

Fortunately, we had *The Lumberman's Actuary* by John W. Barry, a well-used eighth edition. The book was a blessing when it came to doing estimates that had a multitude of lumber items to price. During the dreaded yearly inventory, the tables greatly sped up the calculations for quantities and pricing of lumber items.

As material prices rose, the books were issued in later editions with newer tables. I eventually acquired a twelfth edition in 1959. Shortly before I retired, I found a fifth edition printed in 1909 in an antique store in Nanton. It is a treasure, with all sorts of tables related to the amount of time needed for the various stages of construction, from form work to finishing, as well as giving a quick price for "cheap box, good house, better house, and well-done house." It's a time capsule that shows the changes in the industry since the time Norman and Tom started. [43 (p. 219)]

Pre-fab homes

The idea of component, also called pre-fab or pre-cut, homes wasn't new. In one form or another they had been in the Canadian marketplace from at least 1905, when Aladdin, a U.S.A.-based company selling a completely pre-cut house package, set up a branch office in Canada. Eaton's also sold a packaged home, but it was not pre-cut. We, like many others, put our take on the idea, and entered the market with a component home package, thanks to my father's foresight.

I think my father knew I wasn't interested in the machinery side of the business, and was probably relieved that I enjoyed the building supply side. In 1959, he became aware of the opportunity to get into component housing. He figured we had better get in the game or end up losing building material sales. By this time, there were at least a couple of pre-fab housing plants, including Muttart in Edmonton and Nelson Homes in Lloydminster.

The earliest example of a component home in what is now Canada, is when Sir Martin Frobisher (1535-1594) brought a knocked-down structure to house his crew during their search for gold around Frobisher Bay.

For $500, we obtained a franchise from Inter-Provincial Component Homes, an eastern-Canadian organization. That fee got us a manual, sales literature, and one set each of architect-sealed plans for ten different house designs. The iron components necessary for a four-foot-wall section jig were also supplied. A great deal of the material was useless, as it was from the parent organization in the U.S.A. and many of the items were not available in Canada. Still, there was enough information to get me started. The first thing I did was get the jig assembled onto a plywood base, as instructed in the diagram.[44 (p.220)]

Then the crap hit the fan.

Our first job was on the north boundary road for Gordon Dahl. It was built under the Veterans Land Act (VLA) on one of the large lots which Norman had surveyed in 1948. But, the architect-sealed plans were rejected by the local VLA office without explanation. My father and I talked it over and decided that it was likely because the plans were not sufficiently clear due to background shading. So, I taped the original plans to a large office window with drafting paper on top, traced them, and had them copied. Once again, the VLA rejected them and wouldn't tell us what the issue was. My father had a small wood-framed, linoleum-covered drafting board, a wood T-square, a 30/60 triangle, and a three-sided architect's scale ruler. We decided that I would draw new plans, using the originals as a guide for layout and measurements. Once drawn and blueprinted, we sent them off to

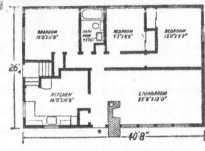
Among the material supplied by Inter-Provincial Homes was this ad for one of the home plans, called "The Lady Jane". We placed it in the Red Deer Advocate in 1959 or '60. The Lumber Research Council of America created the component system and we used their Lu-Re-Co designation as the name for our component home packages.

the VLA, and this time the plans were accepted. We were in business, and I was suddenly the fellow in Penhold who could draw plans.

The original panel system for Inter-Provincial Component Homes was based on an unusual framing system featuring a ninety-one-inch-high stud-framed wall capped with a vertical two-ply 2x6 continuous header, lag-screwed to the stud-frame wall below. The thinking was that the continuous header would allow doors and windows up to five feet wide to be placed anywhere along the exterior wall. However, this wasn't adequate for the large picture windows used in our area. I believe we used the system on only a couple of houses before switching to a standard 97$^{1}/_{8}$" wall using a 92$^{5}/_{8}$" stud.

By the numbers

When I started, lumber was still being sold by the "per thousand board foot" (MBF), the same unit measure as we purchased it from the wholesalers. The stock question from the customer was: "How much is your lumber per thousand?" This question would vary to state the dimension and species: spruce or fir, 2x4, 2x6 or whatever. It didn't matter if they wanted a couple of boards or a couple of hundred pieces. The answer told them whether you were competitive with the other yards.

Lumber in the price list in use when I started was broken down into the various lengths for each dimension, with a different MBF price. In the case of locally produced spruce the 8' and 16' lengths were higher priced because of their popularity, and the 20' because of their length. The difference was small, usually between $2 or $4 per thousand. Mountain fir and larch from the British Columbia interior had a greater cost spread; in the narrower widths, it was around $15. The interior mills also had 22' and 24' length stock available, with a length premium above the 16' stock as high as $35.

Lumber use was diminishing with the introduction of plywood for floor, wall, and roof sheathing, but we were still selling 1x6 boards for roof sheathing until the mid 60s, primarily because that's what the customer wanted.

An interesting item in the price list is Spruce Well Cribbing. It was used for shallow hand-dug wells. I remember cutting the bevel on some 2x6 for a two-foot diameter set of cribbing. The math for calculating the number of pieces and the bevel needed on the lumber is interesting:

> (Diameter x 22/7 equals circumference)
> (Divide circumference by 5 equals # of pieces)
> (No. of pieces times 2, divide into 360)
> (Will be degrees of saw cut)

Within the decade, plywood replaced lumber subflooring, wall, and roof sheathing. Shop-assembled window frames and sash were replaced by factory built windows and pre-hung exterior doors. Cedar shingles were no longer a stock item, replaced by more affordable asphalt shingles available in many colours. Affordable exotic wood mouldings, like Philippine Mahogany, coupled with changing consumer tastes, quickly replaced domestic fir and hemlock. Cedar siding was being replaced by products like pre-finished asbestos, which would in turn be overtaken by pre-finished hardboard and vinyl siding.

By the 1970s, we were selling our lumber based on a piece price, which took into account the difference in the dimension and length price. It also simplified the math when making up an invoice, by not having to calculate the board foot quantity, which varied with each dimension, and then the price. In 1980, it all became moot anyway, when inventory was computerized. The pricing was by the piece and the computer did the math. What a relief!

From a sales perspective, marketing a component home or any type of package solved the problem of customers "cherry-picking" each item in a quotation. A "cherry-picker" would bring in a list of materials for pricing. Once they had our prices for the individual items, they would look at the total. If it was competitive, they would go through the list checking the price of each item. Some would decide that our prices were fine but would dicker on the few that were priced a bit higher, which was fine. On a large job quote, they would go home to compare quotes from a variety of suppliers, return to each supplier and purchase only the cheapest items. The only way to combat this nuisance was to show a total without individual prices. Some didn't like it, but I would explain that we used our "total order" pricing, based on our supplying the whole bill of material. Packaged component homes solved this problem. The package price included a list of materials in enough quantities and with the degree of prefabrication defined, and a set of plans to go by.

> During the late '50s and early '60s, fly-by-night sales teams would come through an area. Some were legitimate and did provide the service offered, usually roofing or aluminum siding. Others would get a deposit to cover the cost of the material but never show up to do the installation, having made their money on the product. Our package houses had all the material we could provide included. That generally stopped them cold.

The only risk of package selling was that you had to be sure to include everything in quantities sufficient to complete the package. That meant careful and accurate estimating and a very detailed plan so there were no misunderstandings. I always held that the plan was the contract and strived to ensure that what our standard package included was what I specified on the plan, including the grade, dimension, and manufacturer when applicable. We had very few problems with this method.

The National Lumber Manufacturers Association in the U.S.A., in partnership with Lu-Re-Co, produced a manual dealing with componentization aimed at the house-building industry. It was based on using a four-inch minor module, which fit the standard 12", 16", 24", 32", and 48" construction modules in current use. I purchased the books and found them helpful when designing house plans. While the theory and practice stayed current, the examples using measurement information based on the dressed size of lumber was invalidated when the "green" size-based dimensions used in the manuals were nullified by new "dry" measures of kiln-dried lumber, which quickly became the norm a few years later. Still, they remain excellent publications on efficient use of materials.

The main pre-fab home suppliers, Muttart Homes, Nelson Homes, and Beaver, each had stock plan books. Except for the ten plans that were part of the package we had purchased from Inter-Provincial Homes, we had no catalogue of stock drawings. This didn't hold us back. Our customers would come in with plans from one of the newsstand plan books or from a competitor. I can count on the fingers of one hand the customers who had exactly the plan they wanted. More often, they would say, "This is just what I want…but…," and I would draw a new plan. We were the only building supply in the area that could do the plans in-house, and we offered the service as part of the price. Within a couple of years, I had drawn enough component home plans that I was able to put the floor plans through the blueprint machine and have a portfolio of them handy for customers to look at.

> The plan portfolio worked out well when David and Marcy Pope came in needing a home plan. I made note of their requirements and chose three plans drawn for previous customers, each containing the features and room placements they wanted. The following weekend, we visited each of the homes, viewing the sizes and layouts of the different rooms. With their choices made, I drew the new plans and supplied the materials.

Learning curves

Occasionally, I would have to make a delivery. I was the worst delivery person the business ever had to suffer. I had a bit of a thrill once when delivering a load of material, a mile east of Penhold on Highway 42. The road was loose gravel and quite soft in the spring. I had the throttle full open when the trailer started to fishtail, which in turn started the rear of the tractor to do the same. It was scary, but once I slowed down enough, I regained control. No harm done and I learned a valuable lesson.

I remember taking a load out to the west country. My father had given me directions, but I became completely lost. I was saved by a farmer who fortunately knew the neighbour I was trying to find. On another occasion, one Saturday morning, while transporting a knocked-down side-delivery rake to a farmer near Pine Lake, I fell asleep at the wheel, went in a ditch, up over an approach, back into the ditch, and through a barbed wire fence, side-swiping a spruce tree and peeling off the right fender of the IHC half-ton. I rousted a farmer out of bed to use his phone. The other half-ton came out, we switched the load, some of which was picked up out of the ditch. I continued on my way, and as I arrived late, stayed to help set-up the rake before returning to Penhold.

In 1960, Mrs. Peggy Smith joined the firm. We had become much busier with the expanding building supply now that we had started selling component homes. She was hired to help the bookkeeper and eventually became the Office Manager. "Smitty," as she was affectionately called, was a key employee, particularly for the assistance she provided me, keeping track of the contract jobs and construction crews. A priceless asset, she ran the office in a way you didn't realize it was being managed. She worked with us for eighteen years until her retirement in 1978, when the original store was sold. It surprised no one who knew her that she was named Citizen of the Year in 1980.[45 (p.221)]

An unintended benefit of having Smitty join the staff was the necessity to provide a toilet. My father had me draw a plan for a simple, flat-roofed "His and Her" washroom that was built on the north side of the store. Until that time, those of us who could would walk home to use the bathroom, usually at lunch time. Or, we would relieve ourselves between the lumber shed and saw shop!

Also in 1960, the world leaders were in New York at the United Nations. I decided to see the show and flew down. The highlight was sitting on the main delegates' floor in the

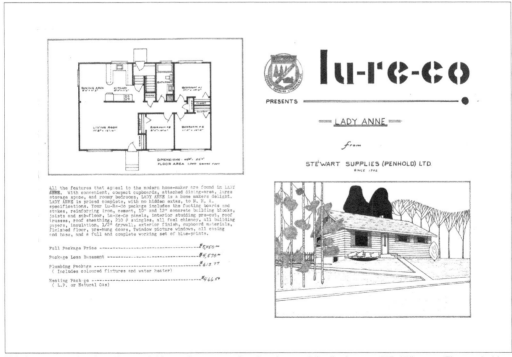

This is an example of my first vanishing-point perspective drawings, originally done on 11"x17" paper. The symbol is a stamp I had made of Lu-Re-Co's emblem, surrounded by our company name.

General Assembly thirty feet behind Nikita Khrushchev as he banged the desk with his two fists. More importantly for my work, I found a small $2.50 book at a newsstand titled, "Mechanical Drafting Self Taught". The chapter that intrigued me most was on vanishing-point perspective. I put the lessons to work. By learning to do photograph-like perspective drawings, I was able to develop our first, albeit amateurish, plan book.

I drew eight plans in this fashion and had the *Red Deer Advocate* print a quantity of brochures. Compared with what our competitors were doing it was rudimentary, but it put us in the game. Already, we were the only firm including concrete blocks for the basement, and I thought

> I picked up useful insights about construction while working with customers. In one case, two brothers were helping a third build his Lu-Re-Co home package. They were having problems squaring the floor framing. They would take diagonal measurements with a hundred-foot steel tape, readjust the framing with a few taps of a maul, and check the result. The measurement would be off again. They finally realized it was a hot day and they were stretching the tape by pulling it too tight.

it would be a good idea to include prices for the heating and plumbing materials. Simpson-Sears was leasing our former implement office in Red Deer and they sold plumbing and heating packages. I asked if they would be interested in supplying packages for our component homes. They thought it was a great idea. As it turned out, our customers preferred that a local trade of their choice supply and do the installation.

Eventually, we stopped pre-fabricating exterior walls. Our competitors were also building interior walls, which was something we were not able to do, mostly because I didn't have the smarts to figure them out. Also, most of our sales went hand-in-hand with carpenters we dealt with and who would build the homes. They were ambivalent about pre-fabricated exterior walls, preferring to build them onsite to get a better fit with the floor. The roof trusses and stairs we continued to supply pre-built.

I was a self-taught draftsman and relied on the help of others to develop my skills. One of our crews was Bill Kirkham of Innisfail and Carl Larsen of Sylvan Lake. They were a great help to me, educating me to leave room for interior-wall finish and trim moulding when placing doors and windows near interior partitions. They also taught me how to calculate the correct headroom for stairs. The other crew I relied on comprised three retired farmers: John Johannson, Louis Kathol, and Steve Raleigh. Customers also often brought plans drawn by others for material quotations, and anytime I saw a better way to present information on someone else's plan, I would adapt it and improve my own.

Plans for a new Royal Bank of Canada building were another of my efforts. The bank wanted the Stewart Supplies account, and in much secrecy, the manager came to see Norman and

I drew these plans for a new Penhold Post Office in 1961, which replaced one destroyed by fire. The floorplans show details of the construction. The building still exists. It was moved and used as a club house in Newton Park, then later sold and moved to 1412 Lucina Street, where it sits today as a small dwelling shown here. A new, larger Post Office supplied by Stewart Supplies replaced it in 1985, the plans for which were drawn and sealed by a registered professional engineer.

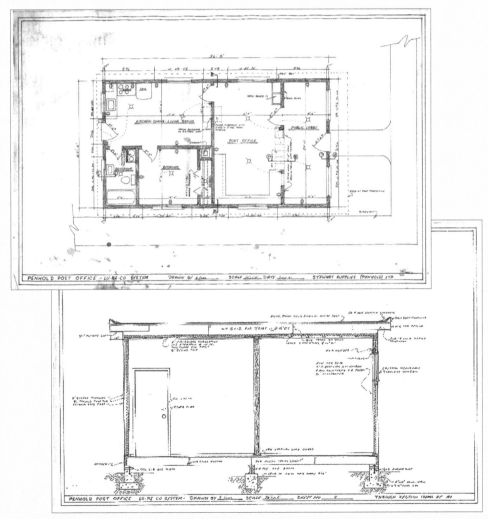

my father about switching from the Canadian Imperial Bank of Commerce to the Royal. There was already a Bank of Montreal at the air base two miles north, and the Royal wanted to get into Penhold ahead of any other. We struck a deal: we'd supply the bank with a building that they would lease for five years. In return, Stewart Supplies switched its account to the Royal.

Spreading my wings

In retrospect, I may have been feeling restless in my twenties. I had never been exposed to life outside of my family and the all-consuming family business. Working in a family business is a wonderful thing, but I didn't know where I stood in the industry or among my peers. I was also protected from the more difficult parts of the business, like collecting delinquent accounts. I reasoned that I could gain the knowledge I needed by spending a few years working for someone else. Our construction season largely came to a stop during the winter months. Crown Zellerbach, the wholesale division of the Crown Lumber yards, was headquartered in the U.S.A. If I could get a job with them in California, where there was no winter slow down, I would be able to gain the experience I needed more quickly. So, I obtained a Green Card and attended a Lu-Re-Co convention in San Francisco, where I had arranged an interview with a Crown Zellerbach representative. Unfortunately, he informed me that they did not have retail outlets in the U.S.A., only in Canada. So much for that idea.

I returned to Canada and talked with the Monarch Lumber manager in Red Deer, Lorne Derksen. He was all for hiring me and checked with his Winnipeg head office. They had reservations about hiring a potential competitor but did so anyway. In 1962, I signed a five-year non-compete agreement and spent a month at the Red Deer yard while they figured out what to do with me. My first lesson occurred when "my" loyal customers came through the door to shop at Monarch! I don't know which of us was more surprised, but I learned that even "loyal" customers shop around.

Soon, I was sent to Grande Prairie in the spring, as Assistant Manager at Monarch's new yard there. Five months later, I transferred to Regina, again as Assistant Manager, and stayed for fourteen months. The first clue I had that things were different in Saskatchewan was when I went into the main branch of Royal Bank to set up my account. Ten savings tellers were lined up on one side (more than double what you'd see in Alberta), and three current account tellers were opposite. In Saskatchewan, you saved for rainy days because most of the time it was dry with poor crop conditions. Another difference, which I learned when making my first sale, was that there was a five percent provincial sales tax, which I forgot to add to the invoice.

Being a city yard, the customer mix was also somewhat different than I was used to. In the winter, we ran basement-development classes, which I enjoyed giving. Regina had an interesting soil condition. The city sits on gumbo, which expands with excess moisture, lifting the basement floors. Any interior basement construction required the framed walls to be built an inch short and fastened at the top to the floor joists with a four-inch spike. This allowed the walls to "float" up and down. A large moulding fastened around the perimeter of the ceiling hid the gap at the top of the wall.

I was used to grain-bin season starting in late June, but in Saskatchewan the inquiries didn't start until around the first of July. Orders didn't start until a week or two before harvest, and then, with the crop virtually guaranteed, they flowed in and there was no turning off the tap. I was there during a one-year-in-twenty bumper crop. We had crews out on farms building plywood bins and even brought a truckload of steel bins back from Alberta to meet the demand. It was a wonderful time to be a salesman.

I would have liked to stay longer, but Monarch was purchased by Revelstoke, an Alberta-based company with yards in Alberta and Saskatchewan. I had no desire to work for Revelstoke and returned to Penhold in mid-September of 1963.

The last photo of Norman (eighty-nine) and Tom (eighty-four) together, on a once-in-a-lifetime vacation to Jamaica in 1962.

1962

Business celebrates its sixtieth anniversary.

IHC awards five long-service pins, to Norman, Tom, Jack, Norman Jr., and Graham.

1963

Penhold farm expands with new grain elevator and feed lot expansion.

Stewart rejoins business in Penhold.

Sale of first four-way leveling IHC combine in Canada.

1964

Stewart becomes a shareholder with shares from his grandfather, Tom.

Norman Stewart Jr. constructs new home on quarter section of company land south of Penhold.

Company purchases first fork lift, a Ross.

Chapter 6:
Sixty Years in Business

In 1962, IHC marked the sixtieth anniversary of the founding of Stewart Brothers by sending executives from its Alberta office to Penhold. They awarded the five active shareholders – Norman, Tom, Jack, Norman Jr., and Graham – long-service pins. Three of these were gold with a ruby dotting the I, presented to Norman, Tom, and Jack. It was the first time IHC had awarded three 30-year pins at one dealership. A fourth pin was gold, presented to Norman Jr. The fifth pin was silver, presented to Graham.

The dealer years-of-service pins presented by International Harvester Company.

Later that same year, Stewart Supplies was honoured in the Christmas issue of *The Harvester* with an article about the company, reproduced in the Appendix.[46 (p.222-225)]

Aside from brief breaks at the summer cabin in Sylvan Lake and a trip to Florida in the 1920s as Laura convalesced after a cancer operation, neither Norman nor Tom took holidays. So, it was quite an event when, in 1965, Laura organized a trip to Jamaica for Tom, herself, her Ontario relatives, Norman, and his daughter, Irene. Norman died of heart failure later that year.

1965	1966	1967	1968
Entry into construction business with first building supply sales flyer.	Trigger year for mass-introduction of archrafter shed buildings in the area.	IHC contract surrendered after sixty-five years.	Auction sale to clear used machinery inventory.
Svend and Patsy storm move from Toronto to Penhold and join Jack on the farm.	New 48'x102' archrafter building materials warehouse constructed.	New retail store and office for building supply added to front of new archrafter warehouse.	
Tom, Norman, Laura's Ontario relatives, and Norman's daughter, Irene vacation in Jamaica.	Construction of farm barns, archrafter sheds, and houses takes off.		
Norman Stewart dies of heart failure.			

Deliverance

Unloading anhydrous ammonia fertilizer onto a tank truck for delivery to customers, 1965.

Stewart Supplies had been a major dealer for Elephant Brand Fertilizer since the 1930s. When Jack Stewart's son, Michael, finished his degree in Agriculture, he joined his dad on the farm. He also helped with fertilizer sales by doing soil analysis. This involved testing the soil from the fields to determine which of the fertilizers would provide the best results. We dealers made equipment available to spread fertilizer pellets and inject liquid anhydrous ammonia.

My involvement with the fertilizer side of the business was limited to unloading the boxcars at our fertilizer and cement shed on the CPR siding. The shed was raised so the floor was level with the floor of the boxcar. We used a metal plate to bridge the gap. We'd stack the eighty-pound bags of fertilizer seven high on a wheeled cart, roll it into the warehouse, and tip it against the previous stack. The fertilizer was brought in during the winter and we would have around three hundred tons in stock, much of it pre-sold and pre-paid, ready for the spring rush. Anhydrous ammonia fertilizer, a nitrogen-rich product shipped under pressure in tank cars, was of course handled differently. It would be off-loaded onto a tank-equipped delivery truck and taken to the farm.

Bagged cement from the Canada Cement plant at Exshaw, west of Calgary, was handled the same way as the bagged fertilizer. We brought it in by rail rather than truck because the CPR paid a five-cent-per-bag subsidy to encourage dealers to get their cement that way. We reverted to truck deliveries after we ceased to handle fertilizer. By then we had also purchased a forklift, which solved the handling issue, the cement being on pallets.

Prior to the construction of the fertilizer and cement shed on the CPR spur, we stored the bagged cement in an old garage. I remember unloading a four-hundred-bag, forty-foot truckload of cement by hand, just me and the truck driver. The driver backed the trailer as close to the door as possible and handed the bags down to me one at a time. At first, I was walking with an eighty-pound bag about thirty feet to the back of the garage and stacking it eight high. As the truck emptied, the driver had to carry the bags an increasing distance from the front of the trailer, while I had a lesser distance to travel. It was punishing work and the necessity of having a forklift was finally recognized.

We purchased our first forklift in 1964. It was a rough-looking Ross that had apparently been with the American army in Korea, somehow ending up in Canada. It had a peculiar carburetor that was a constant source of aggravation. Fortunately, Percy Lunt, the local B-A service station owner, had the gift to keep the thing going. It served us well until 1968, when we purchased our first new Hyster. Once we had a forklift, the lumber beds had to be removed, and from that time forward, all storage was done in lumber lifts stacked in the opposite direction to the hand-piled stacks.

The forklift created an unanticipated challenge. The storage yard had previously been the location of a row of buildings destroyed by fires, the last in 1921. Driving the back-end-heavy forklift over this property ensured that we found every original out-house hole! We would pull the forklift out with a W-9 tractor, fill the hole with gravel, and carry on. After surrendering the IHC contract, we rebuilt the front lot along Highway 2A in 1968, removing the black soil and building it up with clay and graveling the surface. After that, there were no more difficulties with hidden holes. Eileen and I later purchased the original lumberyard storage property along Fleming Avenue and built two fourplex rental units. Three of the lots at the north end along Lucina Street were sold to a young couple for their new grocery store.

A Danish perspective

During the 1960s, with Jack in charge of the farm, several additions were made to its infrastructure. The feed lot was enlarged to eight pens, enabling it to accommodate six-hundred head of cattle, with each pen sharing a waterer. A 40'x180' bunker silo with concrete floor was constructed, followed by a traditionally designed wood-crib, metal-clad grain elevator with a thirty-thousand-bushel capacity. It featured a scale and eight-inch horizontal auger going from the pit under the dumping grates over to the vertical cup elevator "leg" to the

I had the elevator on the farm torn down in the '80s. Some local fellows asked to salvage the crib lumber, which consisted of oversized 2x4 and 2x6 dimension. They were a bit embarrassed because I was in the business of selling lumber, not giving it away. But I was happy to have them clean up the mess and to see the material used.

distribution head. From there, the grain would be distributed to the eight large storage bins. The arrangement worked well until the combine harvesters got so big and efficient that the eight-inch auger and slow leg couldn't handle the input fast enough.[47] (p.226-227)

Jack's daughter, Patsy, had married a Dane named Svend Storm. They were living in Toronto where Svend worked with a landscape gardening firm, and in June 1965 they came out to Alberta. This is Svend's recollection of their years in the business:

"We arrived in Penhold in early June of 1965 and attended the dedication of a stained-glass window in the Anglican church in Penhold, donated by Norman Stewart (Pat's grandad) in commemoration of Pat's grandmother, who had passed on a few years earlier. On that Sunday we were invited in for a cup of coffee at the Norman Stewart house, next to the lumberyard and store, where I met my father-in-law, Jack Stewart and his sister, Irene. I had a good talk with them, and especially with Pat's grandad, about the country around Penhold and its people, and I came away with a good feeling about him and the whole family. They were good, honest folks. That Sunday proved to be his last, as he died of heart failure a few days later. So, the next Sunday, we went to his funeral.

> The winter of 1968 had a forty-day spell of below-freezing temperatures, which saw farm-hand Svend on his knees at the waterers, pouring boiling hot water slowly down rags wrapped around the standpipe while thirsty cattle sniffed his back.

"The next day, Monday, we were shown the farm. It had been a late spring and people were still seeding. Pat's grandfather drove us around and my father-in-law was driving a doubled-up – that is – on two WD-9 International tractors driven from the rear tractor, pulling 20 feet of cultivator. We also met Phil Tweten who was driving an IH 660 tractor pulling 24 feet of seed drills. To me, coming from farming on several different farms in Denmark and with an education in farming, that was pretty impressive, size-wise. I discovered later that, with the short growing season here, what you can grow is limited and it takes more land to do it. Here, you might get 100 frost-free days and nights; in Denmark it was more like double that.

"The next week I went to Taber and got a job hoeing/thinning sugar beet; this was something I was used to from Denmark. I went into a hardware store and asked if they had one of the sharp Danish hoes with blades of saw-blade steel, and sure enough, he did, and I paid $7.50 for that hoe. But he said he wasn't really making any money on it because he had to buy them in lots of 25 to make it come out even for him, as only Danes asked for them. Then he asked me if I had a job yet. Well, no, I was hoping he could tell me if he knew of anybody who could use a guy who knew one end of a hoe from the other.

"Well, he sure did, and a few minutes later I was on my way out of town. About 12 miles North-East of there I met the family of Norman Hall. Norman said he could sure use me, alright. He had several native families doing the thinning, about 20 adults and a lot of kids. This was my first experience with indigenous people. We all did piece-work, earning so much an acre. I glanced a bit at what they had thinned and asked Norman if I could have my "own" beets for the second time through, and that was fine with him. The result was that, in one day towards the end of my stay there, I made $105. Sure, it took me 15 hours to do it, but still … that was a lot of money in those days. You could easily buy a good meal with dessert and coffee for $3.00, even though coffee had just gone up 100% from a nickel to a dime.

"One day, Hall came walking across some of 'my' rows as I was thinning, and he said to me, 'I think you're doing almost as many acres as the others, and the job you're doing is better, to boot. Well, that really warmed a lonely soul because there were over twenty of them and just one of me."

In June, at the end of beet-thinning season, Svend returned to Penhold and joined his father-in-law on the Stewart Supplies farm. He continues with his story:

"Pat and I rented a house about a block from the farmstead in Penhold and my first job there was ploughing a 30-acre field of sod which Jack had started on. We used the two WD-9s and a four-bottom plow. Those tractors had the front axels taken off and were hooked up in line to each other with hydraulic steering. Steering was easy enough, but the clutches were hooked up to each other too, and you really had to use all your leg power to step that pedal down. After a day in the field, your knee couldn't take much more. Anyway, I sure enjoyed the feeling of all that power. This tractor also never got stuck, because if one set of driving wheels was in soft ground the other was on dry land because of the distance between the axles.

"We were feeding around 800 cattle a year, heifers, steers, and older cows, mainly on grass-silage and grain. The feedlot was on the west side of the railroad running

Svend's story reminds me of another. My first matrimonial home was in our fourplex on Fleming Avenue, directly across the railway from the feedlot. Apparently, our neighbours – twenty-eight of them – signed a petition requesting that the smelly feed lot be shut down and presented it to the Village Council. Council reminded them the farm was there before their houses were built, and no action was taken. We were unaware of any of this until some time later when Cy Little told me about what had taken place. I told him that we lived right across from the feedlot and I didn't notice any smell. Cy's response was classic: "You don't smell your own money."

through town, and I'm sure the people living in town would rather not have had it there, as in the warmer seasons of the year it could be quite aromatic.

"Some of the cattle were taken as payment for lumber or implements and after a while I got to go and buy these cattle from farmers who owed money to the firm. I soon cottoned on to the fact that farmers would rather sell them with an "overnight stand" (meaning without feed and water overnight before getting weighed in the morning) rather than a 2% shrink on the recorded weight. That's because, with an overnight stand, they would sometimes loose up to around 4% and the farmer would be none the wiser. I later checked up on this and found it to be true. Later, I got to go to auction marts to buy cattle in the slow season. This had been Phil's job to do but, if memory serves, he was 71 years of age when I arrived, and would have liked to slow down a bit by then. After a couple of years, he bought a house in Red Deer and did just that."

Pat and Svend really wanted a place of their own. That opportunity arose when Pat's father, Jack, was able to purchase a quarter-section farm from the business near Withrow in the west country, which the business held a mortgage on. Jack paid off the mortgage before selling the land to Pat and Svend. It illustrates how the business dealt fairly with those who were unable to meet their obligations. The back-taxes and unpaid interest on the mortgage were paid, and an additional $7,354.54 added to compensate for the increased value of the property over the six-year life of the mortgage.

Svend and Patsy Storm (née Stewart), in their retirement years.

Archrafter bonanza

By the time of Norman's death in June 1965, I was managing the Penhold building supply, selling building packages, estimating and quoting jobs, and drawing plans. Farmers were doing well and the Farm Credit Corporation was making low-cost loans available for the purchase of land, farm equipment, and buildings. The archrafter shed had been on the market for some time, but for whatever reason, 1966 was a trigger year for its mass introduction.

Low-cost money was available; barley, the principal crop, was $2.50 a bushel; and labour was $2.50 an hour. There was a pent-up demand for new buildings, machine and grain storage, and animal shelter. The archrafter was the least expensive structure to meet all those needs.

Erecting the archrafters for Stewart Supplies' 48'x102' warehouse. George Leusink is standing on the scaffolding – can you spot his brother, Benny, on the ground?

I decided to run an eight-page flyer for insertion in the *Ad-Viser*, a local print mail-out.[48] (p.228) Home plans drawn with perspective views and matching floorplans filled three of the pages. The remaining five pages featured ads for residential fencing, garages, pole-framed buildings, rigid-frame buildings, archrafter sheds, cattle feeders, grain bins, summer cabins, and truss rafters.

That flyer got us into the construction business, first with archrafter buildings, then barns and houses. Murray Pointer wanted an archrafter for his farm east of Innisfail. He'd already selected the carpenters and ordered a 32'x48' package. During construction, I drove out to see how things were going and met the carpenters, George and Benny Leusink, who farmed near Olds. I was particularly impressed with their work ethic and we agreed they'd do more buildings for us.

The second archrafter building we did was for Alvin Hoffos, in the Knee Hill district. George and Benny were again the carpenters. Alvin told me that when they arrived early in the morning, he would hear the car doors slam closed and immediately the hammers would start pounding. When the two brothers went to work, they really worked.

We weren't the only ones getting in on the archrafter bonanza. Wilson Archrafter, located in Calgary, with crews in Alberta and Saskatchewan, was the main competitor.

The United Farmers of Alberta (UFA) operated across the province, and the line yards – Beaver, Revelstoke, Crown and local Co-Ops – were all vying for a piece of the action. Wilson used an upgraded arch designed for 32" o.c. spacing, which was very difficult to compete against using the 24" o.c. arch from our supplier. I developed a unique archrafter design that reduced material costs without sacrificing structural stability of large buildings. At the time, the two principal arch manufacturers, Western Archrib in Edmonton, and Dring in Manitoba, offered 24" o.c and 48" o.c. options. Wilson Archrib in Calgary, with its unique 32" o.c. arch, had a competitive edge against the standard 24" o.c. rafter. My solution incorporated 48" o.c. arches with 2x4 blocking, which we pre-cut in the shop from economy grade studs, placed between the rafters at 24" o.c. from the base to peak. The construction crews agreed to this system, as it took no extra time to build, and with lower material costs, we were competitive, and customers were happy!

An unforeseen advantage to that design revealed itself about twenty years later when the shingles needed replacing. Metal roofing was by then the material of choice and the 2x4 cut-in purlins were ideal for holding the screws to fasten the metal, with the plywood sheathing providing solid backing.

By 1966, we had grown significantly and needed to expand our storage and office areas. We were very busy supplying and constructing archrafter buildings. Handling material with a forklift demanded a proper storage shed for drywall, plywood, and finish material. The old bin-storage lumber shed had outlived its usefulness. An archrafter fit the bill! Not only did it allow us to keep our plywood and drywall inside, but it also provided an all-season fabrication facility for grain bins, cattle feeders, and fertilizer bins. None of our competitors had that ability. The new 48'x102' building used barn arches to get the maximum wall height possible and were the largest that our supplier, Dring, could build.[49] (p.229)

It was my custom to check job sites on weekends. If I travelled east on Saturday, I would go west on Sunday or vice-versa. Customers welcomed the visits and I could manage any issues before they became a major problem. I maintained this practice

In 1967, we supplied an archrafter for Charles Warke, who farmed in the Pine Lake area. Fifty years earlier, he and a neighbour had loaded up a wagon with four steers and driven it to Penhold, where they corralled the steers to have them shipped by rail. He said the steers spent more time out of the wagon than in it! Warke then caught the train from Penhold to Red Deer to visit his mother in the hospital and returned the next morning to pick up supplies from Stewart Brothers before heading back home. Now, fifty years later, he made the trip again under somewhat different conditions. He and his wife came in a car on the paved highway, stopped to see me about the archrafter, drove into Red Deer for lunch and shopping, and were home later the same afternoon.

throughout the following decades. My children fondly remember these road trips just as I remember the working drives I took with my father and grandfather.

With business booming in archrafters and package-home sales, we were hopping. I was run off my feet with the volume of construction, the drawing of plans, and keeping up with ordering stock. Of the company's three parts – building supply, machinery, and farm – the building supply portion was becoming the primary profit generator.

Building supply expansion

In the fall of 1966, after talking things over with Jack and Norman Jr., my father informed IHC that Stewart Supplies would surrender its IHC contract at the end of the next business year. After sixty-five years, it was the longest-held IHC dealer contract on the North American continent.

There was a general feeling of relief about the decision. Norman Sr. was gone, two small strokes had put Tom into full retirement, Norman Jr. wanted to strike out on his own, Jack

> Many of the farm homes were completed in the late fall, in time for a Christmas move-in. The word would go out that New Year's celebrations would be in the new home. Within a couple of years, the late-built farm homes didn't get finished until January, as the owners didn't appreciate the wear and tear of a New Year's party.

was content on the farm, and IHC had a dealer in Red Deer that couldn't reach its full potential while Stewart Supplies was still in the game. For my father, it was a chance to cut back on work and enjoy his fishing. He continued to keep in touch by selling the short-line equipment for a few more years. Although it would take some time to wind down the machinery end of the business as far as book-work and collections were concerned, the day-to-day pressures were off.

The used equipment, along with some odds and ends of building supplies, were auctioned off.[50] [(p.229)] My grandfather attended the auction and enjoyed visiting with many of the customers who remembered him.

It is said that what you focus on expands. By the end of the 1966 business year, we had sold and built over thirty archrafter buildings, many Confederation-series component homes, hog barns, cattle feeders, grain bins, and truss rafters. The increasing sale of building materials necessitated a purpose-built retail store and office. It was time to complete the transition to an efficient building supply facility. When the new archrafter warehouse was built, we knew we would no longer be handling a major line of farm equipment and had made provision for the addition of a store dedicated to builders' hardware and supplies at the front.

We obtained a custom retail store plan from MacMillan-Bloedel, a major wholesale supplier of building materials that made the service available to its dealers. The new store was designed

Three views of the 1967 retail building supply store: during construction, the interior, and the finished exterior. In the exterior photo, Stewart (left) and Larry Miller (right) are seen with a selection of the grain bins for sale.

with a box-beam roof system that created unobstructed floor area for the showroom and an airy interior under a sloped ceiling. The showroom included a sales counter with a glass-front showcase. My office was in a raised area with room for a drafting board and my second man, Allan Johannson, and later Larry Miller. We moved in late fall of 1967.

Finally, I was out of the saw shop, meaning no more sawdust or paint overspray from the attached combine shop on my plans! I updated my drafting board from a parallel-edge to a drafting arm, with the board mounted on an adjustable metal stand. It sped up the drawing process and I eventually bought a second one for my home so I wouldn't have to return to the store to work in the evenings.

We hosted a Penhold Bonspiel Curling Club dance in the late winter of 1968. We moved the stock outside, swept the floor, and set up a couple of two-hundred-fifty-thousand BTU heaters outside the north end, with tubes running heat into the building. It was a great way to show off our new digs and have some fun, too.[51] (p.230)

Bin-building season

Bin-building season began around the end of June when, with long evening light and mild weather, we wouldn't have to tie up the warehouse.[52] (p.230) By late September we would move into the warehouse, building both 1,300-bus. and 2,500-bus. bins in runs of five. We would organize into crews of two or three and prepare the piece parts in advance: build a stack of five floors, cut roof sheets, construct ladders, and cut the

The bins had 1-1/4" steel banding. One year, we fell heir to a bunch of it when carloads of pipe were delivered to Penhold by rail for unloading. I went over and inquired if I could have the banding and was told it would cost a bottle of whiskey, which I willingly paid. It was a great bargain!

Four bins Stewart Supplies constructed for a customer.

bin clean-out parts. The rigid wall-rafter frames for the 2,500-bus. bins would be built in a jig on the saw shop floor next door, while the rafters for the smaller 1,300-bus. bins were precut. The pre-drilled twenty-four-inch steel centre ring for the roof was pre-ordered and in stock. With the parts ready, we'd pull a floor into the warehouse and start building. This process was repeated over and over until the end of the season, which could be as late as the end of November. One weekend, Mike French, a school teacher from Innisfail, and I built five 1300-bus. bins ourselves using this method. Debbie and Lynn Bouteiller did much of the roof tarring while perched on a pallet raised up with a forklift. It was a messy job. Lynn also worked with Russ Morton building hopper-bottom fertilizer bins.

Grain bins and other pre-built structures were great for "cleaning house", as we could use crooked and twisted planks for the floor. This caused no structural issues, and we got the material to lay flat by using long spikes to fasten it to the skids. The plywood overlay took care of the cracks.[53 (p.231)]

We constructed our 2,500-bus. bins differently from the competition, saving on time and material. I was a fan of rigid-frame construction, and we would componentize the wall stud and rafter into one member by fastening them together with a plywood gusset. We could set up the wall and pre-built roof in a matter of minutes. Setting the frames at 30.5" rather than 24" centres reduced materials. The plywood on the walls could take the strain, and the steel banding held the walls together anyway. We never lost a bin to a wall blowout.[54 (p.232)]

In 1970, the Federal Government rebated the manufacturer's tax on materials used in the construction of grain storage. All the yards in the area had a 2,500-bus. bin, but we promoted ours with a tax-back rebate and a weather-resistant tarred roof. I kept track of customers we sold the bins to and at the end of the season made up a list of the materials used and applied to Revenue Canada for the tax rebate. We had special cheques printed on orange paper, larger than normal, and mailed them out, keeping our promise to rebate the tax and doing some good customer relations along the way.[55 (p.233)]

During the winter of 1966-'67, Casey den Boer arrived in the area from the Netherlands.[56 (p.233)] He occupied an acreage a mile north of Penhold. Casey wanted to raise hogs, and like so many before him, he came to us in need of material and credit. Casey had construction experience and could pay off the material bill by working in the building supply. So, between Casey selling hogs and working off the debt, we were paid, and he prospered. It was the beginning of a thirty-five-year working relationship. Casey built plywood gusset and later air-nailer-fastened metal gusset plate trusses, grain bins, cattle feeders, bulk bins, and just about anything else I would dream up, or that a customer required. We were a great team, feeding off each other's ideas.

One project I'll always remember was using a galvanized steel metal corner cover to reinforce the join of the 2x10 trough face to the end wall. The galvanized metal was bright and shiny. Casey remarked, "People are like crows, they like shiny things." I was fortunate to have him available, as anything Casey built lasted.

Home construction

Red Deer County was having trouble attracting teachers to its schools in Spruceview and Delburne, a couple of smaller villages without available housing. So, in the spring of 1967, the county decided to construct four teacherages: two houses in each village. The County Councillor for Spruceview asked one of our construction crewmen, John Johannson, if he was interested. John got a hold of me and we decided to have a go at it.

There was no specific plan to bid on, just a request for proposals for a two-bedroom dwelling, with or without a full basement. I came up with a plan, took off the material bill, and contacted subtrades to price the foundation, excavation and backfill, plumbing, heating, electrical, painting, and floor coverings, while John priced the construction labour. Our bid was accepted and the houses were completed in time for the start of the 1967- '68 school year in September.

Looking after the construction of four houses on a fixed-price contract was much more involved than an archrafter shed job. What made it doable was the quality of the crews involved, including Gary Landin, who did the block foundations, John and his crew of Steve Raleigh and Louis Kathol, and the electricians from Spruceview. All worked as a team, which made my supervising responsibilities much less demanding. The contract came in on time and under budget.

That's the only house contract I can recall in which we were responsible for the sub-trades. After that I stuck with "closed to the weather including exterior finish", which

The teacherages in the photograph were built at Spruceview. Those built in Delburne were of the same design.

95

required much less management. We didn't have to worry about things we weren't selling and could focus on what we did best. We typically worked in rural areas with farmers who already had their preferred sub-trades, anyway.

Once we got involved in component construction, an engineered design for roof trusses became necessary. The roof design for the first Lu-Re-Co dwelling we sold, a twenty-six-foot-wide house, was overkill unless the house was built in the mountains with much higher snow loads.

I located a more practical design for the same span using 2x4 construction and 3/8" plywood gussets. That worked fine for simple span houses, but as business picked up we needed designs for longer spans, not only for houses, but also for the wider farm buildings. I retained Moriarity and Associates Ltd. of Calgary to create designs from twenty-four feet to forty feet, later adding forty-eight-foot and sixty-foot designs. We used these for all our housing and farm buildings. I also developed some beefed-up designs for 48" o.c. trusses, which could be used on farm buildings.[57] (p.234)

Farm-building construction

Farm building sales were brisk from 1966 to '69 and well into the '70s. My favourite of all the archrafter buildings was the forty-eight-foot-wide model. It was the best choice for machine storage, the wider building being more efficient. The six 8x10-4 light sash windows over the 20'x13'6" door were a hallmark of the design. The three-panel door could open within the width of the end wall without needing to extend the track beyond the edge, making for a clean appearance as no track rail protruded past the end-wall roof overhang.

A late-1960s "selfie" that I took with the Taylor dairy barn archrafter behind me.

A 48'x80' archrafter with 4' centres.

We used a heavier concrete foundation than our competitors, opting for a twenty-inch-wide base and twenty-four-inch height. Each spring, Carl and Bill would come into the shop and build a set of forms enough for a 48'x80' building. These forms would be shared by all the crews. When one crew was finished, we would pick them up during the material delivery and take them to the next job along with the foundation reinforcing steel, steel door sill, and anchor bolts. By the end of the year the forms would be worn out.

Our most challenging archrafter job was the dairy barn pictured earlier, built for Dan Taylor, who farmed north of Leslieville. The hillside site required a buttressed foundation, a most difficult aspect of the job. Russ Morton and Jack Beer, the builders, overcame the difficulties presented by the site and by the late fall/winter build.

Homes for hogs

For a period during the 1960s and '70s, grain sales were restricted by a quota system. This meant that surplus grain, which couldn't be shipped, was used as a barter or "trade-in", the same as for an implement sale. Most of us selling to the farm community had to figure out ways to accept the grain and turn it into cash. Fortunately, there were several feed lots

Hog barns had a considerable amount of material buried in the ground, so the initial construction cost (concrete foundation, gutter(s), and slats) was high.

As I tracked the expenditures against the full material supply, it could be frightening – more than half of the budget was spent before the building was out of the ground!

A particularly satisfying job was supplying a rigid-frame structure for Murray Stauffer. It was set on top of the original eight-foot-high concrete walls of a bunker silo. A few years previously, Murray had me draw a plan and construct a pavilion for cattle sales. Now, he needed a clear-span roof on raised side walls to cover the 50'x100' silo. A rigid frame would meet these requirements. I consulted my MacMillian-Bloedel workbook and priced the project. These photos were taken forty or so years after the structure was built. I liked rigid-frame buildings because they didn't sag over time, had vertical walls, and were constructed of plywood and dimension lumber from in-stock material.

that needed barley for their animals. Some came from farmers who had cattle on feed with them, but fortunately for us and others, they still required considerable quantities of grain. We dealt with a local lot owned by Bill Janssen who, with his partner, Norman Corrigan, had owned the feed mill in Penhold. The other was Morningside Feeders, which had purchased a grain elevator on the Morningside CPR siding north of Lacombe.

As I recall, barley was selling for between ninety to ninety-five cents a bushel. The bargaining point was always the cost of hauling the grain from the farm to the feed lot, five cents a bushel. We had a good relationship with the feeders. It wasn't unlike the bartering that Norman referred to in his story of the early years of the business. It had to be done and we got on with it. Fortunately, within a few years the quotas ended, and we got back to a "cash" basis.

The glut of grain created a market for hog barns. Loans from the Farm Credit Corporation provided much of the money for their construction. We sold numerous hog barn packages, usually with labour supplied. The barns were large-ticket sales, as they had expensive concrete foundations with side or centre manure gutters covered with concrete slats, metal pens, and air circulation systems. While they were large for their day, I know of only one still in use today. Many of the customers were grain farmers who didn't want to raise pigs but were forced to. As soon as they were able to move their grain without putting it through a hog, many of the barns were emptied and remained so. It's sad to drive by and see the abandoned barns, just like the hip roof barns from previous generations that dot the rural farmscape.[58] (p.234-235)

Prairie giants

In addition to material sales, my drafting skills brought in an unusual project. Clay Rasmussen, an elevator builder who farmed near Delburne, was contacted by a group of Southern Alberta grain farmers to see if he would supervise the construction of a grain elevator and feed lot complex at Warner, just north of the Canada/U.S.A. border.

The grain farmers had formed Dryland Feeders Association to get rid of surplus grain by feeding it to cattle and selling the livestock. Clay asked if I could draw the plans. I agreed to do so under his direction and with the provision that Stewart Supplies would supply as much of the material as we could be competitive on.

With Clay's guidance, the elevator plans proved surprisingly straightforward to draw. It was a simple structure; the only demanding

> Drawing vanishing-point elevation plans involved detailing the view with a sidewalk, hedge, trees, clouds, etc. When I did this work at home, our two children would often watch, and when Eileen would ask, "What's Dad doing?" they would reply, "He's landscaping".

The grain elevator we designed and supplied in Saskatchewan, during construction.

work was detailing the distribution head at the top of the elevator. The project honed my drawing skills and educated me about an aspect of farming that came in handy when dealing with rural customers.

The success of the venture was such that a group of grain farmers from Assiniboia, south of Swift Current, Saskatchewan, decided to do the same thing. They contacted Clay and he and I came to the same agreement as before. Saskatchewan had a five-percent Provincial Sales Tax (PST), so we made the group aware we would be collecting the tax and remitting it to the Saskatchewan government. Upon completion of our work, we wrote to the government in Regina inquiring where to send our cheque. They were not very polite, informing us that we had not followed proper procedure. Nevertheless, they happily accepted our cheque.

The directors of Dryland Feeders were invited to the official opening of the elevator, and Clay invited me to come along. It was quite an affair, with three provincial cabinet ministers and the local MLA in attendance along with more than a hundred members of the community.

Once the speeches were over, the local feeder association directors wanted to meet with the Alberta directors, so Clay and I followed along. The Saskatchewan farmers got right to the point: "How do we go about selling the cattle?" The Albertans managed to keep their composure and explained how it worked: when the cattle were ready, you'd pen them out, call the buyers from slaughter houses in Moose Jaw, Regina, and Saskatoon to let them know what you had, they'd make an offer over the phone or come out and inspect the animals.

Incredibly, they had spent a significant amount of money without having researched how to market the cattle.

Eileen and me during our courting days.

1970

Publication of first plan brochure, ADVENTURE '70 HOMES.

1971

Stewart Ford marries Eileen Chizmazia.

1973

Stewart and Eileen's first child, Esther Maria (Maria) Ford, born

Business joins the Tim-BR-Mart buying group.

Red Deer implement office sold to Hudson's Bay Company.

Preserved Wood Foundation (PWF) enters the Canadian Building Code.

Tom Stewart dies.

Chapter 7:

Moving Forward

In 1963, Norman Jr. had a new home built on NW ¼-S24-T36-R28-4, which the company owned a mile south of Penhold. He moved out of the farm house, making it available for his brother, Jack. After the death of his father in 1965, Norman Jr. decided to take over the quarter section he was living on, acquire cattle from the business, and make a living that way. It didn't work out, and in 1968 the company did a property deal with Mike Eckenswiller whereby he purchased Norman's house and land, plus traded additional farmland and Red Deer properties of sufficient value to allow the remaining shareholders to buy out Norman Jr.'s shares.

In 1970, Norman Jr. and his sisters, Betty, Kaye, and Irene, ceased to be shareholders in Stewart Supplies (Penhold) Ltd. The total number of shares in Stewart Supplies was reduced by one third, reflecting the new circumstances.

At that time, I was courting my future wife, Eileen Chizmazia, while continuing to grow the business. In the spring of 1971, I was chosen as the first President of the new Penhold Lions Club. On July 17, we got married and settled into a one-bedroom suite in a new fourplex that I had designed and built on the corner of Fleming Avenue and Aberdeen Street in Penhold.

1974

Stewart Supplies begins to design, sell, and supply the new PWF system.

Sale of Red Deer lumber shed property to Dr. Allard Company is initiated.

Jack and Gwen sell their shares to Graham, Muriel, Stewart, and Eileen.

1975

Stewart and Eileen's second child, William Thomas (Tom) Ford, born.

Penhold machine shop and saw shop sold and moved off property.

50'x144' warehouse and truss rafter plant constructed.

Original 1908 Penhold store sold.

Balance of block of land between Highway 2A and Windsor Avenue purchased.

Final auction of short-line machinery, odds and ends.

Former Penhold Farm Supply building and property acquired.

The first fourplex Eileen and I built and moved into on the occasion of our marriage.

Great planning

In the 1970s, it became more difficult to survive as a small player in the building supply industry. Even the line yards had increasing difficulty finding competent staff for their smaller outlets. Better roads made it easier for customers to travel to larger centres that had better selections of building supplies, hardware, and other services like banking, clothing, groceries, and entertainment. Several small rural yards closed in our area, most notably a Revelstoke yard in Delburne in 1970. I wrote a letter that we sent to the postal addresses in the Delburne and Elnora area, reminding them that Stewart Supplies was still there to serve them.[59] (p.235)

1976

40'x100' dedicated truss rafter manufacturing facility constructed.

Eileen becomes a shareholder.

Stewart Supplies once again becomes Pine Hill Colony's materials supplier.

Stewart families donate $10,000 to Red Deer and District Museum to fund Stewart Room.

1977

Stewart gives All Weather Windows its first purchase order.

1978

First picker-equipped tandem delivery truck acquired.

Earl Smith and Pat Schmidt join sales staff.

Stewart and Eileen make $10,000 donation to furnish Stewart Room at Red Deer and District Museum.

Development-ready thirteen-acre parcel of land at the south of Penhold sold to UCM Properties.

Stewart joins board of Western Retail Lumbermen's Association (WRLA).

We were a minor player in the package-house field, too, although we held our own and out-sold several neighbouring suppliers. Our custom plan service set us apart. It was a personal service that brought customers back, and we'd usually supply the job as well as future building material needs.

The winter months were the best time to promote the plan service. As we were slower in that season, customers weren't as rushed by the need to break ground and they could get their trades booked ahead. I came up with the phrase, "The least expensive change is with an eraser.", to remind potential clients that good planning would save them money and grief by sorting out their options before the walls went up. Once I started doing plans on the computer, I changed the message to, "The least expensive change is with a key stroke."

The biggest issue with drawing a plan would occur after a client had everything settled and took a copy home to share with family and friends who would then throw in their two-cents worth. Most often, customers were confident in their choices, but occasionally we'd need another session at the drafting board. I drew the plans at no cost, provided that the customer purchased the building material package from us. When the service started to be abused, I introduced a $500 plan fee, later raising it to $1,000, which was refunded after we supplied the materials.

I made it a practice to draw plans for our pre-built items. It made costing a breeze and ensured the crew, or the individual building the product, had a plan to follow. By 1970, I had drawn enough plans in the fashion required for a plan brochure – all had vanishing-point exterior views with landscaping, and solid-filled walls on the floor plans including basic measurements. I had noticed that the plan books of other component home manufacturers contained advertising from (and paid for by) their material suppliers. Our suppliers were happy to do the same, and our first real plan book became a reality. The *ADVENTURE '70 HOMES* publication contained twenty-eight plans, all named after Alberta towns and villages.[60 (p.236)]

1979	1980	1981
Company dedicates 211 acres of wetland to Ducks Unlimited as a nesting habitat.	Original 1938 farm house sold; Stewart and Eileen's new residence constructed on the adjacent farm property	Sale of Red Deer property to Dr. Allard completed.
	Stewart appointed as delegate to the Metric Commission, Sector 5.04.	Dedicated floor truss machine built.
	Business begins to computerize point-of-sale and inventory. Stewart Brothers Land and Livestock Ltd. formed.	Interior of 48'x102' archrafter warehouse insulated to enlarge retail floor space.
	Stewart Brothers Holdings Ltd. formed.	

This is my mother's favourite photo of my grandfather, taken in 1962 at age 81. Grandfather Tom lived to see our first child, Maria, born in 1973.

Tom Stewart: 1881-1973

1973 was a bittersweet year. My first child, daughter Esther Maria (Maria), was born on February 13 and my grandfather, Tom Stewart – one of the original Stewart Brothers – died a few months later.

He had been important in shaping my life. During the summer school holidays, I would hang around the machine shop with him. Patient and soft-spoken, his nature is symbolized for me in the way he went about re-conditioning the older farm machinery. It was not a prestigious job, but he seemed to enjoy it. Starting in the fall, he would paint the working parts of the machine, usually a binder, with kerosene, letting it soak in over the winter months to soften the dirt-caked oil on the bearings and to loosen the nuts on the bolts. In the spring, he would begin cleaning the machine for reconditioning. The square-cut nuts used on the bolts generally could not be turned off without the wrench slipping, risking a bruised knuckle. A ball peen hammer and cold chisel were the only alternative, and that risked a battered thumb. Come fall, though, the machines were ready for the field. He was in the shop or making calls to farms, fixing problem machines until his eightieth year. He was ambidextrous, a great advantage for a mechanic, and the only mechanic I know who had clean hands. He wore a pair of thirty-five-cent cotton gloves, and when they wore out, he would switch them around so the palm of the right-hand glove became the back of the left-hand, and vice-versa.

> The only time I heard my grandfather swear was when he hit his thumb while trying to split a nut with a cold chisel. I had distracted him, causing him to give his thumb a solid whack, and he said: "Ffffffff-ish hooks!" Even at ten years old, I knew what he had wanted to say.

My grandfather once gave me a lesson in up-selling by telling me the story of a customer who came in for dressed 2x4. He had piled some of the shipment inside the lumber shed, with the rest being outside. Tom showed him the ones in the outside yard, but suggested he had some nicer stock piled inside the lumber shed for $5 more per thousand board feet. The customer agreed and paid the extra for the inside stock. The only advice he ever gave me about dealing with prospective customers was this: "Beware of Psalm singers and finger waggers." – and I've found it to be true.

The *Red Deer Advocate* commemorated Tom in two articles on November 6, 1973. The first gave a brief history of his life and time in the district. The second was an editorial penned by Fred Turnbull, Honorary Chairman of the Board, relating the sweeping changes that had occurred during Tom's lifetime in Central Alberta:

> "And will a man's lifetime ever again span such a monumental span in this region: ponder the time of Thomas Stevens Stewart, brought here as a three-year-old youngster in 1884 – a decade before even the railway was punched through Central Alberta?

"The first summer they camped along the Edmonton-Calgary trail near today's Penhold. They lived in a sod-roofed log house at the Crossing that winter. They fled to Calgary the next spring when the Riel Rebellion flared (south of town, you still see the marks on a hillside where they hid and buried some of their provisions...)

"When they returned, his family began work improving the homestead – which ultimately became part of CFB Penhold. In his lifetime, 'progress' saw the advent of the train and its near-obsolescence; the age of the horse on the Prairies and its virtual oblivion; and the era of the aircraft, which ultimately consumed the old homestead, and which hadn't even been invented when the family came here. In later years, as part of Stewart Bros., of Penhold and Red Deer, machinery and lumber dealers, he had an influence on development for fifty miles or more in all directions. And that doesn't begin to touch the social change in that time.

"Family man, community worker, businessman, a figure in history, he was being mourned today, dead a few weeks short of his ninety-second birthday."[61] (p.237)

1973 also saw the former Red Deer implement office building sold to Hudson's Bay Company. More significantly to the future of the business, the Preserved Wood Foundation (PWF) system entered the Canadian Building Code, and we were invited by Barrie Sali to join the Tim-BR-Mart buying group.[62] (p.238)

Joining Tim-BR-Mart was the most profitable and best business decision I ever made. Group buying power put us on a purchasing level equal to the large multi-branch building supply yards like Beaver, Revelstoke, Crown, and Federated Co-Op. Barrie Sali put it all together, grew it, and kept it together. He was a tough negotiator who made his dealers wealthy and did well for himself as well.

> Over the years, the partners in Stewart Supplies discussed a bonus system for employees. This was in addition to the usual yearly salary increases. The Tim-BR-Mart rebate allowed us to make it happen, and a portion of the rebate was paid out as a bonus.

Wooden you rather

By the early 1970s, I was becoming known as an eager beaver, a guy who was going places in the building supply field. I never felt that way myself, but looking back now, I can see that the way our suppliers treated us indicated that we were batting above our league.

When MacMillian-Bloedel wanted to introduce the PWF system into the province, their Calgary manager and a sales rep came to see me. I went for the idea like a mouse to cheese. At the time, concrete block was our only option to sell a foundation, as we didn't own a concrete plant. Nor, for that matter, did most lumberyards. PWF would get us into the foundation business, and lumber was our stock-in-trade, easier to handle than blocks.

Preserved wood foundations for UCM Properties development.

PWF construction required sealed engineered plans. I drew a set showing the structural details which, with notations about specific elements, could be applied to an existing plan, then had them sealed by Colin Campbell, the same engineer who had sealed our plywood gusset truss plans. I also became a "delegate" under George Billings P.Eng., enabling me to conduct the final inspections of the foundations for which we had supplied material. I did this for several years.[63 (p.238-240)]

Strangely, the first PWF we did was the basement under a caged laying house for chickens on the Alex Richards farm. It was a renovation, requiring the excavation of the ground under the existing building to create a pit for the manure from the caged birds above. Upon completion of the project, Alex told me that the PWF foundation was the only way the job could have been done.[64 (p.241)]

I added a PWF system using a post-and-plank design to our archrafter sheds and made up a set of four-page sales folders.[65 (p.241)] We sold a number of these, including one for a 32'x48' building to the Salvation Army Camp at Pine Lake. The PWF led to faster construction and lower cost. The only special requirement was a bank of earth against the outside of the side walls to brace against the outward thrust of the archrafters.[66 (p.242)]

Ready-mix woes

The ready-mix cement companies weren't too happy with the entry of PWF, but there was room for both systems. In rural areas, PWF saved customers money by eliminating the delivery charges associated with ready-mix. With no forms required, a PWF foundation was as straight-forward as building a wood frame wall, which in many cases was done by the owner.

One of the first owner-built PWF foundations was for one of the tenants in the first fourplex that Eileen and I had built. Terry and Christine Chapman wanted a home of their own and I designed a triplex for them based on my original fourplex design. The two upper suites became a single residence atop the two lower suites, which they rented out. A PWF foundation was the other change, ideal for bi-level foundations such as theirs. The 2x6 wall provided far superior insulation and eliminated the ledge between the lower half of the eight-inch block or concrete wall in normal bi-level foundations. The concrete footing was replaced with a six-inch crushed-rock base. Terry, Christine, and her dad were able to do all the construction work, a considerable saving for them.

At the time, six-mil polythene was used on the outside of the walls as a moisture barrier, but it tended to tear during backfill. We solved the problem by switching to the asphalt coating used on concrete foundations for the below-grade portion of PWFs.

I believe we were the main supplier of PWF within our local trading area. I liked to sell them, I believed in them, and we had our own engineer-sealed plans to accompany the house plans. Later, regulations changed and a specific set of drawings for individual PWF plans became a requirement. Even so, the system was competitive, and it was fully insulated without the need for a secondary interior wall.

PWF sub-divisions

One of our larger PWF projects was a residential sub-division that my father almost developed. Stewart Supplies owned a thirteen-acre parcel at the south end of Penhold between Highway 2A and the CPR railroad. On the opposite side of the highway, Reg Newton had developed a trailer court on his property, then developed the balance for residential lots. My father decided to do the same with the parcel we owned. He had a sub-division plan prepared and approved for single-family and multi-family lots. Reg shared the frustrations of dealing with the multitude of trades and individuals involved in the process of turning raw land into building lots. Graham was semi-retired and didn't need the hassle, and he knew my plate was full running the building supply. We had spent $17,755.29 to ready the property for development. We sold it for $50,000 to someone who knew what he was doing – Al Sprecker from Grande Cache, owner of UCM Properties. He began work on the project in 1979 and agreed to use PWF foundations.

The first houses fronted Grey Street and were all bi-level designs. Half were pre-fab packages from a British Columbia supplier Al had done business with in Grand Cache. We supplied the rest as stick-built material packages. Most of the lots were sold to various contractors with whom we dealt. The fourplexes were also constructed with PWF foundations that we supplied, using a plan called the Grenada that I had drawn for our own rental property built in 1976. It was a very successful design and was used elsewhere as well.[67] (p.242-243)

110

Preserved wood foundations used in subdivision development.

Serendipitously, the PWF led to one of my favourite coups as an amateur historian! I made MacMillian-Bloedel aware of the UCM Properties' development in Penhold. Their publicity department in Vancouver sent a photographer to take photos of the project for use in PWF promotional materials. It was an inordinate amount of money to spend for the small image of three walls of a PWF foundation they chose for the poster.[68 (p.243)] However, I learned that they had the ability to print images as large as 4'x8', so I had them enlarge two circa-1921 exterior and single interior photos of the original store. It took three 48"x96" photos to make the total 144"x96" image of each picture. I mounted these on half-inch plywood and set them up in the store, and donated a second set to the Red Deer and District Museum.[69 (p.244)]

New products sometimes raise unexpected concerns in a customer's mind. When I suggested a PWF for a new home I was designing for Norm and Margie McPhee, Margie had reservations and asked if she could see the material. I took them into the yard to a lift of PWF lumber and Margie put her nose close to the wood, sniffing it. Being on a farm, she was familiar with the smell of Penta and Creosote treated wood, and wasn't going to suffer that in her home. It passed her "doesn't stink" test, and they built with PWF.

PWF innovations

We continued to innovate with the PWF system. In the late 1980s, an article in an American trade magazine with a photograph of a "Bowen Frame" caught my attention. It combined a PWF foundation with the floor system of a crawl-space residence. I thought it was an excellent way to simplify the construction of homes that didn't require a full basement. Soon enough, I would have a chance to use it – I called it an E-Frame design, essentially a componentized PWF.[70 (p.244)]

Gil Clement wanted to build a small summer cabin using a slab-on-grade foundation. I showed him the E-Frame system, which he agreed to use. The cabin was a simple twenty-four-foot-wide building, ideal to cut our teeth on using the new concept. We built the frames in our shop using plywood gussets to connect them. Gil assembled them on the jobsite and liked the result.

Our second opportunity to use the E-Frame system came when Walt Miller needed plans for a large single-story residence alongside the Red Deer River, just west of Penhold. He didn't want a basement, so an E-Frame system was ideal. Angle braces between the wall leg and the floor joist reduced the span, allowing for lighter floor-joist framing. That was important because the system was designed for 24" o.c. spacing, which would normally require larger dimension joists. By keeping the total leg and joist height with bottom plate at forty-eight inches, the treated exterior plywood sheathing allowed for maximum backfill to the subfloor and permitted a single step up to the house-floor level. It also happened that we were able to purchase 4x8-1⅛" T&G Oriented Strand Board flooring. Used on Walt's floor, it was like walking on the deck of a battleship.

Property matters

In 1974, the City of Red Deer began to build a bypass that would require part of the company's property on 51st Street, which was then occupied by the planer shed and rented to Pine Tree Lumber. The bypass would cut up the property into several disconnected pieces from various adjoining lots. The City's offer for the land was far less than my father felt was fair. He suggested that the city take what it needed for the new road and, after completing the project, consolidate the remaining properties onto our title. Three mayors and seven years later, we ended up with more land than we'd started with. The

A Bowen Frame, also called an "E"-Frame, ready to deliver. The building with the three windows in the background is the one I later purchased from Bill Larratt as my first retirement office.

delay was due to the number of titles involved. The CPR spur abandonment had been improperly done, causing a year's delay. The Royalite Oil land had been sold to Shell Oil and their land office in Vancouver wasn't too concerned about rushing to switch the title. After I had a conversation with their land agent in Vancouver, the title switch was done in a couple of weeks.

About the same time that the city began work on the new bypass, a land company in Edmonton, owned by Dr. Allard, expressed an interest in the property. My father sold the property to him, taking a $100,000 deposit, with the balance due once the final amount of land was settled and the new titles issued. With nothing settled by the start of the 1980s, and the economy getting dicey, my father obtained another $100,000 payment as assurance that the sale would proceed. Finally, in 1981, after a further hold-up caused by incorrect titling, the land was registered and final payment of around $300,000 was made. We had gained about eighteen-hundred square feet of property. At $15 per square-foot, Graham had made a good deal and the wait had been worthwhile.

At that time, we separated the company into three divisions: the building supply, the farm lands, and the inactive town properties in Penhold that were not essential to the business. We incorporated the farm lands as Stewart Brothers Land & Livestock Ltd., and the inactive Town properties as Stewart Brothers Holdings Ltd., with Stewart Supplies (Penhold) Ltd. retaining the building supply division. The Red Deer property was placed on the Stewart Brothers Land & Livestock Ltd. title prior to selling it. This left the new farm company owing the business money for its assets, a debt paid off by Stewart Brothers Land and Livestock Ltd., newly flush with the proceeds of the Allard sale. The farm company was debt-free and Stewart Supplies (Penhold) Ltd. had the capital.

We made our last payment on the RBC loan on November 1, 1974. The loan had been taken to buy out Norman, Betty, Irene, and Kaye's shares in the business. Graham, Muriel, Stewart, Jack, and Gwen were the remaining shareholders.

Our son, William Thomas (Tom), was born March 31, 1975. In preparation for the big event, I designed a two-bedroom fourplex based on the same layout as our first one. It was constructed on Fleming Avenue, a block and a half north of the first fourplex, on property purchased from the

Son, Tom, a few days old, with his grandmother, Laura Stewart, in 1975.

The new 1975 warehouse, truss machine, and saw shop located in the "lean-to" building attached to the new archrafter, which was built over top of the old building.

Bill Coyle is on the saw, with Harold Lee waiting to put the lumber on the cart.

business. I named the plan Cascade and added it to our plan book, and we moved into an upper unit.[71 (p.245)]

In 1975, Parker's Machine Shop in Red Deer was sold to Bob Parker, for whom we had built and rented it, providing him a new workplace after selling the machine agency business in Red Deer. The original Stewart Brothers store in Penhold was sold to a couple of fellows who operated A-1 New and Used. With the $25,000 from that sale, the business purchased the remainder of the land along Highway 2A that lay between our existing property and Emma Street from Bill Janssen and Norm Corrigan. The same year, we sold three lots at the north end of Block 1 Plan G.F. to Bob Thomas and his wife for a new grocery store.

The 50'x96' lumber shed built just after the Second War sat on the Red Deer property that had been sold to Dr. Allard's company. It was demolished by Bonanza Movers, whose owner, Swede Tronnes, offered me the fifty-foot bowstring trusses for $3,000 delivered. We had been contemplating a new warehouse, so I agreed and drew the plan for a 50'x144' facility with twenty-foot walls using post-frame construction. I set the four-ply 2x10 laminated post columns at twelve-foot centres and placed the trusses directly on top of them.

The new warehouse was constructed right over the top of the existing saw shop, and once the roof and walls were finished, Bonanza Movers took the old building out and delivered it to the farm of Harry Morton.[72 (p.245)] We then leveled the ground inside the new structure, poured a concrete floor, and finished the interior walls up to eight feet. A 14'x144' lean-to shed on the west side held the Speed Cut zero-point radial arm saw specifically designed for cutting truss rafter components. Twin 18'x18' metal overhead doors in the south-end wall could be opened independently or together. Removing the centre post provided a thirty-six-foot-wide opening, designed to allow for construction of ready-to-move (RTM) houses.[73 (p.245)] For the convenience of the outside staff, a washroom was included.

The truss machinery consisted of a C-clamp hung like a pendulum from a beam and track between the bottom cords of the roof trusses. Ten movable pedestals, resting on tracks fastened to the floor, supported the truss lumber and metal gusset plates ready for pressing by the C-clamp. The system was eighty feet long. We had previously constructed air-nail fastened metal-plate trusses on an old forty-foot jig. The new trusses were much superior because of the tightness of the pressed plates.

There were two other truss plants in the area, a shoe-string operation south of Penhold, and a well-run one in Red Deer. Within a month there were just the two of us locally; other suppliers were the large plants in Edmonton and Calgary. There was business enough for all of us.

With the building completed and the truss manufacturing equipment installed, we held a grand opening on the evening of June 20, 1975. The Penhold Lions Club catered a BBQ followed by a dance. It was a great way to show off our new facility, support the Lions Club, and have fun.[74 (p.246-247)]

The truss rafter machinery was supplied by the manufacturer of the metal truss plates, Tested Truss Systems in Calgary. They also supplied the necessary engineering for the trusses, which meant that we had to invest in a computer to run the engineering program. That familiarized us with computers, and when the time came to update our accounting and point-of-sale systems, we had some basic computer knowledge.

It quickly became apparent that our new 50'x120' building was better used for storing building supplies than for building trusses. So we purpose-built a 40'x100'-12' structure to house the Speed-Cut saw and C-clamp truss press and jig. It was a post-frame structure with three-ply truss rafters set directly on top of the 8' o.c. posts. Insulated and lined, with infra-red heaters, it was a pleasant workplace even on the coldest winter days.

Taking ownership

We held another auction, this time to clear out the last of the short-line farm equipment and some odds and ends. With the last of the machinery gone, my father could fully step back, travel with my mother, and make the weekly bank deposits for the business. Within a couple of years, the rest of our Red Deer properties were sold off and the monies borrowed from the bank to buy out Jack and Gwen were cleared.[75 (p.248)]

Aware that the third-generation children of the Norman Stewart families were not going to be involved in the business, my father put forward a proposal to purchase the shares of Jack and Gwen.[76 (p.249-250)] After a bit of negotiating, the deal went ahead. This avoided the possibility of third-generation shareholders, who were inactive in the business and not necessarily interested. It also ensured that should the companies sell, Eileen and I would be fully rewarded for our efforts. The deal was completed in 1974, and Eileen became a partner.

Commemorations

The families of Norman and Tom Stewart had been searching for a way to commemorate the lives of the two brothers. An opportunity arose in 1976, when the Red Deer Museum Society launched a fundraising drive for a new museum. The families made a $10,000 donation and the Red Deer and District Museum's boardroom was named the Stewart Room in the brothers' honour.[77 (p.251)]

Eileen and I also made a matching gift to furnish the new Stewart Room. This included a twenty-foot-long walnut table with lectern, built at the Bowden Institution, and twenty chairs from the Drumheller Institution. Stewart tartan lined one wall, and oil paintings of each of

A Scene from the 1975 auction of the last of the farm machinery. The auctioneer is Keith Sim, seen in the Stetson hat and holding the microphone.

The new expanded retail showroom and hardware section, 1976. These photos are taken from the same spot between the two sections, each photo looking in the opposite direction.

the brothers hung in the room. The excellent paintings (featured on the cover of this book) were the work of Esther Freeman, an artist from Edmonton, who used photos as her guide.

We built our third fourplex in 1976 on Fleming Avenue, next to our second one. With Jack no longer on the farm, my family moved into the vacant farm house. It had been updated and was much larger than our suite in the fourplex. It had a wonderful yard with mature hardwood trees, ideal for raising our two children.

Business was picking up and we desperately needed more room in the retail store. Moving the truss machinery out of the adjoining shed gave us cold-storage space for plywood, waferboard, drywall, cement, and related products. We then insulated and lined the archrafter, painted the floor, installed unit heaters, and gained close to five-thousand extra square feet of showroom.

I put the outside staff to work in their spare time and the renovation of the archrafter was complete in a couple of months. I think the only outside hiring we did was for electrical and drywall. We now had more room for prefinished paneling, mouldings, and finish, plus an expanded hardware selection, all available inside a customer-friendly showroom.

It's always been a point of pride that the business never laid anyone off that I know of. I did not, nor do I recall, my father or Norman doing so. There was always work to be done in slack times.

In the driver's seat

We were the first retail building supply in the area to have a picker-equipped truck, a brand-new IHC tandem diesel. The decals hadn't even been applied before we had it loaded for a jobsite in north Red Deer.

Our brand-new picker truck loaded up with deliveries, 1978.

I wanted to try out the new truck. Although I didn't have the correct driver's license, I had signed the cheque for the rig and was determined to make the first delivery. Earl Smith, our newest sales staff member, rode along. I mentioned previously that I was surely the worst delivery driver in the firm's history. My "luck" was about to continue. I had never driven a fully loaded tandem before and I came off the 67th Street overpass into Red Deer a bit fast and had to "English" the truck around the curve.

Arriving safely at the jobsite, it was time to learn to use the picker. The nylon tie-down straps were also used as slings to lift loads off the truck. We slid the straps under the product bundles, then brought the ends up to the hook on the picker boom. I lifted the first bundle, 2x10-14 Douglas fir floor joists, swinging it out too quickly. It swayed back and forth like a pendulum. Then, one sling slipped backwards, and the bundle fell forward toward the ground at an angle, hitting the ground about six inches from my feet. Next, the top of the bundle bounced up, causing the top sling to come free. The lift dropped to the ground with a resounding crash! Really, it was a perfect unload – there was no damage and the slings weren't trapped under the 2x10s. With great care, we slowly unloaded the rest. Sometime later, I realized that if the metal bands had broken on the bundle, I would have had two smashed legs. Back at the store, I didn't go into any detail, but I made sure the drivers knew to take it easy when using the picker.

We originally got the picker-equipped truck because it would help with truss deliveries, but it was just as valuable for making regular deliveries. We serviced a large area and multiple jobsites. With hoist-equipped trucks, making multiple drop-offs meant having to unload everything except the last delivery by hand. This took time and effort. Unless extra help was sent or was available onsite, some larger or fragile items couldn't simply be "bombed off" the truck.

The picker solved these problems. We could load material for five or six jobsites in a single haul, all of which could be handled by the driver. Sometimes, we were able to place a bundle of precut studs right onto the house floor, saving the builders time. Reverse deliveries (when we had returns to bring back) were also easier with a picker. Placed in a pile on bunks, they were quickly picked up and set on the truck deck. Customers preferred deliveries with the picker because the materials were bundled, and unlike dumped loads, always ended up where intended.[78] (p.252)

We acquired another picker-equipped tandem a few years later to keep up with deliveries. I never understood why none of our competitors got picker trucks until years later. They more than paid their way in time saved.

Staffing up

In late 1977, my father approached Earl Smith, manager of the Crown Lumberyard in Red Deer, offering him a job at Stewart Supplies. He accepted on condition that he bring his assistant, Pat Schmidt, with him. They joined our staff on January 2, 1978. Earl stayed with us for five years; Pat was still there when I retired.

The following is Pat's story of her time with Stewart Supplies. We were very fortunate to have her. She was a

Pat Schmidt at 1988 WRLA convention, during her time on the Board of Directors.

true "Jane-of-all-trades" and mistress of them all. Her humour added a great energy to the store, and it shines through in her writing, too.

"When Stewart first asked me to write this I thought it would be a piece of cake 'cause there are so many memories from the nearly 25 years I was in their employ. Putting those memories on paper took some thinking, though. My memory cells seem to fail in the chronological order of these memories so I will share them as I recall them.

"In late 1977, Earl Smith, who at that time was my boss at Crown Mart in Red Deer, told me he was going for an interview with Stewart Supplies, in Penhold and they wanted me to come, too. I had worked for Earl for two or three years and I knew he thought highly of my work so I didn't even think about the questions this might, and did, raise. There were a few whispers about 'who was this girl Earl was bringing.' We went down to Penhold one evening and I thought no more about it until I got a phone call asking me to start on January 2, 1978.

"The first person I saw as I walked through the door was Larry Miller. I didn't know Larry, but I knew his brother George and they looked so much alike there was no question who he was. It was a relief to see someone I knew, or almost knew, in this new adventure. I have often heard the expression, 'this was a life changing experience' and I often wondered if that is an overstatement, but in this case, this truly was a life changing experience. Finally, I was in a workplace where I was respected for what I knew, even though I was female and at that time the lumber industry was very much a man's world.

"For several years when I answered the phone I would hear, 'Is anyone there?' or, 'Let me talk to someone who knows something.' It took time to convince some of these seasoned contractors and farmers to believe that a woman might know something about lumber or building.

"Pete Bouteiller, an old timer in the community, would come in and I would ask if I could help him and his reply would always be, 'No, I'll wait for one of the guys.' Then he would purchase a screw driver or a flashlight battery, or something that anyone could write an invoice for. Four or five years later, shortly before he passed away, he made my day when he let me sell him some lumber and plywood. I had made it in the lumber world!!!

"Customer service was always the priority at Stewart Supplies. One day I was in the store alone at noon hour. An older gentleman came in the back way and, after looking about, asked if any of the guys were around. I said, 'No, but, could I help you?' He told me his wife had passed away a few days before, and her funeral was that day, and she had always tied his tie. I told him I was raised with brothers and

I could help him with that. He left ready to go to the funeral. That put a whole new meaning on customer service, and I was glad to be able to do it.

"At the time I started at Stewart Supplies, there was a large new sub-division going in on the East side of the highway. San Jan Homes had a few lots. They built homes with a cottage roof which were entirely 'stick built'. I had learned how to do a take-off for a stick-built roof, but it was much simpler to figure out pre-built trusses. The contractors on these homes were a father and son, both named Don Stearns. One day they needed a box of nails, so I went across to the warehouse and brought over the 50-pound box. Don Jr. (who was close to my age) said, 'that will improve your bust line.' His father was shocked and embarrassed by this comment. I simply looked at them both and said, 'No it won't do a thing for my bust line, but it will improve my biceps, so I can deal with smart alecks.' I thought Don Sr. was going to die laughing.

"I had taken a couple of courses in estimating through the WRLA, taught by Darling Estimating. I was the first female to take one of these courses (with 78 fellows of all ages). Bill Darling and I became fast friends over the years and he would often suggest that if someone needed help with something during the course they should talk to me. Stewart Ford was very generous about sending me to these estimating and blue print reading courses. I think I took all the courses that were offered, including a speed-estimating course.

"The speed-estimating course taught a 15-minute method to provide an estimated price for a home. There was no material list as it was based on many formulae with current pricing included in each. Stewart tested me by taking-off a print the regular way while I did the estimate using the speed method. This was for a customer who we knew would purchase his materials through us. I was about $1500 higher and Stewart pointed out that he would have got the job. It was several months later when this house was built that Stewart discovered he had missed the sub-floor plywood in his take off (about the amount I had been high). I don't remember if I reminded Stewart of how he would have got the job by being the lower bid, but knowing me, I probably did.

"Working the sales desk and doing blueprint take-offs was not my only 'job' with the company. A few times during the first couple of years, Eileen would call and ask me if I could babysit, as she was stuck for a sitter. I never minded helping out.

"During the late '70s and early '80s, we were booming. Stewart and Larry and the yard guys would make up loads in the evening while the truck drivers were still on deliveries, and I would take home blueprints to estimate. There just weren't enough hours in a day. One of the reasons we were busy was a Government program called C.H.A.P., for home owners who wanted to be their own general contractors. I think this program lasted for two or three years and for at least one of those years I did all the C.H.A.P. estimates. Many of those homes were built here in Penhold by military personnel who hoped to make C.F.B. Penhold in Mynarski Park (about two miles north) their retirement base.

"Also during the early '80s, I took over the scheduling for the truss plant. It was my job to get the engineering for the truss order, put that order into the schedule, and make sure it was built and delivered to the customer on time. The latter didn't always happen, but we tried hard. When there was a call for trusses the fellows would tell the customer they should talk to Pat. I would pick up the phone and usually have a conversation something like this: 'Pat here. May I help you?' 'No, I want to talk to the guy who runs the truss plant.' Then with a grin I would reply, 'You've got him.'

"In 1984, things were slowing down some and we were a little overstaffed. The bookkeeper, Frieda Bragg, retired so there was a vacancy in the office. Stewart and I agreed that I would take her position. I never admitted it, but that was a steep learning curve for me.

"Once I was in the upstairs office, I would get a daily visit from Graham Ford. He would come to borrow a cigarette and to chat. We smoked the same brand of cigarettes, but he always forgot his, and besides, mine always tasted better. When cigarettes went up in price he would go all over town to buy up all his brand before the increase. He did always bring me a pack once or twice a year. Listening to Graham was always a pleasant way to spend a few minutes. And, of course, a visit from his four-legged babies Sally and Fiona was always fun as well.

"It was about this time that Stewart began to work with a local fellow, Ron Bunn, to develop an inventory control and bookkeeping software. Our first computer was purchased, and the software was installed. Back-up was done on floppy disks —not unusual, except these were 8" floppies. Ron was local, so things could be addressed quickly. It wasn't long, however, before Stewart realized we needed a more extensive software. We went to a company called Advanced Solutions out of Texas.

"The software was new to Western Canada, and the retailer who sold it to us was just learning it themselves. Their software trainer was learning the software about one step before she trained me. The software was a nightmare to set up. There was a glitch somewhere and I would spend all day entering data, only to have that data destroy a linked set of data when the back-up was done in the evening. I was often on the phone with Texas. While getting this system set-up and working the way it should, I spent many evenings at the store. In fact, it became a nightly custom for the local RCMP officers who were on patrol in Penhold to pop in for coffee about 10pm.

"Finally, the system was up and running, but I was the only one who knew the accounting end, and much of the non-Point of Sales workings. I went on holidays and, unfortunately, there was a mix up with the young lady who was to come in as temp and she left after a couple of days. This was long before the cellphone, so I was unreachable. They did manage to find someone to fill in and, by using the notes I had left, she was able to carry on. That was when Stewart decided that I should have an assistant who could do some of the things in the office, but most importantly, who could take over when I was away. From that point on there were two people in the office.

"There was another 'first' in my life during this time. Stewart was approached by Mike Kearney, Executive Director of WRLA, to ask for the company's permission for me to sit on the Board of Directors of The Western Retail Lumber**men's** Association, as it was then, later shortened to Western Retail **Lumber** Association. Stewart gave his permission and I met with Mike Kearney and Dwayne Thomas, the presiding President of the Board. When I told Graham that I had been asked to sit on the Board he said, 'Well, you've broken into the Old Boys Club.' I was the first woman to ever sit on the Board, and I reached the position of Vice-President under Mike Westrum. During my tenure, the WRLA had its hundredth anniversary, so it took about 98 years to bring a woman on board. It was also during this time that Stewart was awarded the 'Mr. Lumberman' award for, among other things, his work on the metric guide for the lumber industry.

"Before the goods and services tax (GST) there was federal sales tax (FST). Lumber purchased for the manufacture of trusses was FST-exempt and other goods were purchased at different rates. When the Government implemented GST, there had to be a record of materials purchased exempt and materials purchased at the varying rates of FST. Through the computer system I could set up parameters for these various areas, and when the time came, print a report of these to present to the Government for the change-over to GST. I was leaving soon, and I had to make sure that this report would be complete and not cause problems for the company when I was gone. One of the last jobs I did was to file the GST report. Stewart Supplies was one of the first companies to get its report filed, and unfortunately that caused an audit, but everything was in order.

"Thinking that the grass is greener on the other side, I headed for new pastures, only to find that the grass was not only greener at home, but sweeter as well. I left for two years and when I came back to Stewart Supplies, it was as the hardware person. That was hard and heavy work. Anita Layden, the bookkeeper who replaced me, never liked to work Saturdays and I think maybe she was a little threatened by me being back. After about a year she decided that she would leave. Once again, I was up in the office and happy to be there. That's where I spent the remaining years as an employee of Stewart Supplies (Penhold) Ltd."

Over the years, I had the help of several excellent yard staff and drivers, as well. Bill Campbell began as a driver, became the yard foreman, and later, the first manager of the truss shop. I have mentioned his successor, John Page, who was invaluable in the yard, with customers, and at the drafting board. After John returned to England and became a publican, Bill Lawrence took over. The last yard foreman was Don Armstrong – he was the best tandem driver and picker operator we had.

A home for the ducks

My mother was a nature lover, so when Ducks Unlimited (DU) approached Stewart Supplies about establishing a nesting habitat for water fowl on the Fleming Slough property, she championed the project. Under the agreement, DU constructed a nesting habitat on the portion of the wetland that was in Red Deer County. It is a boon to myriad species of ducks and other waterfowl, and the road at the south end of the property is a favourite of dog walkers and bird watchers alike.

The *Ad-Viser* wrote an article about the project, paying tribute to the company and the Ford family. Several other district landowners participated in the program by setting aside land for wildlife. The Participating Landowner awards were made in the same year the DU project was completed at Fleming Slough.[79] (p.253)

Habitat Program, 1979. L to R: Norm McGee (behind Graham), Graham and Muriel Ford, the Honourable Bud Miller, Nigel Pengelly M.P.P., and Warren Mabb, Deputy Mayor of Red Deer.

The Metric Commission of Canada

In the 1980s, Canada committed to "going metric," with the timetable for conversion of building supplies scheduled for November 30, 1980, six months after Sector 5.04 was belatedly formed. It was wishful thinking. Things were not moving forward, and the WRLA was tapped for representation from the retail sector. I volunteered.

Part of the executive of the W.R.L.A. meeting in Calgary in late January-early February (l-r, front): Gordon Schramm, vice-president of W.R.L.A., Beaver Lumber, Wpg.; J. D. Lee, CrownMart, Calgary; R. E. Patterson; Stewart Ford, Stewart Supplies, Penhold, Alberta; second row: Ken Huber, Boychuck Lumber, Saskatoon, Sask.; Norman Lawrence, past president, Allied Lumber, Regina.

Members of the W.R.L.A. executive, including Stewart Ford, far right, 1980.

With the help of our government liaison in Ottawa, Carl Rockburn, semi-annual meetings brought together all the regional building suppliers and major wholesalers at various locations across Canada. Those of us from the prairies and British Columbia liked to meet elsewhere in Canada rather than near home. Our airfare and hotel for the day were paid for. We thought, "Let's take the opportunity and see Canada!" The meetings started in the morning and ended just after a sandwich lunch. In this way, my family (at my expense) and I, got to see Halifax, Quebec City, and Ottawa.[80] (p.254)

The Canadian Construction Association was the main proponent for change in the building materials sector. The association primarily represented large commercial and industrial builders, with their members pushing for change. The housing sector and the retail building supply sector were different, with many small players and no guarantee that everyone would switch. No one was going to go to the expense and hassle of stocking two different sized products, particularly when the metric panel and lumber lengths were smaller in the former and shorter in the latter.

The government refused to legislate the change, the public was disinterested, and the building material dealers and their suppliers were indifferent. The U.S.A., Canada's largest trading partner, was in an economic recession and backed off the change. By 1982-'83 it was apparent that the conversion to Système International (SI) metric in the building supply industry was not going to happen. It had become a political hot potato and the commission was shut down. However, I did get a nice letter form the Chairman of the Metric Commission, D.R.B. McArthur. The one thing I took away from the process was that the civil service tells the minister what the minister wants to hear.

Thinking that I should practice what I preached, I switched some of our package-building advertising to metric units. We also purchased an electronic metric hardware scale, and as far as I know we were the only building supply to advertise in metric units or to sell nails and screws by the kilogram.

Other sectors switched successfully. Road speed signs changed on a weekend and fuel pumps went from gallons to litres just as quickly, as did the measurement for temperature from Fahrenheit to Celsius. Education began to teach metric units, phasing out inches and feet, only to have to switch back a few years later.

Our sector had asked for a metric-use manual, which I ended up putting together. Another Alberta committee member, Vic Roskey, from the Revelstoke building supply company, was supposed to help but his boss seemed to have other things for him to do. My manual was one of the last things the commission produced.[81 (p.255)]

Beaver Lumber Co. had donated a couple of its home-owner plans for use by dealers, and I converted these to metric measure and the commission published them, along with the manual, for distribution to building-supply dealers. The *Metric Use Manual* was published in English and French, as were the home-owner plans of a picnic table and garage package. The latter two were a hit in Quebec, as apparently French language plans were not readily available.[82 (p.256-257)]

The plans I drew for our new home were the first I did using metric measurements. I drew them in "soft" metric, knowing that we would be using non-metric sized material. It was an exercise to familiarize myself with using the new numbers. I found metric easier to use than foot-inch and fractions.

One builder in Penhold was doing smaller homes and, like myself, was gung-ho for metric measure. To supply him, we trimmed 4x8 sheathing down to 1.2x2.4 metric and shortened the studs by 1¾" to accommodate the smaller sheathing panel. He built four houses, and after the first one, we noticed that in sheathing the roof, there was a small space left to finish at the peak. For the last of the homes, we trimmed only the length of the roof sheathing and left the width of the sheets full size, a hybrid solution that took care of the small gap at the peak. I found it remarkable that, while the height had been reduced by just 1½", it was noticeable when you entered the house. I did one other plan in hard metric for a customer south of Innisfail, but that was all.

Our new home in Penhold, built in 1980. The stationwagon parked out front is Bill McEwan's – see Chapter 9 for more about him.

Some interesting CHAPs

The Co-operative Housing Action Plan (CHAP) was an Alberta Government initiative offered through the Alberta Home Mortgage Corporation (AHMC), intended to aid families who wanted to build their own homes. Assistance included a low down-payment, organization of qualifying clients into purchasing groups, and guidance on financing and selecting suppliers.

Geared to starter homes and first-time owners, CHAP stipulated that house plans could not exceed a certain square footage, and were limited in the number of perks, or luxury items, allowed. For example, you had to choose between a patio door, a fireplace, or a half-bath. These rules made for some interesting construction. If a homeowner wanted a patio door but had already chosen another "luxury" item, a window would be installed, usually in the dining room, the same width as a patio door. After the final inspection, the window would be removed, the opening deepened, and a patio door installed.

Building material outlets, plumbers, electricians, and so on were invited to make presentations to the CHAP buying group. The first-year group didn't quite gel, and some purchased from different suppliers than those the group had agreed upon. There were difficulties getting group members to keep their accounts current, and in a couple of cases, the challenges of overseeing the construction of a new home without previous experience put a strain on marriages. We got our share of the CHAP business and several of the homes were built in Penhold. But, the overall experience wasn't enjoyable, as most of the customers saw us as an adversary rather than as their partner to help them get into a new home.

When the second-year CHAP group came looking for estimates, I told their leader that, given our past problems, I would rather not deal with them. Somewhat taken aback, he hastened to assure me that would not be the case this time around; he was in charge and would make sure the dealings were handled properly. I relented. An RCMP constable, he was true to his word. That group of ten couples was well managed, and we supplied all the houses, each in the order of one thousand and forty square feet.

Canada's interest rates in the 1980s crippled the home-buying market and forced many homeowners to return their homes to mortgage companies:

1980: 14.15%
1981: 19.29%
1982: 18.18%
1984: 12.16%

The same cannot be said of the third CHAP group. Rather than the usual collection of young couples, this was a more mature group consisting mostly of women, and my usual presentation didn't seem to be what they wanted to hear. My eyes opened over the next few days when they started to bring in their plans – luxury homes up to two thousand square feet! I remember unrolling a set of plans and exclaiming, "This isn't a CHAP home plan!" The woman replied: "We just took the course so we would know how to deal with people like you." A doctor's wife, she (and her peers) intended to be general contractors, hiring trades, selecting and purchasing material, and supervising subtrades. They were not going to get their hands dirty.

The sales office in 1981. L to R: Earl Smith, John Page (yard foreman), and Larry Miller.

We didn't do any business with them, largely because they weren't looking for help from a supplier, and because a new player had entered the marketplace. A former builder opened a building supply in Red Deer and aggressively pursued their business and that of the major builders. He was very successful, eventually becoming the major building supply outlet in the city.

There was no fourth CHAP group. High interest rates put AHMC in a difficult situation. Foreclosure rates were climbing, and they had no money to loan even if there were customers who could afford to buy and pay the interest. In Penhold alone, more than thirty AHMC dwellings went into foreclosure. People just walked away, sometimes taking the appliances or light fixtures with them.

Truss me

By 1980, I wanted to start building floor trusses and needed a specialized machine. The C-clamp jig set-up was no longer adequate. The truss design we wanted to use had the lumber set on edge, making for a wider nailing base for the sub-floor. The shorter spans used 2x3 lumber and the wider 2x4.

Bob Bilton, an employee since the late 1970s (and later founder of Alberta's Bilton Welding and Manufacturing Ltd.), was mechanically inclined and built the machine. We were in the floor-truss business! One of the first jobs was our new family home in 1980. The flat floor trusses eliminated the problem of shrinkage, which in turn meant fewer cracks in the drywall, and prevented sticking doors as the structure dried out and settled. Their use was much appreciated by the plumbing and electrical sub-trades, as the copper lines for the hot

The new floor-truss machine in the truss shop, 1981. Rob Dyck is watching Bob Bilton adjust the jig.

water heating system could be routed through the open webs. The same was true for the rest of the plumbing lines. For the electrician, there was no drilling of holes in floor joists, a significant saving in time.

Still, floor trusses proved to be a hard sell. No one disagreed with the advantages and features of the product, but price was always an issue. Also, the trusses had to be ordered well in advance to make sure they were on the jobsite when required. Before the decade was out, the wood 'I' joist system became available, eclipsing the use of floor trusses and lumber joists.

We supplied an eighteen-suite apartment building constructed by UCM Properties in Penhold.[83] [(p.258)] The three-story structure had two sets of floor trusses plus a set of flat-roof trusses. It was an involved job, with cantilevered balconies. Sadly, this building burned down in 2015.

The truss side of the business was computerized, but all other aspects of the business still used traditional methods. I became concerned with the price books, as it was challenging to keep up with the increasingly frequent cost changes from wholesalers. We had five flip-page price lists – one on the counter and one on each of our desks. I would note changes, change the price in my book, and usually also in the one on the counter. I'd let the others know so they could make the changes in their books as well. Sometimes, the message was missed or forgotten and there would be an embarrassing episode when the price on an invoice didn't match what was quoted. The obvious solution was to computerize everything, accounting and point of sale.

I took the plunge and ordered the system in 1981. Pat Schmidt's earlier story recalls the implementation hassles. The change was also stressful because we were all learning on the go. As the first retail building supply in our area to computerize point of sale, we were the guinea pig.

But it was wonderful. The system contained our price list, so all the computer monitors showed the same prices. Material estimates could be printed from the computer as well. Two weeks after switching to the new system, one of our estimates caused a stir in Edmonton at Nelson Homes. They probably thought we were using an estimating program; we weren't (yet), although I was keeping my eyes open for one. For the time, we continued estimating by hand, then keyed in the product codes to the computer, which created the quote.

Computerization changed our brains. Very quickly, we came to think of items by their product codes instead of their prices. A sheet of plywood or a dimension item was no longer "so much each" or "per thousand board foot", but instead a product code to be entered into the computer.

The Stewart family descendants, taken at our reunion in 1984 to celebrate the hundredth anniversary of the Stewarts arriving in Alberta. Our children, Maria and Tom, are seen in the front row, far right.

1982

Business celebrates its eightieth anniversary.

Crown Lumber chain closes.

1983

Tom's wife, Laura, dies.

First participation in HUDAC Home Show.

New Tim-BR-Frame II building design.

Metric Use Manual for building industry, assembled by Stewart, is published.

Metric Commission is disbanded.

1984

Stewart family reunion celebrates their hundredth anniversary in Alberta.

Truss rafter plant sold to Ron Godbout.

Tim-BR-Frame II post-frame building design begins to be widely used.

Chapter 8:
Eighty Years in Business

In 1982, we celebrated the business' eightieth anniversary. It was recognized in the *Red Deer Advocate* with an article by George Yackulic that paid special tribute to the brothers' families: "From $600 loan Stewart Supplies has grow into million-dollar venture."[84 (p.258)] In fact, our retained earnings at the end of 1981 were $855,918.07. But, our yearly profits had started to decline and would continue to do so. It was a drag and occupied my mind more than it should have.

Tightening margins and unpaid bills certainly contributed to the decline. We had also become more reliant on smaller contractors and builders working in towns and cities, at the expense of our rural customer base. This shift wasn't premeditated; rather, it happened over time as the trades sought us out and kept us busy. Not running construction crews in rural areas like we used to, we were no longer as close to our traditional customer base.

At the same time, the rural base was changing. The generation of farmers for whom I had built archrafters, hog barns, and houses in the 1960s and '70s had retired, or were planning to, and in many cases were not succeeded by family. Often, their land was absorbed into larger farms and new buildings were not required in the short-term. We began to sell them packages for retirement homes in town.

1985
Supplies plans and building materials for 50'x80' addition to the original Penhold Memorial Hall.

Graham donates $10,000 to construction of new curling rink in his hometown of Castor, Alberta.

1986
Sponsors Pepsi Challenge Canadian Juniors Curling Competition.

1987
Transfer of accounts to Alberta Treasury Branch (ATB).

High interest rates were a major factor in the failure of several small builders in the '80s. In many of those cases, the builders worked hand-to-mouth without bridge financing or savings, relying on their suppliers to carry them between draws. In hindsight, I was too lenient. In the good times, with quick sales, we'd had few problems. But now, builders began to find their draws closely monitored to ensure everything was completed before money was advanced. If they couldn't finish the job because they lacked the funds to pay their trades, the lender would often foreclose, leaving trades and suppliers unpaid. The only recourse was to purchase the property once it was in the hands of the receiver, finish it, and hope to be able to sell, which I recall doing just once.

Showtime

The Red Deer branch of The Housing and Urban Development Association of Canada (HUDAC) invited us to put a booth in its February Home Show. We joined as members and, in a ten-foot-wide space, we displayed the cross-section of a dwelling. This included floor trusses with a sheathed floor, two framed side walls, and roof trusses. I drew a perspective view of the display for our end-of-February ad, inviting readers to visit our booth at the show. It was an interesting experience, but I don't recall any great response other than to let the city attendees learn who we were and what we offered.

Me at the 1983 HUDAC Home Show, beside one of the scale-model buildings we created to showcase the extent of our offerings.

Figuring out what to do for our annual display in the HUDAC Home Show was always a challenge. It had to tell our story and attract attention. For the 1983 show, we built scale models of the various types of buildings we sold. We were even able to cut all the "lumber parts" on our big table saw. Our scale models included the framing detail of a residence on a PWF, a garden barn, a pole cattle shed, a pole machine shelter, and an archrafter shed. We also promoted our truss rafter plant with display boards from Truswall, our truss plate supplier.

The 1987 HUDAC Home Show was the last we participated in. It featured an outdoor theme with a covered cedar deck, a fence backdrop, and beams supporting different roof coverings. Inside the deck we placed our sales and product information. It was a complete failure. People saw a deck and thought we were a deck company. Home Hardware did it right: they cleaned up one of their delivery tandems, loaded it up with various construction materials, and made that their display! It illustrated, in the simplest possible way, what a building supply is.

After that experience, I decided that print advertising was the best use of our advertising money. In retrospect, I also came to see that the market was changing. In the city, housing was controlled by land developers, and their lots were purchased by construction companies that had their own plans. Any product we would feature likely had a supplier that specialized in the item, with a display booth of their own.

Rebuilding with Pine Hill

It was thanks to our truss rafter plant that we again started to do business with the Pine Hill Hutterite Colony. In 1979 the colony began reconstruction with a new dining/kitchen/bakery building, for which we supplied the truss rafters. (At the time, we didn't yet build floor trusses – they were supplied by Alberta Truss from Edmonton.) Our break came when Josh Hofer, the carpenter boss, placed an order for a set of forty-foot truss rafters.[85 (p.258)]

Once we had settled the truss specifications, I offered to quote on the sheet metal they'd be using for roofing. Josh's face said, "You're likely wasting your time," but his voice said, "O.K." I knew I had to sharpen my pencil and knocked off two cents a linear foot. I got the nod to order the steel, and from that point on, we were again the colony's building material supplier of choice. It was the beginning of a long business association, and a warm personal relationship between Josh, Katie, Eileen and me and our children.

The colony's kitchen/dining/bakery was soon followed by new residences consisting of four or five suites each measuring 32'x40'. Each unit had a covered open porch on the one side with a step and entry on the other. The basement plan was similar to the main floor, allowing the basement to become a separate suite if necessary. Because colony meals are eaten communally, the kitchen in a residence unit is more of a snack bar. There were vaulted ceilings over the sewing and sitting room areas.[86 (p.259)]

The colony continued rebuilding its infrastructure in 1983.[87 (p.260)] I drew plans for a new 36'x94' church and school. Plans for a kindergarten and bookbindery, a unique building consisting of two separate structures connected by a roof over a ten-foot-wide centre breezeway, followed. Into the late '80s, the colony continued to grow and again found itself short on living space.[88 (p.261)] Not yet prepared to split, they needed additional residences, for which Josh and I designed less-expensive bi-level town house units.[89 (p.261-262)]

At this time, we also upgraded our 48'x112' archrafter shed, which we had renovated two years prior. We strengthened some of the arches, increased the thickness of the insulation using rigid Plastispan bead board over fibreglass batt insulation, and finished it with drywall.

New products, new challenges

One of the challenges over the years came from the development of new materials and products. A couple of examples come to mind. The first involved vinyl floor coverings and new adhesives. When coupled with the plywood manufacturer's development of paste filler in lieu of the traditional wood 'boat' patch to fill knot holes in the top veneer, problems arose.

We had sold an order of good-one-side ¼" fir plywood to a customer as the underlay for his vinyl floor covering. Within the industry, it was considered superior to the particle board alternative. A few months later, after they had moved in, the owners came by to report that random yellow splotches had started to show up in their floor. Representatives from the flooring retailer and manufacturer had looked at the problem, concluding that the issue wasn't with the vinyl flooring.

In the end, a section of the vinyl flooring containing the stain was cut out, revealing the stain to be over one of the paste filler patches. The issue was now one of who was going to pay, as the cost was in the $1,800 range. Neither the seller, nor the installer, nor the manufacturer felt they were responsible; the problem was in the plywood. It turned out the vinyl flooring manufacturer was aware of the issue with the glue. They claimed to have sent out a bulletin to the sellers, making them aware of an issue with the paste filler.

Looking at a $1,800 hit, everyone would be running for cover, so I proposed that, if each of us took some responsibility, the customer would get a new floor. In the end, we took responsibility for a fifth of the cost, the floor covering seller took a fifth, his installer took a fifth, the plywood manufacturer took a fifth, and the customer, as general contractor, took a fifth. I was responsible for collecting from CANFOR, the plywood manufacturer, and handed their cheque to the customer. It all turned out well. In the spirit of English common law, this was what was expected of two reasonable people – in this case, five reasonable people.

Another example is oriented strand board (OSB), a less expensive alternative to plywood, which became very popular for subfloors. As with plywood, it was a tongue-and-groove product, ⅝" or ¾" thick. The OSB was prone to edge swelling, which on subfloors was managed by sanding the edges before installing an overlay sheet. One of our builder customers asked me to visit a newly occupied house he had built to look at an issue with the vinyl flooring in the kitchen and dining room. He had arranged for the installer and supplier of the flooring to meet on site, and he wanted me there as well, since we had provided the building materials.

The floor was showing a series of shaded lines about six inches wide, every four feet or so apart, across the floor. The supplier and installer denied responsibility. We all got together in the dining area and stood around looking at the floor. Finally, I said, "Cut it open and let's have a look." The flooring fellows cut open the vinyl in an eight-inch or so square, exposing the plywood sub floor, where it met up with the next sheet. There was a distinct mound about six inches back of the plywood joint. I had the contractor measure the distance from the outside wall to the joint between the two sheets of plywood. It was a bit over 16'. I suggested we go down into the basement and have a look at the sub floor. Sure enough, at the 16' point was the joint of the subfloor. With that knowledge, we went back upstairs and cut out the overlay, revealing a subfloor joint with swollen edges that had not been sanded down. The problem was magnified by the installers starting the sheets at the edge of the exterior wall rather than using a partial sheet to ensure the overlay seam was a joist space (16") past the underlay joint.

The builder had to tear up the flooring, sand the subfloor seams, and replace the overlay and vinyl flooring. He asked if we could help, which we did by providing half of the underlay. I don't know if the flooring supplier and installer were as generous.

As I recall, we didn't have problems with the various particle boards used for underlays. We did, however ensure, when we were the supplier, that the customer made sure he was buying what the flooring supplier wanted.

Fence me in

The store's security alarm was connected to the phone at our house. I'd had the system installed after a break-in through one of the side windows in 1981. The alarm had a microphone so when it called our telephone I could hear what was happening at the store.

Around 3:00 am on March 7, 1983, the phone rang at the house, and when I picked it up I could hear the bi-fold door on a storage closet in my office being roughly opened. I asked Eileen to call the Innisfail detachment of the RCMP, got dressed, and headed out. I parked on a side street and walked to the store. The front door was not damaged, no street-side windows were broken, and everything looked okay around the back, too. As I unlocked the front door, a fellow jumped from behind the service counter, ran to the back, and

A panorama showing the Stewart Supplies properties in 1980. The UGG elevator is seen in the background.

leaped through an opening in the overhead door. I returned to the front just as the police arrived. I gave one of the constables the store keys and went home to bed.

Soon, the police called me back to identify a man that a police dog had found hiding upstairs in the mezzanine above my office – but he wasn't the same person I'd seen. Another officer noticed some tracks in the snow at the rear of the store, which led him to a car in the lane. Crouched inside was the fellow who had run away from me.

Shortly after that incident, I received a call from the RCMP detachment in Stettler asking if we were missing any Loewen windows. Stewart Supplies' name was on some windows they had seized from a suspected thief. They gave me the order numbers that were printed beside our name on the stolen items, Loewen Windows checked them against our invoices and found the match. In the same raid, the police found stolen items in an archrafter shed belonging to the suspect's uncle – plywood stolen from the Revelstoke yard in Eckville that had since been closed, a patio door from an Anglican minister's new home in Airdrie, and a furnace taken from a building site in Alix. The thief had been gathering materials for a new house.

These incidents were a wake-up call for me. Our yards had never been fenced and until the theft it hadn't even occurred to me. Now, I had Bob Bilton and his brother build fences around all the business property, a project that also cleaned up our inventory of off-grade cedar board.

Note the fenced lumberyard.

Having a fenced premises saved us from a lawsuit a couple of years later, when a local youth broke his leg while playing on our bundled trusses. Our insurance company was served with notice of a lawsuit in the order of $75,000, which our insurer denied. The yard had been properly fenced and the chain gate had been closed. The law suit never came to trial. Years later, we replaced that first fence with chain link. "Good fences make good neighbours", as the saying goes.

Back to our roots

The historical benchmark for white settlement in Central Alberta is 1884, and was the year of the Stewart family's arrival in Alberta. To recognize the 100th anniversary of both, the *Red Deer Advocate* published an article titled, "Stewarts' first home a half-finished log shack with sod roof." Meanwhile, Eileen and I decided to hold a Stewart family reunion, pictured at the beginning of this chapter. With Gwen Calverley's help, we contacted family members and sent invitations. I ordered red-and-white caps embossed with the Stewart badge that Norman Sr. had used on the cover page of his family history, *Children of the Pioneers*. Eileen organized a barbeque in our garage. Norman's eldest son, Jack, led a visit to the original homestead a mile west and two-and-a-half miles north of Penhold, pointing out the location of the original log home.

I commissioned a silkscreen print by Dennis Moffat. Reprinted on the back cover of this book, it depicted John Hay Stewart, with his wagon-load of settler's effects and the rise of Antler Hill in the background, checking the survey marker to confirm the location of his homestead's quarter. Each member of the seven Stewart families was presented with a print. Local historian, Michael Dawe, presently Red Deer City Councillor, gave a talk on the history of early settlement in the district.

Catching up

Business-wise, we were catching up and working at getting back to our roots – rural customers. We also maintained our major contractor, Seibel Construction, which was building townhouse units I had drawn the plans for. While we were no longer running crews ourselves, we had two or three smaller builders whom we would recommend for construction. They, in turn, sent customers our way for material supplies.

> The beauty of drawing plans for Gerry Seibel was that, unlike individual home plans, his were built time and time again. One plan earned me numerous building supply sales.

It was a help that Pine Hill Hutterite Colony continued to rebuild. They constructed a 38'x100' dairy-calf barn in 1985, followed by a 46'x42' addition to a hog barn.

While we were well capitalized, we were in the midst of a three-year period of losses. We had an operating line of credit in the order of $500,000 and an equal amount in non-pledged certificates with the bank. We were in no danger of going under, and I knew we simply had to work our way through the current difficulties.

At the same time, the banks were having their own problems, like the oil patch and troublesome foreign loans. I got nervous about having all our eggs in one basket. Accounts were protected up to only $100,000, so I decided to break up the deposits into $100,000 amounts and spread them between five banks. Just before closing on the day I moved the funds, a panic-stricken Royal Bank account executive called. I think he was worried that we were going to pack up our tents and disappear. I explained why I had taken the action I did, but he wasn't mollified.

Two weeks later, my father and I were called in to meet with the banker, who informed us that the interest on our loan would be increased, and that we'd need to make personal guarantees on it. It was an invitation to take our business elsewhere, so we did. My father spoke to John Ireland, the manager at Alberta Treasury Branch (ATB), and arranged for the Stewart Supplies account to be transferred. On March 27, 1987, Graham and Muriel put up $400,000; Eileen and I, $100,000; and the Treasury Branch provided us with a $125,000 operating loan.

While I was upset with the Royal Bank's move to punish us for protecting ourselves, and especially for not believing in our ability to turn things around after all those years, I understood their thinking. We were a closely-held personal corporation, as were many of their oil-patch accounts. They would often declare bankruptcy, keeping their money in the owners' pockets, leaving the bank with millions of dollars of equipment at a few cents on the dollar. Unfortunately, we were judged by the same measure.

Both Stewart Brothers and the RBC survived, and within three years we were in the black, operating with our own money. Our business association with the ATB continued for thirty years, until the voluntary dissolution of Stewart Supplies (Penhold) Ltd. in June 2014.

Community spaces

In the 1980s, I had the opportunity to draw plans for some of the community buildings for which we supplied the materials.

In Penhold, I drew the plans for a 40'x80' addition to the north side of the Penhold Memorial Hall, including washrooms, a full kitchen, and 40'x50' banquet room. This left the original hall, which had a gorgeous hardwood floor and stage, free for dancing, shows, and orchestras. The two spaces were connected by removing the original north wall and re-supporting the roof with gluelam beams. I persuaded the decision-makers to use a Preserved Wood Foundation for the new addition. It saved money and the basement was fully finished.

For the new Pine Lake Crossroads Community Centre, I drew the plans and we supplied the materials. In Elnora, we supplied the materials for the Fire Hall and for the Elnora and District Community Hall. Floor trusses of our own manufacture were used for the floor system of the hall.

A new building design I developed in the '80s, the Tim-BR-Frame II, came to be used for several halls and commercial structures. The design was inspired by an aesthetic consideration

The original Penhold Memorial Hall with stage and hardwood floor on the right, and the new addition on the left.

that had been bothering me. The wood-frame farm and commercial buildings we were doing were all metal clad. We owned an all-metal building, the former Penhold Farm Supply Centre. It was an American Steel product with a low-pitch roof and no side-wall overhangs, except for the extended roof sheathing. That's what a metal building looked like, and I figured that our exterior metal clad, wood-framed buildings should look the same. The standard four-on-twelve roof with overhangs and soffit didn't fit the picture.

The challenge was the need for a roof system with a very low pitch that could span up to seventy feet. I gave Truswall, our plate supplier, my requirements. They told me what could be done: a 1.5-on-12 pitch truss with heel heights of 24", 30", and 36", depending on the span. With that information, I designed, drew, and branded our new building: the Tim-BR-Frame II.

> I received a very special gift at this time in the form of two tickets to the final game of the 1983-1984 NHL season, played in Edmonton between the Edmonton Oilers and the New York Islanders.
>
> Murray Finkbiner, manager of the Northwood branch in Edmonton, had company tickets to the final game, but it was his son's bar mitzva. Knowing I had a son near the same age, he offered me the tickets. It was a once-in-a-lifetime experience for Tom and me. Sitting in the best seats in the house, ten rows back on the centre line, we saw Wayne Gretzky play, and the Oilers win the Grey Cup.

I drew the plans in 1984 and ran an ad featuring the new building. While slightly more expensive because of the extra-strength low-slope truss design and greater wall height, it had a cleaner, more attractive appearance. We could also include sliding side-wall doors of ceiling height. The high-end heel roof truss provided enough height for a flat girder truss or laminated beam entirely within the depth of the truss heel. From a construction point of view, the deep low-slope trusses were much more stable, and, with no overhang, the time-consuming installation of soffit and fascia was eliminated.

The Tim-BR-Frame II came to be used widely as a farm building and as a commercial building (with upgraded specifications). There are three in the industrial subdivision in Red Deer on the south side of Westerner Park. A fourth is in north Red Deer, and one is in the Belich subdivision in Red Deer County. All are laminated-post construction and, according to the owners, very energy efficient.

One of the first public or commercial uses of the new design was for the Crossroads Agricultural Society pavilion at Pine Lake. Judy Dreeshen was in charge of the organization and explained what was needed: a building with a roofed outside area, an enclosed hall, bathrooms, and a kitchen. The new hall was to be built on the playing fields adjoining "The Hub" Community Centre.

A new restaurant in Penhold, on Emma Street and Highway 2A (it's still there today), is also a Tim-BR-Frame II. Under the Alberta Building Code, such an occupancy needed an engineer's seal, so George Billings did the plans with a PWF below-grade foundation, and we supplied the materials.

Our Tim-BR-Frame II also fit the bill at Pine Hill Hutterite Colony. I rarely dealt with the colony boss, Dave, as Josh the carpenter was the point-man for building. But Dave himself, very agitated, came into the store one day, told me what he wanted, and said to just get it done. The building was for storing the colony's farm equipment. My suspicion was that there had been some costly weather-related damage to expensive machines. With machine doors in both ends and one sidewall, it was the largest Tim-BR-Frame II we ever sold: 60'x160'.

It is always interesting to look back at the changes in materials and building designs over the years. One that stands out is the "pole building". What started as a simple shelter with round pentachlorophenol-treated posts eventually improved, first with rough-squared timber posts treated with ACA or CCA dry-to-the-touch preservative; later, with laminated lumber columns combining treated bottom sections with standard dimension lumber. In the process, the building became stronger, more readily insulated and lined, and engineered to commercial standards, thereby expanding its use and acceptance.

A community use of the Tim-BR-Frame II design: Pine Lake's Crossroads Agricultural Society pavilion. The 70-foot Tim-BR-Frame truss rafters were produced at our truss rafter plant. The yard foreman, John Page, can be seen third from the right.

As is evidenced by the Tim-BR-Frame buildings, we were one of the early users and developers of the squared-post wall system. Our first was the four-ply laminated 2x10 columns for our 50'x144' warehouse built in 1975. With the structural wall column acting as both foundation and roof support, these were the most economical wood-frame building systems available. "Price sells" was never truer when a post-frame building was compared to its stud-wall counterpart, requiring a perimeter foundation. The building material package for a stud-wall was less, but with foundation costs added in, the finished cost was significantly higher.

> My involvement in laminated-wood post-frame construction first started in the mid 1960s, when one of our supplier's salesmen mentioned the UFA was developing a building using nail-laminated wood posts. I thought it was a great idea and came up with my own version, which I named "Column Wall Buildings". The system was before its time, largely because of the cost of the laminated post and the truss rafter designs of the time. It could not compete with the archrafter building. My idea died on the vine but would return to dominate in the 1980s.

Good sportsmanship

My father was an avid sportsman; both he and his dad were keen curlers. When the opportunity arose to support the construction of a new rink in his hometown of Castor, Alberta, he and Allan Mathias, a childhood friend and local businessman, arranged to donate to the building fund in a manner that would attract press attention by bidding up the price of a very expensive pumpkin to $10,000. Their intention was to bring other contributors out of the woodwork.

A year later, Graham was honoured as the largest private contributor to the building fund for a new curling rink in Innisfail. This giving back to the community, particularly in support of organizations that had been part of his life, set an example for me. [90 (p.263-264)]

In 1986, the Red Deer Curling Club was looking for sponsors for "The Pepsi Challenge", the Men's Curling Championship. We provided sponsorship and welcomed the guests. Eileen (who had been a French-language teacher) gave part of the welcome in French, which was a big hit with the Quebec contingent. For my part, I challenged all the teams to see which province could donate the largest selection of pins for my collection. Quebec won! [91 (p.264)]

Penhold's New Post Office at 1221 Windsor Avenue, circa 1986, now a used-car dealership.

Going postal

Since the early 1950s, the business had supplied Penhold's various post-office buildings. The first one was located in the former old Odd Fellows Hall. The business purchased the hall, and moved it onto our property along the south side of Lucina St. at the corner of Windsor Ave. When it burned down, we constructed a new building at the same location, and when that became too small, Canada Post approached us about supplying a new, larger structure.

We had other property available on Windsor Avenue and agreed to provide the site, draw the plans, and supply the building. Public Works Canada was responsible for construction. They had recently completed one in another town, and this became the basis for the one we provided. George Billings did the plan using an insulated PWF grade foundation. We owned the building until 2004, when it was sold. Canada Post moved out in 2017 and the site, along with adjoining properties, is presently a used-car dealership.

Receiving the WRLA's Mr. Lumberman award in 1988.

1987

Contributes child's playhouse to the Red Deer Women's Shelter fundraiser.

Provides plans and materials for new Rainbow Hutterite Colony near Wimborne.

1988

Contributes second playhouse to Red Deer Women's Shelter Fundraiser.

Revelstoke Company building supply chain closes.

Stewart Ford named WRLA's Mr. Lumberman.

1990

For its hundredth anniversary, WRLA publishes a special book for which Stewart compiles a brief business history (a precursor to this publication).

Chapter 9:
Computer Savvy

By the mid 1980s, our operations were completely computerized. A big focus for me was to make estimating and costing as easy and accurate as possible. With the computer system, once an estimate for one of our standard package buildings was created, we could make corrections and save the material package for use later. Any changes in price would automatically update the whole package. It made preparing ads much easier.

Most of our building packages fell into three categories: residences, stud-framed buildings, and post-framed buildings. I devised an estimate form for each category. The material quantities were hand-calculated and entered onto the printed form opposite the applicable item number (SKU), solving the problem of having to look up SKU numbers or suffer manual errors.

Residential estimates were much longer, as they included interior and exterior finish, all with different SKU numbers. For items we supplied but didn't stock, such as truss rafters, "wood-I" floor systems, and window packages, we'd obtain a cost from the supplier and generate a SKU number so the item could be entered into the system, handwritten on the estimate form, and keyed in with the rest of the estimate items.

1993
The Crown in Canada grants business badge.

1994
Stewart computerizes drafting with Chief Architect software.

More farm land acquired.

1995
Stewart Supplies is gold patron of the Karcher's World Juniors Curling Championship in Red Deer.

Several computer estimating systems bypassed the manual step of filling in a form. Even the Chief Architect drafting program, which I started using in 1994, had one. But none of them impressed me, as none could produce a usable materials list. Volumes and square footages still had to be converted into sheets or specific lengths of lumber, bags, or whatever. Our system worked for us, and that's what mattered.

My shift from hand-drawn plans to computer had to be immediate. I couldn't take time off to learn a new system. Chief Architect allowed me to make the transition almost overnight. I downloaded a free trial of the Chief Architect 0.2 release, and within two weeks knew I could handle the change. We ordered the new system (on two 3.5" floppy disks) and I started drawing.

In the beginning, it was a hybrid system. I would draw floor plans on the computer and print them off on a pen-plotter printer, but I continued to do elevations and cross-sections on the drafting board. Both sets of plans would be reproduced using our ammonia fluid-based Ozalid printer. Within two years, Chief Architect upgraded to a 3D system that could generate roofs, elevations, and cross sections from the floorplan design. After that, my drafting boards were retired.

We began to print our own plans, doing away with the malodorous Ozalid. Our first printer was a used large-format machine that employed a series of pens, which would be selected as required by the drawing arm, with the paper moving back and forth. It was an awesome sight to behold in action, hugely entertaining! Later, we purchased a new large-format printer using ink-jet technology. The excitement of watching a plan print off was gone, but the quality and quietness was welcomed.

Now, we could show the customer a three-dimensional coloured image of the finished project on the computer screen, do changes quickly and in real-time, right in front of their eyes. The plans could be printed in colour, at various scales, on different sizes of paper, or could be attached to an email in an electronic format.

A lesson in advertising

We did a lot of advertising during the 1980s. Not all of it was successful.

In 1986, our Tim-BR-Mart group developed a sixteen-page catalogue sales flyer for dealers. We were doing our own regular ads, but the idea of a seasonal flyer was appealing, so I signed on. The participating dealers were provided with a list of the items in the flyer so we could order non-stock items ahead of the sale date. But, there were numerous items we didn't deal in: light fixtures, most of the power tools, the cabinetry, and the electronics. We could have brought in a token number of the non-stock items, but I thought most of them would just take up shelf space and gather dust. I also wanted to see building material package items like garages and pre-builts in the mix.

In one of the flyers there was an electronics item, a cord of some sort, priced at a couple of dollars. I had passed it over when ordering the flyer material. We could have sold ten of them! Very frustrating. As it was, things came to a head when we received a back-ordered $120 item that had missed the main shipment. Of all things, it came via CNR express with a freight charge of something like $90! Even the fellow delivering it was shocked and suggested we not pay the fee and send it

Cover of the Tim-BR-Mart group flyer.

back. I did. I got a phone call from a very displeased Barrie Sali. He and I mutually agreed that Stewart Supplies would no longer participate in the Tim-BR-Mart flyer program.

Mr. Lumberman

It was an honour to be named Mr. Lumberman by the WRLA in 1988.[92 (p.265)] The annual award recognized my work with the Metric Commission and my service while on the WRLA board of directors.

I nearly didn't attend that meeting, as the day-to-day of the business was holding my attention. Pat Schmidt, our bookkeeper and a member of the WRLA board, was making noises that I should attend, but I wasn't listening. She finally broke down and informed me I had better go, as I had been chosen to receive the award. So, I drove to Calgary, made my acceptance speech, collected my Mr. Lumberman badge and mantle clock, and came back home the same evening.

After some hours, the honour finally sank in, and the following day, I decided to take Larry Miller, my second man; John Page, the yard foreman; and salesman Ross Stewart to the wind-up banquet. If we got away promptly at 5:00 pm, we could get there just in time.

Alas, we got away late and I still had to stop in Innisfail to pick up Larry. When my silver 1986 Audi came charging around a corner on Highway 2A on the way to Innisfail, I was greeted by a set of blue-and-red flashing lights! The constable asked for my driver's licence, pink-slip, and registration. After looking over the documents he asked, "Do you own Stewart Supplies?" I was startled but confirmed that I did, and thought to myself, "Just take it easy, this is going to be alright." The constable then asked, "How fast were you going?" I answered, "130." He countered, "133." Then he noticed that my rear license plate lacked the yearly registration sticker.[xii]

"You don't always drive this fast, do you?" the constable finally asked. I explained that I had a supper meeting in Calgary and was late, still having to pick up another passenger. He handed back my documents with the admonition to watch my speed and to get the current license plate sticker.

The previous year, I had sold a double-car garage package to a corporal at the Innisfail RCMP detachment. When he came in to pay, he mentioned that the top rafter member of the trusses had a dip in them. I apologized for the quality of the trusses and offered a Stanley automatic door opener as recompense. Though surprised, he gladly accepted the opener. I'm quite sure I didn't get a speeding ticket because word had gone out that if the occasion arose for Stewart Supplies to be given a break, we deserved one.

After picking up Larry and getting on Highway 2, I set the cruise control to the speed limit of 110 kph. Every vehicle was passing me so I nudged it up to 120, and was still too slow to keep up with traffic. Finally, I set the cruise control at 130 and stayed with the natural flow of the traffic all the way to Calgary, making the dinner on time.

Cutting losses

Through my relationships with other WRLA members, I knew that we were not alone in slugging our way back to profitability, although we were perhaps one of the few doing so with money in the bank.[93 (p.266)] The British Columbia dealers were in the same situation. The mood at the 1988 WRLA convention was muted and the meet-and-greet rooms weren't bustling like usual. Despite the subdued tone, I recall a general sense of optimism that things would pick-up. And, they did.

The truss-rafter plant required a considerable staff, and because the work was repetitive, also had significant turnover. Truss rafters had become the norm for roof framing,

---

xii The licence plate sticker error turned out to have occurred during a vehicle trade-in. We had two consecutive plate numbers and had cancelled the wrong one. I got that fixed right away.

replacing stick-framing that required bearing walls, limiting design options. Having a truss plant kept us in touch with several of the surviving builders but did not guarantee the sale of materials for the rest of the building.

Needing to focus on areas producing a profit, I had our accountant separate the truss plant operation from the rest of the business. That exercise showed that the plant was losing money. It was not an enormous amount, and it did bring in other business. However, I decided to close it down. Ron Godbout, the truss plant manager, took it over, staying for a few years on our premises before moving to his own facility.

After I made the decision, a family-owned building supply in Ponoka that also had a truss plant called me. The owner congratulated me on being "brave enough" to get out of the truss-rafter manufacturing business. I guess I wasn't the only one having problems trying to run two businesses.

In retrospect, if I had not made that decision, I would have had to make it later when "Wood-I" engineered-floor systems became dominant. Like roof trusses, Wood-I systems required dedicated staff to design, quote, fabricate, and deliver. Roof trusses and floor systems were specialized, needing to be run separately from the regular building supply operation.

Back in black

By the end of 1990, we were back in the black and operating on our own funds. The support of the ATB had enabled me to concentrate on getting back to profitability, knowing we could meet our obligations. Things felt good!

We were busy with custom plans and supplying those jobs. We also supplied materials to customers who had their own plans, and shed packages to customers with their own labour, as

The Goods and Services Tax (GST) was introduced in 1991. I made a mess of our first ad showing the GST, but soon got it sorted out. It was unfortunate that the government was timid and did not permit businesses to simply include the tax in the selling price, as was done in European countries.

well as those to whom we recommended crews. The guys in the yard were busy building garden sheds and animal shelters. We tried to keep a few of these on hand to satisfy immediate needs, particularly calf shelters (or, as we had started to call them, small animal shelters). It always amazed me how many of the shelter purchasers waited until a storm to place an order.[94] (p.267)

Building boom

A good number of large-scale jobs came our way in the '90s. Subdivisions brought significant business. When the Roman Catholic Convent in Red Deer downsized in 1993, Gerry Seibel acquired a sizeable parcel of its land for development. He had a duplex plan he wanted made into a three-plex so I came up with a design he liked. What he and his real-estate agent didn't like was my idea to name the development "Grey Nuns", after the Sisters of Mercy who had run the convent. The agent handling the sales thought the name would turn away Protestant buyers.

A three-plex that we designed and supplied for Seibel Construction.

Cy Little, who rented our farm land, developed some of his property in Penhold on the north side of Lucina Street east of his farmyard, and asked if we would support his project by purchasing a lot and building a home on it. I agreed, and asked a builder we were supplying in Innisfail, Finn Max Construction, if they'd be interested in the joint venture. Penti, the owner, was happy to join forces. We agreed on a plan that I drew, taking advantage of the grade by including a walk-out basement – the only home in that part of the subdivision to have one. The window supplier provided LoE glazing at no extra cost, and our upgraded product sold quickly. I also drew plans for other local builders' homes in the subdivision, including Penti's, and we supplied the material.

Large-scale commercial opportunities came our way in the '90s as well. The Tim-BR-Frame designs continued to pay dividends. Andy Buruma, one of the fellows who had drywalled and stuccoed our first fourplex, was now a property developer in Red Deer, with a post-frame commercial building project for Kello-Built Industries. Mike Richards drew the engineered plans, Larry Barker of Apple Builders did the construction, and we supplied the material. It proved to be a very low-energy building and Andy built another close by, to lease out.

Two years later, we again worked with Andy on the Moose Lodge to be constructed on the southern outskirts of Red Deer. He needed a coloured 3D view of the building for the development permit, showing the proposed building as it would look upon completion.

New Kello-Bilt Laminated Post Tim-BR-Frame II framing view.

Completed Kello-Bilt office and shop.

The Kello-Bilt owners were so pleased with post frame construction that their new larger building, pictured above, used the same type of construction.

I was able to produce that using Chief Architect, and the Mike Richards/Apple Builders/ Stewart Supplies team was at it again. The post-frame construction system for commercial/ industrial rated buildings consisted of four-ply laminated 2x8 lumber columns.[95 (p.268)]

Our team worked together again about two years later, when Kello-Built Industries purchased land in the Belich subdivision of Red Deer County, west of the city, to accommodate its expansion. Happy with their first building, they used the same post-frame construction for the new building, twice the size of the original.

An interesting job during this period was a building in Red Deer's Riverside Light Industrial Park. We ended up doing a "hybrid" steel column and laminated-wood-post building to contend with Red Deer's development requirements. The owner had understood that the city's development permit approved a laminated-wood-post-frame building. Unfortunately, when it came time to get the building permit, he discovered one side wall could not be constructed with wood framing and meet the fire rating required. This was not a problem for the Mike Richards/Apple Builders team, as they were more than familiar with steel construction. Their solution was to build a steel-frame wall on the side that required superior fire rating and use the wood framing on the other three walls as originally intended. We adjusted our part of the material package and construction proceeded.

One of our major trading areas was in the west country, particularly with some builders in Rocky Mountain House. This seemed strange. I always said that, if we were supplying out of our normal trading area, something was wrong in that local business area's market. Rocky Mountain House had both a large Federated Co-Op yard and a Home Building supply. The local mill we dealt with told me that one was "an old-folks' home" (referring to the staff) and the other was unpleasant to deal with. We supplied several local builders, including plans and materials, and did a large industrial building thanks to a very detailed and thorough material bid that I spent a weekend putting together. The same customer also purchased materials for his new residence from us.

I drew and supplied the new Rainbow Hutterite Colony's common building, with kitchen, dining room, and church.

Pine Hill Colony had finally grown large enough to warrant a split, and construction of the new colony – called Rainbow – got underway in the mid 1980s. The first structures were a large commercial metal-frame, all-purpose building to house the carpentry, mechanical, and wash-bay facilities, followed by the hog barns. In 1989, I started plans for the "hub" building of the colony: the church, kitchen, dining hall, and bakery. This "T"-shaped building was the largest plan I had ever drawn – 44'x188' + 50'x72'. I would not have been able to do it had I not switched to drawing plans on the computer and printing on our large-format roll-fed printer. Although large, the plans were easy to do, as everything was simple rectangular rooms. Construction continued in 1997 with a 44'x153' barn for chickens, geese, and ducks plus a slaughter house.

With the working buildings complete, residences were next on the list. These were different from those done when Pine Hill Colony rebuilt, so we needed a new plan. The buildings were constructed with five suites in a row, each measuring 40'x44'. The heating, while independently controlled in each unit, was a centralized hot-water system contained in a building at one end.[96 (p.268-269)]

Once the residential units were complete, the colony would officially split. To do so, the Pine Hill Colony families had been divided into two groups – one group would stay and the other would move. Each group had a preacher, a colony boss, and bosses responsible for each of the various operations of the colony: land, dairy, cattle, hogs, carpentry, and so on. Each group loaded all its members' possessions into a forty-foot trailer. A straw-pull determined which group would move. Then one group would start unloading while the other drove to the new colony. The assets (equipment, animals, cash, investments, etc.) were divided as well.

Rainbow Colony became a hive of activity as relatives from colonies in Alberta and Saskatchewan converged to help finish the interiors of the residential suites. The big workshop provided interior space for pre-finishing interior doors, jambs, casings, and baseboards. Every porch had a chop saw for trimming mouldings, and the trailer was unloaded as various rooms were completed. It was a sight to behold.

Dave Dransfield was the building inspector. I had worked with him since the 1970s and we had an excellent relationship. He helpfully explained and interpreted various sections of the Alberta Building Code, enabling me to get a plan drawn correctly the first time, without revisions. When he saw the foundation for the new building, he said it was the straightest concrete wall he had ever seen – one hundred and eighty-eight-feet long, at that![97 (p.269)] The colony's builders were good; they built for the long haul.

Our largest contractor, Gerry Seibel, started another group of townhouses in the Kentwood area of Red Deer, just behind the Totem lumberyard. They needed a new plan similar to a previous one I had done, but with some updates and modifications.[98 (p.269)]

I drew and supplied this design for a Seibel Construction development in the Kentwood area of Red Deer.

By this time, Gerry's son, Craig, had started working with his father, and would build a house each year, to be sold, while he had another in planning stages, always a different design. I drew all those plans, all well thought-out modern homes. The Kentwood townhouse units were the last large set of plans I did for Gerry before he switched to building warehouse units in Red Deer County.

Sales award

We sold a lot of formed-steel roofing and siding. In our area, we were likely the largest or second-largest volume dealer. Our supplier was Vic West Metal, which provided a rebate to Tim-BR-Marts. Two of their sales personnel joined a competitor, Westman Steel, which had a plant in Airdrie. They offered me a better deal, including a private rebate. I made sure to confirm that they were also rebating to Tim-BR-Mart and moved our metal purchases to Westman Steel.

1994 Tim-BR-Mart Award.

When it became apparent I had moved our purchasing, the Alberta manager of Vic West called Barrie Sali, the Tim-BR-Mart CEO, and verified Westman Steel was paying a rebate, specifically on the purchases made by Stewart Supplies.

I got a call from Barrie asking if my deal with Westman Steel included the Tim-BR-Mart rebate. I told him that I had been assured by the Westman Steel manager and salesman that they

An often-repeated bilevel home designed for Harvard Park's Springbrook development on the former BCATP airbase near Penhold.

were rebating to Tim-BR-Mart before I changed suppliers. That satisfied Barrie. The "private" rebate was no one else's business. It allowed us to take control of our local market as far as metal roofing and siding, which, combined with our sales of Tim-BR-Frame buildings, resulted in a spike in our sales figures for 1994.

At the annual Tim-BR-Mart dealer meeting, I was sitting at a table near the front, beside a new dealer with a yard in Black Diamond. As Barrie was making his remarks about the winner of the largest percentage of increase in sales, it sounded to me like my seatmate was going to get the award. As it turned out, Barrie called out my name. I was surprised to win the award. So was Barrie!

Word of mouth

Despite a reduction in advertising, our prebuilt sheds and shelters continued to sell. We were still busy with custom plan work and supplying customers referred by builders, mostly in the west country. Some builders who had been inactive for a few years came in for plans for their retirement properties and workshops.

Lorne White was a Kelowna, British Columbia accountant who set up Harvard Park Developments Ltd. to develop a tract of land on the former wartime BCATP airbase north of Penhold. The residential portion was renamed Springbrook. About thirty lots were ready for construction. They had an excellent series of plans developed by a Calgary architectural firm, and All Weather Windows had been selected as the windows and doors supplier.

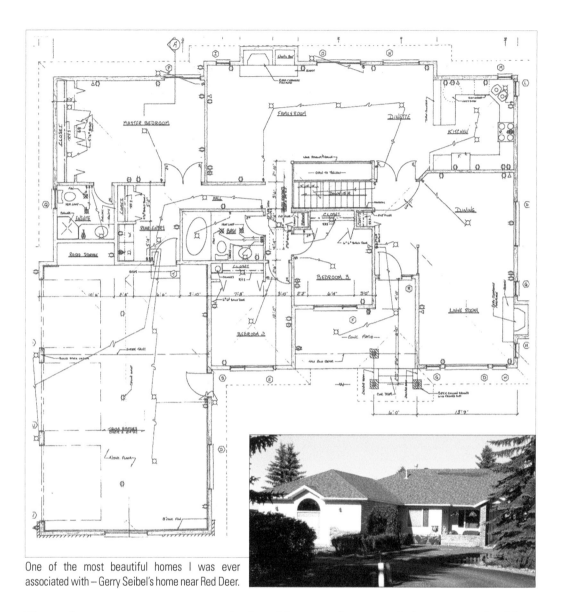

One of the most beautiful homes I was ever associated with – Gerry Seibel's home near Red Deer.

The project manager was an eccentric chap. He was unhappy with the Red Deer building suppliers. He claimed the Red Deer Co-Op had poor lumber; Executive Building Supplies (HOME) had handed his plans over to another developer to use; and he simply didn't like Revelstoke. All Weather Windows sent him our way. We got along fine and struck a deal. The manager left to winter in the southern U.S.A., and in the spring Lorne came out to run the job with his wife Wendy; his brother Doug, a retired roofer with whom we had dealt; and Doug's wife, Ruth. Things were in something of a mess, and they were concerned about needing a revised plan for one of the lots. I fetched one of the plans I'd redone for the original manager and it turned out to be the one they needed. The look of relief on their faces said it all! After that, I did several plans for Harvard Park, until they sold the project.

Special projects

I always had some interesting "one-off" projects to work on, in addition to the bread-and-butter farm buildings, sheds, garages, and package homes. Certain projects are memorable because they require innovation, are challenging, or because the finished project is special. These are a few I recall from the 1980s and '90s:

After Gerry Seibel had completed his subdivision, he came to see me with the rudiments of a house plan for himself and his family. It would be one of the most desirable designs I was ever associated with, not only for its features and layout, but also the beauty of the finished exterior, which included a feature window in the front-facing garage gable, shown here.

I had an idea for a new type of door for our garden sheds. I had seen an overhead door on a farm shed that used a counter-balanced weight to allow the door to tilt open and felt we could do something similar, using formed metal on a light-weight wood frame. I made the top of the door behind the end gable out of 1⅛" OSB sheathing. To the sheathing, we strapped concrete paving stones as a counter-weight, allowing the door to be opened by lifting it, using a handle at the bottom. To open, the door rotated on a bolt through the two angled side arms. We did several of them in garden shed sizes but principally as single car garages. They were much less expensive than regular site-built standard garages. The design caught the eye of a customer who had three collector cars, and three of our 14'x24' tilt-door garage sheds filled the bill at a considerable cost savings.[99] (p.270)

We were supplying a residence west of Sylvan Lake that required a twenty-four-foot clear-span floor system. The depth of the joist system was a concern because of the limited space available for the stairs. After some research, I found that twelve-inch deep "C" section galvanized steel joists at 16" o.c. would work. To solve the insulation problem on the end-wall, I suggested they increase the height of the end wall to match the top of the joist. At the joist ends, over the side wall, we designed the system two inches short of the exterior wall to accommodate a band of two-inch rigid insulation, isolating the steel header joist from the cold exterior. The electrician loved it because "C" sections had pre-punched holes suitable for running the wiring through.[100] (p.270) A few years later I had occasion to use the same system again on a job at Cremona I had drawn the plans for – this time to span a twenty-two-foot ceiling over an attached double garage.

My redesign of the standard open-face cattle shed to remove the centre post was ahead of its time.[101] (p.271) In the 1960s, I had come up with a new design using a twenty-four-foot sloped box beam from front to back spaced sixteen feet apart. With no centre posts, it could be more easily cleaned with a tractor and loader or with a bobcat. We built one on the Dick Newton farm two miles south of Penhold, but it was a one-off because the cost of hand-nailing the beams made it pricey. By 1988, we were using air-nailers and staplers, bringing the cost below that of the centre-post design. We began to promote and sell the new design exclusively. Three fellows from one of the building supplies in Ponoka came in to ask a lot of questions about the design, particularly about the twenty-four-foot box beam. After they left the store, I found them checking out the stack of pre-built box beams we stored out back. I don't know if they came up with their own version or not, but it was an indication that we had something worthy of a competitor's attention, or at the least, our ads were being read.

Our first customer for the "new" design was Frank Johnson, a regular customer from the Delburne area. Upon completion of his shed, the cattle were let back into the pen. The following morning, Frank noticed all the cattle were out in front of the shed. He discovered a breeze coming in from the back of the shed, low to the ground (open face sheds are designed to allow a draft to come in from under the rafters to pressurize the building, keeping the snow from drifting in from the open front). Don gave me a call, so I went out to see what was going on. Sure enough, the breeze coming in over the rear wall came up against the first rafter, which directed it downward over the animals.

The previous shed design had the rafters running back to front, allowing the air to move between them at roof level. Our new design had the rafters running side to side, blocking the air movement and directing it downward. I had to do some quick thinking on my feet. The air had to be directed forward at roof height. I reasoned that a twelve-inch-wide piece of plywood, stiffened with a 2x4, facing forward on top of the wall would direct the air towards the front of the shed. Don also thought this would do the trick. I told him I would send out the necessary material. The following day, Don said the cattle were all back in the shed. The new detail was added to our plans and bill of material. It was a not-so-small detail I hadn't thought of.

In 1994, Union Carbide celebrated its tenth anniversary by gifting $10,000 to the Ellis Bird Farm for the construction of a gazebo. Some years prior, I had done the plans for

The gazebo I designed and we supplied for Ellis Bird Farm.

I designed the facility for Meijer Brothers honey farm – a Tim-BR-Frame II stud-wall design.

the Medicine River Wildlife Centre (MRWC) visitor centre and hospital. MRWC was run by Carol Kelly, whose husband, Grant, was a carpenter. Myrna Pearman, the site services manager at Ellis Bird Farm, asked him to build the gazebo and he came to see me. We decided that the gazebo should be large enough to accommodate twenty people and have a protruding deck with outward-facing seating shaded by extended roof eaves. I recommended a frame design like our smaller three-metre gazebo. Grant could prebuild the frames in our shop and jig them for accuracy. The cutting could be done on our large saws and the material was on hand. The final product, pictured here, was sixteen feet in diameter at the framing posts, with the deck extending a further four feet to allow for seating, with a walkway all around the exterior.

Pre-builts were a steady business, and we experimented with a few designs of barn sheds. But none made any difference in the cost to build them. One of my innovations for garden sheds was to add a "window" panel made from clear plastic scrap from our skylight supplier. It was very unpopular. Anyone could investigate a shed and see if it was worth a night visit. Later, I tried a light panel in the roof, but it was fussy to make waterproof. Sometimes, extra features just aren't worth the time.[102 (p.271-272)]

As machinery became larger, we upgraded our 72'x30' machine shelter with a 72'x42' version. A long-time customer had purchased the shorter version, but no one thought to measure the length of his combine which, when driven into the new shed, protruded about five feet. It was apparent that the new larger machines also required a larger building to accommodate them. The design had to maintain a clear interior height at a fourteen-foot minimum. A forward-sloping roof met that requirement and gained an extra twelve feet of depth. Vertical framing above the rear wall accommodated two rows of metal placed horizontally over wedge blocking to provide a wind release. They were a popular, economical alternative to the fully enclosed Tim-BR-Frame I and II buildings.[103 (p.273)]

For the Meijer Brothers honey farm near Delia, I designed a warehouse to accommodate storage, extraction, and offices. It was a Tim-BR-Frame II stud wall with fourteen-foot high warehouse walls. In the office and extraction machinery area, the walls were twelve feet. Fully metal clad, it was an impressive building.

The first children's playhouse I collaborated on with Rob Dyck, for charity, was a hit in 1997 – but for the next fundraiser, we pulled out all the stops with an EMS vehicle design.

The same year, we also designed and supplied an eighteen-foot-high vehicle storage rental facility for Jack Hill's farm east of Innisfail. His brother, Ken Hill, was responsible for the construction, which was done using four-ply 2x8 laminated lumber posts to provide eighteen-foot-high walls.[104 (p.273)]

In 1997, Rob Dyck, who'd worked for us in the 1970s, asked if I'd be interested in supplying him with the material to construct a child's playhouse in support of the Red Deer Women's Shelter. He didn't have a plan but knew the specs, and I came up with a design for an 8'x12' house that was insulated, lined, and had a prefinished exterior ready for the back yard. In total, about six play houses were sponsored by various businesses. The money was raised by shoppers who purchased tickets and used them to vote for the playhouse they liked best. At the end of the event, a ticket was drawn from each ballot box and the ticket holder was awarded the playhouse. Rob told me that our entry had the most votes cast!

We did it again that fall, but wanted to do something that would really get noticed. We toyed with the idea of a playhouse in the style of a steam-train engine, but eventually settled on an EMS vehicle design. It had a large rectangular play space, lots of light from the polycarbonate windows, and an outstanding appearance. It was built with good-one-side plywood inside and out, and one-inch rigid insulation sandwiched in between. A couple I had drawn house plans for won it and gave it to their grandchildren.

1977-All Weather Windows
1st Order!

Harry Buhler, Gord Wiebe receive first order from Stuart Ford

A celebratory photo of me presenting the All Weather Windows owners with their first order, in 1977. Note the misspelling of my first name.

Breaking bread

I was brought up with stories of travelling salesmen joining my grandfather and great-uncle's families for dinner if the occasion arose. The tradition continued into my lifetime and it never seemed strange that I would feed the fellow looking to make a sale rather than the other way around. I didn't do this as a matter of everyday practice, but several of the salesmen were interesting to talk to and dinner was a good time to do it. It didn't hurt business either, as being on their "favoured-dealer" list often paid off.

The longest lasting of these relationships was with Bill McEwan, a salesman for Canadian Forest Products (CANFOR) who'd been transferred to Calgary. CANFOR had a plywood mill in Grande Prairie, and Bill's job was to promote their pine plywood to retail yards. He started in Calgary with Revelstoke company, a large line yard, and worked his way north, eventually arriving on my doorstep in Penhold. I liked what he had to offer and enjoyed talking to him. Pine plywood sheathing was less expensive than fir from the coast and could be used anywhere we used fir sheathing. Once CANFOR got its distribution centre

In 1991, I wanted an up-to-date picture of our store and staff, inspired by two taken in 1921. We staged this photo with a large window order on one tandem, a lumber order on the other, a large animal shelter on the one-ton, and the two forklifts, all lined up on the street in front of the store. Each of the female staff sat on a forklift, just as the 1921 picture had a woman on the Titan tractor.

and offices set up, Bill became the western region sales manager and no longer called on us, but remained a close friend.

Bill was a guest at our wedding in 1971. He had become involved with the Calgary Opera board, while Eileen and I attended the opera in Edmonton. Bill convinced us to switch to Calgary, and opera became the basis for our personal friendship. We attended his wedding to Teresa in Montreal, became godparents to their third son, Neil, and enjoyed many family visits at each others' homes. Bill's father was a veteran of the Great War who had fought at Vimy Ridge. In 2007, on the 90th anniversary of the battle of Vimy Ridge, I invited Bill and Neil to accompany me to the ceremony in France. First, we stopped in Scotland to visit my cousins, and Bill was able to show Neil the dwelling his own family had lived in before emigrating to Canada. Bill died that fall; I counted him as my best friend.

Another long-standing, albeit less personal, relationship with salesmen, was with All Weather Windows. Gord Wiebe and Harry Buhler had both worked in the industry

Pictured from L to R: Tony Wilson, Bill Lawrence, Bob Cave, Stewart Ford, Tammy Chatenay, Larry Miller, Brian Smart, Ross Stewart, Anita Lawrence, and Alf Petkau.

VERITAS · TE · LIBERABIT

Just prior to the Labatt Brier, the coat of arms I had applied for a year earlier was granted by the Crown in Canada. With the Arms, a badge for the business was included. The Centaur crest on my arms became the badge, encircled by the business slogan: "Shelter for Man and Beast".

before striking out on their own in 1977. They'd been in Calgary to meet with investors and get the company set up. On their way home to Edmonton, they stopped in at the store to tell me their good news. I had a house job needing windows and doors, so I wrote up the order and gave them their first sale. I had Pat Schmidt take a photo of the event in my office, then invited them to join Eileen and me for supper. They used the photo on the invitation to their fifteenth-anniversary celebration in 1992, an enjoyable event that Eileen and I attended in Edmonton. On their fortieth anniversary celebration in Edmonton in 2018, against the backdrop of the original picture, Gord, Harry, and I recreated that picture. For me, forty years on, it was a moving occasion to celebrate with the success of the largest family-owned window manufacturer in Canada.[105 (p.274)]

I witnessed a phenomenal number of window companies come and go. The advent of off-the-shelf vinyl extrusions lowered the cost for entry. The saying went that all you needed to get into the window-manufacturing business was a $30,000 glass washer for making the sealed units, and a building. I'm sure it was a bit more complicated than that, but compared to the investment for wood-frame windows, it was much easier to get started. But not necessarily easy to keep going.

We had two principal window and exterior-door suppliers: All Weather Windows in Edmonton, and Loewen Windows in Steinbach, Manitoba. Both had quality products; however, Loewen did not have PVC windows, focusing instead on a high-end wood window line. The PVC product was significantly less expensive and particularly attractive to the renovation and replacement market, which formed a growing segment of sales. Our Loewen purchases dwindled, and eventually ceased, as did Loewen itself. Later, it was resurrected by a family member as a specialty wood-window manufacturer selling to builders of high-end housing.

Mixing business and pleasure

One of the things that Norman, Tom, my father, and to some extent their families, all shared, was a love of fun and the idea that business and pleasure should mix. Norman and Tom had their summer cabin at Sylvan Lake. Graham enjoyed sports, brief fishing trips, and after retirement, months each year in Hawaii – but while he was active in the business, it was an all-consuming and never-ending job. I inherited this work ethic and the habit of turning work into fun. Many enjoyable events and opportunities came about because of the WRLA, the suppliers, and the customers.

One of the legacies passed down to me was to use the business to support causes that were fun for us and helped the community. Curling bonspiels are one example. Stewart Brothers had sponsored the Red Deer Farmer's Bonspiel since its inception in 1945. We were asked to be a patron of the Labatt Brier to be held in 1994 in Red Deer. The business

The Edwin and Barb Knight residence, featured on the cover of Westman's 1998 calendar.

went in as a gold-level patron at a cost of $30,000. That granted us ten tickets to all the draws, access to the dining room for two daily meals, one hundred event trading pins, and ten bonspiel jackets.

Knowing that we'd have these goodies to enjoy, I kept track of all our building-package customers during the 1993 construction season. At year end, I began phoning them to offer free tickets to any one of the three daily draws. Being able to offer free tickets to the Brier gained us the sale of a machine shed late in the year, when my offer of championship-game tickets trumped the UFA Co-Op's gift of a jacket!

Eileen and I spent the week at the Brier. I wore my dress-Stewart kilt and official Brier jacket. During the festivities, a young woman approached me, and after some brief conversation, noted that I was wearing a kilt and asked if I was "regimental". "No", I replied, looking down at my kilt, "I'm dress Stewart". She said that she was regimental; I was confused; the conversation died, and she moved on. Later in the year, a former employee came in to the store to place an order. He was a musician and wore a kilt on occasion. I mentioned my kilt story to him and he nearly died of laughter, explaining that the term "regimental" in regard to kilts meant "not wearing underwear" – and that got me wondering exactly what the young woman had in mind![106] (p.275)

A year later, in 1995, we sponsored the World Junior Curling Championships held at the Red Deer Curling Club. We agreed to be drivers for the Scottish teams. Eileen drove the Scottish women and I drove the Scottish men. When their baggage missed its transfer in London and didn't arrive until the next day, I arranged to have one of our drivers collect the bags at the Calgary airport. We opened our home to the Scots the following day while their luggage was collected. As we were returning them to their hotel in Red Deer, our truck crossed the intersection ahead of us, with the missing luggage on board.

Another way of mixing business and pleasure was taking salespeople up on their offers, as I did one day with Bev Fyfe, the sales boss from Westman. Metal roofing and siding continued to be our largest single sales item. It was clean to handle and came properly packaged for our picker trucks to deliver. Bev invited me on a Westman-sponsored fishing trip. Unlike my father, I was no fisherman, but I wasn't going to miss out on a trip to Great Slave Lake! We flew up to Plummer's Lodge for a couple of days of fishing, and on the drive home from the Edmonton airport, I asked Bev to take a detour west of Penhold to the Edwin and Barb Knight residence. White with a red-metal roof, the residence had an attached garage and what we called a "toy-bin." As we crested the hill and the impressive building came into view, I said to Bev, "There's the picture for your next year's calendar!" Westman had a professional photographer take a picture of the building, and the Knights were pleased to see their home featured on the Westman company calendar.

My parents, Graham and Muriel, enjoying their retirement years.

1997

Graham and Muriel Ford die within one month of each other.

Stewart and Eileen become sole owners of the three companies.

1999

Beaver Lumber closes.

2000

Stewart Supplies is gold patron of the Labatt Brier in Red Deer.

2002

Stewart Supplies celebrates hundredth anniversary with publication of special anniversary calendar.

Stewart Ford gives staff six months notice that the business will close on May 30, 2003.

Chapter 10:
One-hundred years in business

My parents, Graham and Muriel, had been in declining health. By 1996, my mother was house-bound with a group of caregivers looking after her; my father was in a nursing home. Mentally, they were both sharp, but their physical decline was rapid. They died within twenty-seven days of each other in 1997 and are buried together in the Horn Hill Cemetery east of Penhold.

Their headstone is a big granite rock that I got from land east of Innisfail near Wimborne, procured with permission from the Pine Hill Hutterite Colony. They'd recently purchased the land and had started work on the site, unearthing numerous granite rocks. After having the names and dates sandblasted into the rock, I took it to Bar-S-Concrete for mounting onto a concrete base and placement at the gravesite.

My thoughts turned to the role that my ancestors, the business, and Graham's keen business mind played in the quality of my life. Graham was responsible for the survival of the business after the Second World War. In the mid 1950s, Jack Stewart chose to leave the Red Deer implement store to run the farm in Penhold. In the 1960s, Norman Stewart Jr. struck out on his own. Norman's four daughters were silent shareholders and not involved in the day-to-day operation of the business. That left Graham, and soon me, to carry on the business.

2003

Stewart Supplies buys Bill Larratt's property on the corner of Windsor Avenue and Emma Street.

Stewart sells the operating business, equipment, and inventory to Ed Stol; leases out the property for five years.

Stewart Ford moves office into former Bill Larratt building.

Stewart Supplies becomes a landlord and plan service.

2004

New office burns and is rebuilt in the fashion of a CPR #2 Station.

Stewart Ford continues to draw plans and wind down the building supply business while supervising the construction of the new office building.

2005

New office building completed and occupied.

Shareholders expect dividends. When we surrendered the IHC contract in 1968, revenues shrank, and the farm was not a substantial source of income. My interest was solely in building supplies, and that business provided a good living for our two families. Graham had the long view and realized that I would be faced with many third-generation children holding their parents' shares, putting me in a minority share position.

Graham engineered the buy-out of the Norman Stewart heirs, and Stewart Supplies (Penhold) Ltd. became the property of us four Fords. I was the largest single shareholder; my parents together were the majority shareholder. It would take another thirty years of hard work and careful attention, but the groundwork my father had prepared created future wealth that enables Eileen and me to spend our retirement years at leisure: traveling, providing for our children and grandchildren, embarking on philanthropic ventures, and supporting causes dear to our hearts.

One of the last things my father said to me was, "Take the money and have fun". But in 1997 I wasn't ready to do that. The business was doing well, and I still enjoyed helping clients with their plans and coming up with new ideas for pre-builts. For several years, I had been reconciled to the fact that I would be the one closing the door on the business my great-uncle and grandfather had founded, that my father had saved, and which I carried on. Our children were making their own way in the world and would not be in the business. I was determined to see the company through to its hundredth anniversary, to celebrate that milestone, and then to retire.

As our children grew into their teens in the 1980s, the business environment was rapidly changing. The line yards were shutting down small-town operations and consolidating in the cities. Then, one after another, they disappeared: Crown Lumber in 1982, Revelstoke in 1988, and Beaver Lumber in 1999. Those of us who remained were successful independents associated with a buying group. Stewart Supplies was a niche player dependent on my design talents, a very knowledgeable front-office staff, and a modern delivery fleet.

Previous generations had hired professional managers for the business. That hadn't worked in the Red Deer building supply after Orie and Nita Thorne left; and, it hadn't worked on

2006
Stewart Brothers Holdings Ltd. sold to Lynn Lee and Debbie King (née Bouteiller), with Stewart Supplies holding a ten-year mortgage.

2007
Stewart Brothers Land and Livestock's eighty-one-acre property in Penhold sold to Penhold Bulk Services, an oilfield fracking sand supplier.

2008
Lease with Penhold Building Supplies Ltd. renewed for five years.

the Penhold farm after Phil Tweten retired until Jack took over. Moreover, I couldn't see myself stepping back and keeping out of the way of a manager.

As it was, the business was doing alright, and I was building a nice retirement fund. At the hundredth anniversary, I'd be sixty-five and it felt like that would be a good time to wrap things up.

Anniversary albatross

By 2000, I was more than ready to retire. But, I wanted to get the business through its hundredth anniversary (2002) – a project that had become an albatross around my neck. In October of 2001, I had an inspiration: publish a commemorative hundredth-year anniversary calendar. It would replace the ones we usually handed out with the generic Alberta scenes.

In writing the thirty-five-page history of the business for the WRLA's hundredth anniversary publication in 1990, I'd compiled much of the information, photographs, business records, and family details to tell our story. I needed someone who could put it all together. Fortunately, that person was our daughter Maria, a writer who owned a marketing firm in Ottawa. I told her what I was thinking and, while she was shocked by the short timeline, she got to work.[107] (p.276-277)

She and her graphic designer created a fourteen-page calendar that divided the hundred years into ten decades. Each month featured a collage of images that helped tell the story of that decade. A timeline summarized the milestones of each decade and told the story of the two founding families and the business. Four hundred copies of the beautifully designed 11"x17" calendars were printed. I picked them up at the Calgary Airport on the afternoon of December 24th, 2001!

I dropped off a few to customers and business contacts on the drive back to Penhold. Each of the staff received one, and over the following four weekends, I travelled throughout the region, delivering calendars to customers and salespeople who had called on us. Acquaintances

2010
Stewart Brothers Land and Livestock Ltd. sells the eastern part of SW ¼-S27-T36-R28-4 to Charles Newton.

2012
Stickland Farms and a partner purchase Stewart Brothers Land and Livestock property on S35-T36-R28-4.

whom I had missed or not yet visited started phoning and coming into the store to ask for a copy. No one was turned down.

Initially, I thought I would close things down on December 31, 2001, but soon realized I needed to complete the 2002 year. Our solicitors advised that six months was adequate for notice to staff, so I continued "business as usual" through 2002, even doing some print advertising. When I handed out the year-end bonuses at Christmas 2002, everyone was told that on May 30, 2003, Stewart Supplies (Penhold) Ltd. would close.

We were not involved in any large multi-unit projects in 2002, but business was steady, with smaller builders and individuals requiring plans. Profits had dropped significantly in the 2001 business year, yet our sales hadn't slipped, and I wasn't able to pinpoint the issue. We bounced back in 2002 and went out on a high note.

This is the last photo of Stewart Supplies prior to its sale, taken in about 2001.

The 2002 WRLA convention organizers were aware that we were marking our hundredth anniversary. Jonah O'Neil, reporter for the WRLA magazine, interviewed me about the business. The article appeared in the March issue of the *Yardstick* and relied heavily on the information in the anniversary calendar. A year later, we rated another article in the *Yardstick*, again by Jonah O'Neil, who seemed fascinated with the Stewart Brothers-Stewart Supplies story.[108] (p.278-281)

2013

Edna Stickland and son Brian purchase balance of Stewart Brothers Land and Livestock Ltd. property, S26-T36-R28-4, and the western part of SW ¼-S27-T36-R28-4 in Red Deer County.

Stewart Supplies (Penhold) Ltd. property sold to Penhold Building Supplies Ltd.

Stewart Brothers Holdings Ltd. mortgage paid off; company voluntarily dissolved.

Stewart Brothers Land and Livestock voluntarily dissolved.

2014

Stewart Supplies (Penhold) Ltd. voluntarily dissolved on June 16, 2014.

Eileen and me, accepting one-hundredth anniversary congratulations from the Provincial government.

Publication of Stewart Brothers
History book.

The business received other accolades as well. The Town of Penhold, the Alberta Legislature and Premier, the leader of the opposition and Prime Minister, and the Governor-General, all sent congratulations on the achievement of one hundred years in business.

Last-minute buyer

I had told the staff that either someone would come along and buy the business, or we would have an auction sale. With no certainty there would be a new owner or a job, staff began to leave, making it difficult to do deliveries. Neither did it make sense to continue advertising.

The business would close on May 30. In April, I got a call from Ed Stol, who owned a hardware and building supply in Blackfalds. He arranged financing to purchase the assets, leased the property, and Penhold Building Supplies Ltd. was born. Ed was in business with a full inventory, two picker-equipped tandem trucks, a two-ton delivery truck, a three-quarter ton truck, three forklifts, and a well-equipped saw shop. Ed had an experienced sales team that knew the business and its systems. Meanwhile, I was collecting CPP *and*

This photo was taken the day before the sale in 2003. I'm posing with a display panel I had created some years prior, featuring Norman and Tom Stewart and a bit of their story.

Welcoming Ed Stol, the new owner, on June 1, 2003.

Back and middle rows, L to R: Bill and Teresa McEwan; Randy and Pat* Schmidt; Sheila and Larry* Miller; Bill* Lawrence and girlfriend, Tammy* Hobbs and daughter, Ross* and Pat Stewart Front row: Dr. Dee Keating; Stewart and Eileen Ford; Brian Keating of the Calgary Zoo (* indicates an employee).

We were (and remain) patrons of the Calgary Zoo. As a thanks to the loyal staff members who stayed to the end, I arranged with Brian Keating at the zoo for a behind-the-scenes, after-hours visit. We travelled in a chartered bus for the event. After a visit to a select group of zoo animals hosted by their keepers, we watched a video and capped the evening with champagne and chocolate-dipped strawberries.

rent! By year-end, Ed was successfully molding Penhold Building Supplies to his way of doing business. The original lease for five years was renewed in 2008 for another five years.

My retirement "home"

Bill Larratt did fine carpentry. He'd done a variety of jobs for me, most notably the custom oak cabinetry and detailing in the library in our 1992 home renovation. His office and shop were at the north end of the block occupied by Stewart Supplies. Shortly before the business sold, he announced that he had just put his building up for sale. I would need a place to carry on my plan work and the administrative details associated with winding down a hundred-year-old business. Stewart Supplies purchased the property for $145,000: a two-storey, 30'x70'-12' metal-clad post-frame building. We were once again the owner of the total parcel of land between the rear lane and Windsor Avenue, from Lucina Street on the south to Emma Street on the north. Bill continued as my tenant, operating from the two-bay ground-floor shop; his daughter lived in the upstairs suite, and I had the main-floor office below.

The new office was perfect for my needs. I had a Konica-Minolta colour photocopier, large-format printer, coffee machine, comfortable office chair, custom-made desk that Tim Larratt built for me, and a private bathroom. I was able to repurpose one of the large panels I'd had printed of the 1921 store for artwork in the new office. Tenants paid the expenses. Life was good.

I stayed as busy as I wanted to be, drawing plans primarily for clients of the small builders we had dealt with and word-of-mouth referrals from previous customers. Now, I was getting paid for my work and not just the material sale. Did I mention that life was good? Former customers and suppliers would often drop by to "chew the fat" and check up on me.

When I wasn't working on plans, I began my "Archives" project, which has since consumed a good majority of my time. This initially involved making copies of documents, photographs, and ledgers tracing the history of the business. In later years it expanded to a custom, searchable database and a physical inventory of original artifacts.

> Pat Schmidt stayed on with Penhold Building Supplies and also did my books for a couple of years. Soon, our daughter-in-law, Rhonda, finished a computer bookkeeping program and kept the books for son Tom's welding business as well as mine.

In the summer of 2004, Bill Larratt and his daughter gave their notice and moved out. A local hairdresser and an environmental consultant both enquired about renting. I said I'd renovate the building for them. So, I drew a set of plans for the building as it existed, opened them in a new file, and drew the redesign with new tenant spaces. I lined up a contractor from Trochu, Randi Gagy, to do the work in December. Materials were delivered and ready for construction to begin on December 28.[109 (p. 282)] Eileen's mother spent that Christmas with us, and as we drove her back to Lethbridge on the 27th, I got a call on my cell phone from Pat Schmidt telling me that my building was on fire. All I could say was, "I'll see you tomorrow."[109 (p.282)]

If you could have a "good fire", I had one. Thanks to an excellent insurance agent, I was fully insured for the loss. My computer was unharmed and none of my photos were destroyed. Content insurance covered my photocopier. The original, and the renovation blueprints I'd done, survived and were used by the restoration contractor to price out the repair or rebuild cost. Rebuilding proved less expensive than repairing the damage.

I took the $150,000 insurance payout, added the same amount of Stewart Supplies money, and replaced the building with a new one. Having always admired the architectural beauty of CPR stations, I decided that my new building would be built using that design. I contacted the CPR archivist in Calgary and asked if a plan of the old Penhold station was available. A few days later, he sent the closest thing available, plans for a #2 station. It was very similar to the original station as I remembered it, and I used the plans as a guide. I paid careful attention to the roof slopes, hardware, window, and door styles, and am proud to have designed a replica that looked so authentic when it was finished that I had people ask me if I had moved the original Penhold station from its location.[110 (p.282-283)]

My new office building, modeled after a CPR #2 train station like the station I knew from my childhood in Penhold. The building caused heads to turn for its beauty and because it sat perpendicular to the rail tracks, which were a block to the west!

The Larratts did the framing and finishing; a myriad of sub-contractors did the rest; and I did the landscaping. All the offices had accessible washrooms with a shower, underfloor heat, five-foot counters with sinks, upper cabinets, air-conditioning, and built-in vacuums. The upstairs apartment was designed with a full kitchen, appliances, single bedroom, bath, living room, and kitchen-dining area, plus a host of storage. At the rear of the building was a fenced private yard, and nine paved parking spaces, for tenants, customers, and visitors.

As fun as it was, the project took a year of my life and the new building wasn't finished and occupied until February 2006. The hair salon occupied two bays and the upstairs suite; the environmental consultant took one bay, and I took the other.

A new feature in my office was a roll-down projector screen with projector connected to my computer. I could project plan drawings for clients, who could watch in real-time as I made changes and showed alternatives. The best part was being able to show clients interior rooms in three dimensions, complete with feature finishes.

Having no staff was an adjustment. I was solely responsible for the upkeep of the building, its weekly cleaning, clearing the parking lot and sidewalks. I no longer had people to attend to snow removal at the post office. Within a year, I approached sisters

Lynn Lee and Debbie King (née Bouteiller) about buying the property of Stewart Brothers Holdings Ltd., which consisted of the post office, a fifty-foot vacant lot beside it, and vacant property across the street. We did the deal and I held the mortgage for ten years.

From the time I sold the business to Penhold Building Supplies Ltd., I continued to draw plans. One of the earliest plans I did for hire was a retirement home for a couple, likely in their late fifties or early sixties. It was a three-thousand square-foot monster with a twelve-hundred square-foot recreation room (the main design criteria for that room was that it had to have one wall large enough to mount a marlin on it), and a multi-car unattached garage with guest rooms above. They must have seen the look on my face as I wondered why anyone would build a retirement home of that size. The husband blurted out: "We've got a big family and they all come home to party."

My CPR station building brought in two jobs plans for two CPR station houses. One is just south-west of Penhold, the other is west of Rocky Mountain House. Other jobs from this period of semi-retirement are a school plan for Rainbow Hutterite Colony, house plans for Craig Seibel, a renovation plan to turn the former Odd Fellows Hall into a daycare, a perspective view of the Harvard Historical Aviation Society's proposed museum, a 40'x72'-16' laminated column building plan for Pinnacle Building Materials Ltd., a couple of residential plans for the Enterprise 203 Holdings First Nations company, and forty or so home plans for various individuals.

Seated in my new office with my printers and computer. The new office also featured a small 'kitchen' counter with sink, refrigerator and storage. The washroom was accessible and included a shower.

Wearing out

When the time came in 2013 to renew the lease or have Ed purchase the building supply properties, I informed Ed that I wanted to sell, and the purchase would include the building I was in as well. That set him back a bit, but by October everything was arranged. Penhold Building Supplies Ltd. owned all the property, and I was now a tenant. I began to say "No" to doing plan work. Although I continued to enjoy the creative part of planning, the detail work and setting up layouts for printing was becoming a drudgery. Things came to a head just before Christmas 2014. I made a solo visit to Ypres in Belgium for a three-day tour to some of the 1914 Christmas Truce locations during the Great War. When I arrived back home I came down with a flu bug, felt lethargic, and just stopped giving a damn. When I was back to my old self, I thought: "Ford, you don't have to do this anymore."

I handed Penhold Building Supplies Ltd. my notice, as I didn't need an office any longer. I gave away the furniture and equipment I had no room for and moved the rest into a room in our basement that became my work space. It is in that room that I continue to archive, sort, and catalog the history of the business and family.

In the '80s and '90s, as I bought up pieces of land around the farmstead on which we lived, I used to make the joke that I liked to know who my neighbours were (i.e. me!). In 2007, I began reversing that tactic, selling an eighty-one-acre parcel of land on the west side of the CPR rail line within the Town of Penhold to Custom Bulk Services. It was intended for a light-industry subdivision, which unfortunately due to the 2008 market crash, is still waiting to be developed. A few years later, I sold a seventy-two-acre parcel on the east side of Highway 2A to Charlie Newton. This left Stewart Brothers Land and Livestock Ltd. with a block of land on the west side of the CPR tracks, consisting of section 26 and parts of sections 25 and 35.

When my parents died, their estates were simple and clean: cash and a house, with my name put on the title with my mother's the day before she died. Eileen and I are determined that our estate should be as simple. Our children would not be farming, so it made little sense to hang onto the land. Although Stewart Brothers Land and Livestock Ltd. still owned the farm, we had not farmed it since 1974, instead renting it to Cy Little, and later to his sons, Scott and Terry. Our children would not be farming it. It did not make sense for us to keep the rest of the farmlands.

When Brian Stickland enquired in 2012 about purchasing land, we sold him and a partner section 35. The following year, we sold sections 26 and 25 to Brian and his mother Edna, keeping the sixty-acre part of section 36 that falls within the Town of Penhold. Within a year of the Stickland land purchase the mortgage on the Stewart Brothers Holdings Ltd. property was discharged. With that, both Stewart Brothers Land and Livestock Ltd.

and Stewart Brothers Holdings Ltd. were dissolved. The following year Stewart Supplies (Penhold) Ltd. was dissolved, officially ending one hundred and twelve years of history – Stewart Brothers-Stewart Supplies: pioneers, entrepreneurs, community builders.

What we give

The stories of our ancestors tell us who we are, where we came from, and what we came from. The characters, events, rhythms, and values all shaped me as a person, just as surely as they have shaped my own children.

In looking back over the stories related here, I'm most proud to know that the Stewart Brothers business provided real service to others for ten decades. Norman and Tom were not born into business. They became businessmen out of need, opportunity, and hard work. It is a testament to them and their families that they lived with such humanity. Their empathy, along with a strong work ethic and great sense of fun, was passed down to future generations. I've always felt that they were men as men ought to be.

As I reflect on what I have learned from the story of Stewart Brothers, some words of my personal hero, Sir Winston Churchill, come to mind:

"We make a living by what we get. We make a life by what we give."

Business Family Tree: Stewart Line

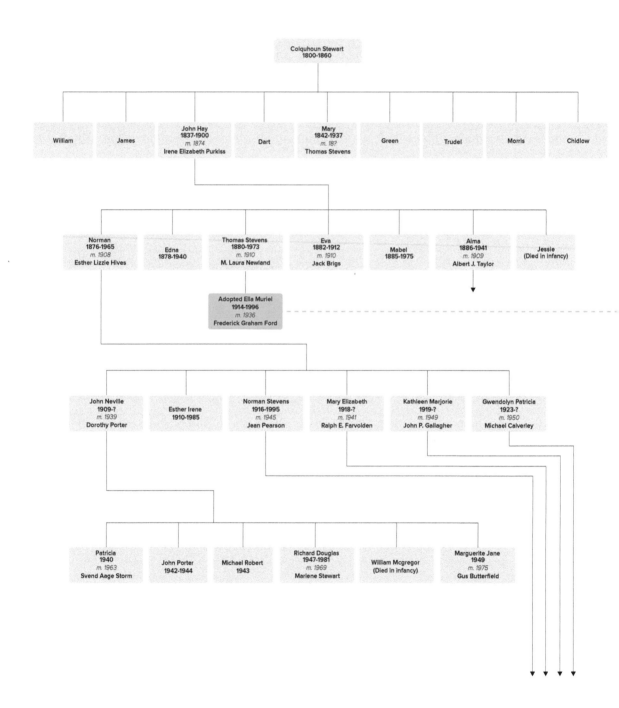

Business Family Tree: Ford Line

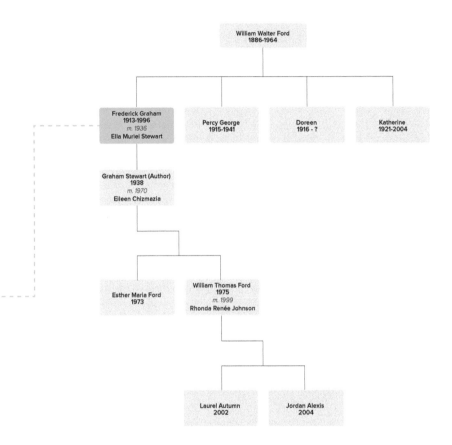

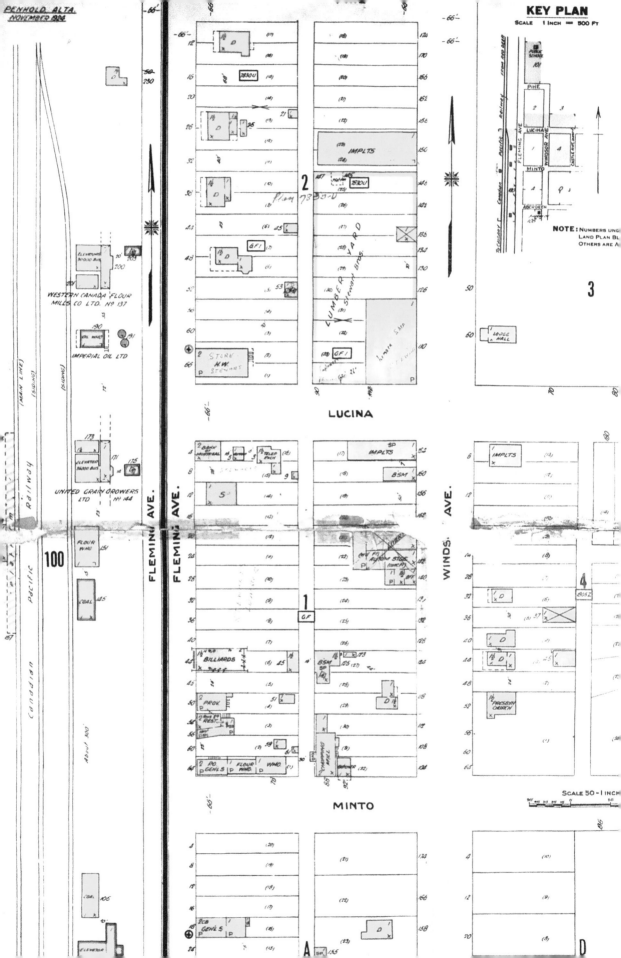

PENHOLD, ALTA.
NOVEMBER 1924

KEY PLAN
SCALE 1 INCH = 500 FT

NOTE: NUMBERS UNDER
LAND PLAN BL
OTHERS ARE A

3

LUCINA

FLEMING AVE.

FLEMING AVE.

WINDS. AVE.

WESTERN CANADA FLOUR
MILLS CO LTD. Nº 137

IMPERIAL OIL LTD

UNITED GRAIN GROWERS
LTD Nº 144

2

1

4

100

MINTO

A   D

SCALE 50 - 1 INCH

HOLD, ALTA.

llage on the Calgary Edmonton Branch of the
fic Railway, 85 Miles Nᵒᶠ Calgary

PRINTED NOVEMBER 1924
ada Fire Underwriters' Association

— REPORT —

Y: 120
Graded, fair condition, not lighted
F BUILDINGS: Electricity, small private plants, Gasoline
systems, Portable Gasoline Lamps and Kerosene

RTMENT -
DE: Volunteer, Unorganized
S: None
RM: Telephones

```
SPACE FOR
REVISION NOTES
```

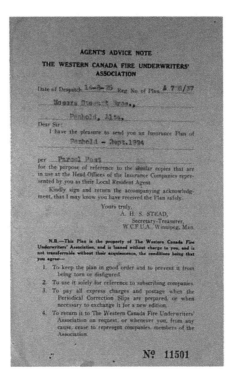

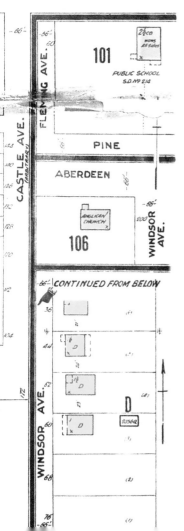

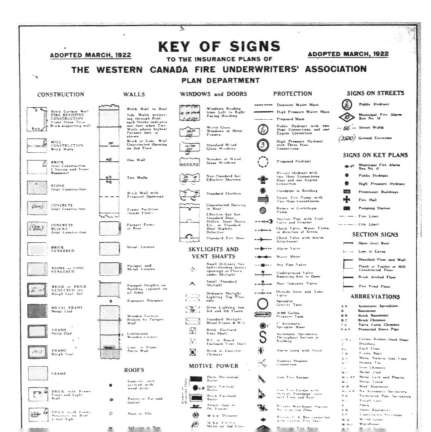

Appendix

1. Colquhoun Stewart, likely in the 1840s.

2. John Hay Stewart, son of Colquhoun and father of Norman and Tom.

3. Irene Purkiss married John Hay.

4. Columbia Lumber Company mill at Beavermouth, British Columbia, where Norman worked as a young man.

5. 1902 ledger page showing the Stewart-Douglas threshing accounts.

Red Deer, Alberta
January 21, 1956.

Mr. Thomas Stewart,
Red Deer, Alberta
and
Mr. Norman Stewart,
Penhold, Alberta

Dear Sirs,

       I have at this point in my lifetime retired from farming and am presently selling all of my farm machinery and livestock to my sons so that they can continue farming. Because I am now retired from farming I feel that it is an appropriate time to express my deep appreciation of the great assistance which Stewart Brothers have been to me in the course of the last 27 years.

       I will never forget the occasion in the year 1928 when you called at my farm at a time when I was completely without funds and severely handicapped in carrying on my farming operations because I did not have the necessary farm equipment. You asked me what item I considered I needed the most and I told you of the great difficulty I was having in watering my livestock because I did not have a pump engine or water tank. You immediately delivered to me a new pump engine and water tank and told me that I could pay for it at such time in the future as I felt able to. I am mentioning this pump engine and tank because to me it is symbolic of many, many ways in which Stewart Brothers have assisted me in the course of the last 27 years. During that time I have purchased almost entirely International Harvester Company machinery and have a complete line of that machinery and also an International Harvester Company deep-freeze in my home.

       It is my personal feeling that, if all businessmen conducted their business and treated their customers in the manner in which Stewart Brothers have over the course of many years, this world would be a much happier place. I feel that both of you can honestly consider that you have fulfilled your purpose in life and have carried out the Golden Rule in the fullest meaning of that expression. In disposing of my assets to my sons I am most strongly recommending to them that all of them continue to deal with Stewart Brothers and that they use International Harvester machinery in all their farming operations.

       In closing, I might say that that I still have the original pump engine which you delivered to me 27 years ago and it constantly reminds me that I could not have made a success of my farming operations without the generous help, assistance and guidance of Stewart Brothers over the many years.

       Very Sincerely Yours,

Les S. Jarvis

(Nellie's Dad)

6. The letter from Les Jarvis to Tom and Norman Stewart.

7. Ledger showing Tom's first pay, 1903

8. Sample of an IHC promissory note.

9. Ledger page 136 from 1903, showing a carload of hay sold to Yale Columbia Lumber Co.

Bridge A/c

	Brought forward from 172.		539 14
	1 pc. 2 x 4 - 16	28-	·30
	" 50' Ship lap	28.	1 40
	" 2 pcs 2 x 8 - 12 32'	25-	·90
	1 " 2 x 4 - 14 10'	25-	·28
Nov 25			542 02
	To 4 pcs 1 x 6 - 16 ship 56'	28-	1 57
Dec 1	To balance a/c		543 59
Mar 20	By mdse... By cheque 541.46		
2	To weighing cord cement		543 59
	for O Hedmark		15
31	Allowance for weighing		15
Jan 30	To 20 pcs 2 x 6 - 18 540'	29	15 66
31	6 2 x 10 - 16		
	6 2 x 10 - 14		
	6 2 x 10 - 12 420'	28	11 76
	By balance		27 42
		27 42	27 42
Feb 1	To balance		27 42
12	To 2 pcs 2 x 6 - 12 24'	28	67
	1 gallon can cyl. oil	1 25	1 25
17	2½ lbs hard oil	20	·50
19	15 pcs 2 x 10 - 16 native s.p. 200'	21	43 00
	69 - - - - 1840'	21	39 56
	2 2 x 8 - 24 - 64'	23	1 50
20	9 pcs 2 x 10 - 16 - 240'	21	5 16
	17 2 x 10 - 16 B.6 fir 455'	23	10 44
	19 2 x 12 - 16 - - - 608'	23	12 98
24	23 pcs 2 x 8 - 22 675'	23	15 53
	7 2 x 8 - 22 B.6 fir 205'	24	5 02
27	113 pcs 1 x 10 - 16 native shiplap 1506⅔	22	33 90
	141 1 x 8 - 16 - 1507'	22	33 84
	2 2 x 6 - 14 native s.p. 28'	21	60
	3130 lbs coal	6 00	9 39
29	By balance		241 76
		241 76	241 76
Mar 1	To balance acct		241 76

10. Ledger page 193 from 1906, showing materials supplied for the construction of the new bridge west of Penhold on the Red Deer River.

11. Eva Elizabeth Stewart

12. Mabel Alberta Stewart

13. Alma (Allie) Jane Stewart

14. Edna Margaret Stewart

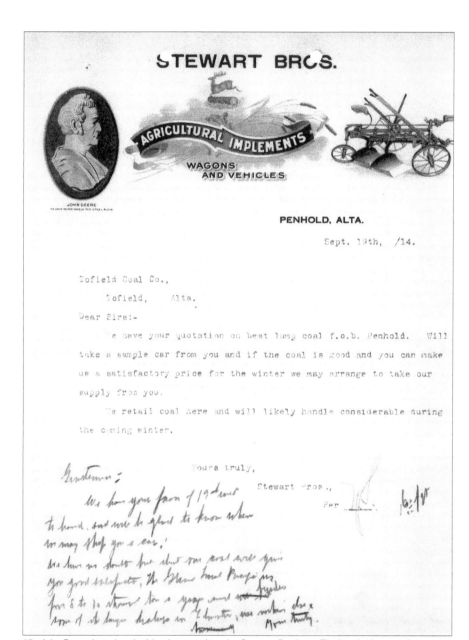

15. John Deere letterhead with a letter written by Stewart Brothers. The handwritten reply says:

Gentlemen:

We have your form of the 19th instant at hand and
will be glad to know when we may ship you same.

We have no doubt but that our coal will give you
good satisfaction. The Grand Trunk Pacific use from
8 to 10 short tons a year and besides some of the
larger in Edmonton use nothing else.

Yours truly

16 A & B. De Laval parts cabinet, circa 1925.

16 A.

16 B.

17. An aerial photo showing Stewart Brothers Coal Shed on the CPR siding, circa 1925.

Though it was Bennett buggies, breadlines and hard times, there was a Central Alberta attraction that drew spectators from all points of the compass. It was the best free show on what was then Main Street Alberta - the Old Calgary-Edmonton Trail.

Started in the late 1920s, construction of the Wright Farm at SW 3-37-28-4 went ahead into the 30s as if the Depression had never been. That was the wonder of it all; economic disaster or not, George Wright was determined, generous with a seemingly endless supply of cash and unstinting in his creation of a fabulous base layout.

conveyors and just about every other gadget out of reach of other contemporary operations. Red shale for the farm roads was freighted into Penhold by CP Railway.

At first quartering Holsteins, the farm went into purebred Jersey cattle with animals coming direct from the Channel Islands. So complete was the setup the federal govern-

master and the other, not much smaller, for the servant, plus a tennis court, all of them extant.

The considerable transactions in building materials was channeled through that sturdy district trader Stewart Lumber Supplies, still flourishing at the same location. Some of the first hired hands plowed wages back into their own

The backing for such an incredible sum those fundless days was a family whiskey fortune founded in Scotland. Since Mr. Wright's death about the end of World War II, the farm was operated for a brief period by his sons. Its break with dairying occurred when another occupier cleared out much of the expensive hardware and converted the big barn to a chicken roost. The holding was subsequently purchased by Miles Pixley, James Lynn and is now owned

PROMINENT LOCATION
...buildings added to, color changed.

It was to be the dairy farm of all dairy farms, and while under construction it was an oasis that supported many a district family and business down in luck.

Highlight of the attraction was the central barn which sported separate steel and concrete stalls, silo, overhead carrier rails, a special liquid manure filtration system, feed

ment allowed an isolated portion of it to be an official quarantine. The farm's products supplied the Wright retail dairy business located in Red Deer between the old Armoury (now the Fire Hall) and the Liquor Store.

Going up at the same time with the barn was a horse stable for purebred draft animals, two houses, one for the

holdings which today form the foundations of a robust agricultural precinct.

Settling in Canada after coming from the Old Country, George Wright bought the Henderson place where the grand design would take shape. The unofficial cost of the dream's fulfillment was around $250,000, cash on the barrelhead.

by Tony Juckes, another Old Countryman, who operates it as it was in the beginning, a Holstein dairy concern.

Originally richly dark brown-light trimmed hue, the buildings now are cream and white trimmed. Other than some additions and improvements, the site has changed little in the 40 years since it bathed weary eyes on old Main Street

18. An article from the Red Deer *AdViser* describing the Wright Dairy and mentioning Stewart Brothers.

19 A-D. 1930 clipping from the *Red Deer Advocate* announcing the purchase of the Red Deer IHC dealership from Ball & Van Slyke.

Strong Firm Coming to Red Deer

Stewart Bros. of Penhold Buy Ball & Van Slyke Implement Business

With the completion of the purchase today of the Ball & Van Slyke implement business by Stewart Bros. of Penhold, there comes to Red Deer one of the strongest, largest and most aggressive implement firms in the province. And they will be warmly welcomed.

Stewart Bros. have been operating at Penhold for the past twenty-five years, and by fair dealing and progressive methods have built up an outstanding business—one that is known all over the province. The firm feel that Red Deer is ever increasing in central services and that they will be able to take care of a wider territory with an agency at Red Deer. They specialize on sales and service. Mr. Jack Stewart, son of Mr. Norman Stewart, will come up from Penhold to take charge. Mr. D. E. Ball will continue his auctioneering and livestock business, and Mr. Van Slyke will look after his farming interests.

19 A.

199

Announcement

We wish to announce that we have purchased the implement business of Ball & Van Slyke, who have been carrying the International Harvester Co. lines of power and farm machinery.

It is our aim to carry a full line of this well-known machinery and also to service it. A fairly complete stock of repairs will always be on hand.

If you are in the market for anything in this line, we should like to have you come and see us.

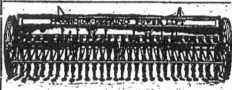

McCormick-Deering Drills

McCormick-Deering Drills are built for years of service. Years of experience and experiment have produced them. There is a McCormick-Deering Drill for every size of farm—large or small. They seed surely and pull light. Come in and talk your seeding problems over with us.

Stewart Bros.

RED DEER   PENHOLD

Red Deer Phone 497

19 B.

Building Sites Sold

Mr. W. E. Lord appeared with further reference to his building plans, accompanied by his architect, Mr. S. Pamely. Mr. Pamely explained in a general way what the building plans called for, and upon receipt from him of a rather more detailed plan, the transfer of property will be made as arranged.

In response to the city's offer of Lots 12-15, Block 8, Plan K, the Bannerman car lot corner, to Stewart Bros. for $3000, the firm offered $2000, half cash and the balance on transfer of the property. Mr. J. N. Stewart was present and submitted to the Council plans of the $7000 building proposed. After some discussion the Council accepted the offer, on the motion of Ald. Halladay and Hogg. A condition is that the building must be finished this year.

19 C.

Stewart Bros. to Build New Brick Warehouse

Plans Being Prepared for 50x100 ft. Structure on Gaetz Ave. South

With the purchase on Monday evening from the City of the southwest corner lot at Gaetz Avenue and Second St. South, Stewart Bros. plans for their new warehouse were carried a stage further. Plans are now being prepared for the erection on this property of a modern brick warehouse building 50x100, with loading platform. There will be a plate glass front on the Gaetz Avenue side and on part of the Second St. South side, and the interior will be arranged to give the speediest and most effective service to the firm's many customers. Showrooms will occupy the front of the building, and behind these will be the offices and repair parts department, with the shop at the rear. The building will probably run $7,000 to $8,000. Stewart Bros. opened their Red Deer warehouse in March, 1930, after having been in business in Penhold since 1884, and their excellent service on I.H.C. implements has built them a large and increasing business. In the new premises they will handle the I.H.C. trucks.

19 D.

20 A & B. Pages from the General Ledger, covering the years 1934 to 1952, detailing the company's fleet of vehicles.

20 A.

20 B.

DATE		DESCRIPTION	FOLIO	DEBITS	CK.	CREDITS	CR. or DR.	BALANCE
Nov	30	1935				79719 22	Cr	79719 22
Mar	30	1936 Prov. Inc. tax	35	87 98				79632 24
Apr	30	" Dom of Can Inc Tax	44	58 50			Cr	79573 74
Nov	30	To Mrs. C.E. Sturtzel		120 00			"	79453 74
	1	By 1/2 Share net profit				974 67	"	80448 41
Apr	29	1937 To Inc. tax	37	16 44			v	80431 97
July	31	By Rebate Dom Inc tax 1935	50			38 63	v	80450 60
Nov	30	To Mrs. Sturtzel		120 00			v	80330 60
"	30	By 1/2 Share net profit				1242 84	"	81573 44
Mar	31	1938 Prov Inc Tax 1937		100 73				81472 69
Apr	30	" Dom " 1937		55 73				81416 06
Nov	30	To 1/2 Share remittances Mrs Sturtzel		120 00			v	81296 06
"	5	" add'l tax Dominion		3 45				81292 61
"	30	By 1/2 Share net Profit 1938				2062 63		83355 14
Apr	30	1939 To Prov. Inc tax	23	129 34				83225 80
		Dom " "		143 34			Cr	83308 48
Sept	30	" " " 1937		20 20				83063 28
Nov	30	To 1/2 share remittances to Mrs Sturtzel		120 00				82943 28
"	"	By 1/3 share net profit				670 26		83613 54
Mar	23	To Dom of Can Inc Tax		160 00				83554 75
	30	" Prov of Alta " "		42 79			Cr	83491 83
Apr	30	" Dom of Can "		62 94			Cr	83443 89
May	31	" Prov. 39 36 Dom 16-53		51 94			Cr	83444 10
Sept	30					4 21	Dr	83444 10
Nov	30	1/2 Share Remittances to Mrs Sturtzel		20 00			Dr	83424 10
"	30	By 1/3 share net profit				971 50		84395 60
Mar	31	To Income Tax	22	34 28				84361 32
Apr	30	" "	28	203 80				84157 52

21. This page of his Capital Account shows Tom Stewart's remittances to Mrs. Sturtzel in the years 1935 to 1939.

22. Two of the company's International Harvester delivery vehicles, a D30 and a D35, in front of the store, circa 1938.

STOCKS & BONDS.

Dominion ofCanada, Conversion Loan,
        $12000.00, 5% due 1941,   @ $99.11 $11893.14

A.P. Cons. Oil Shares,   60 shares @ 30¢   18.00

Calgary Power Co.
        50 shares 6% preferred stock @$81.50 $4075.00   *55 shares are sold for cash + in sample lot*
        3   "   6%   "   "   86.00   258.00
        $6000.00, 5% 1st Mortgage Bonds
            due 1960   @   85.50   5130.00   9463.00

Power Corp. of Canada;
        $6500, 4% Debentures due Mar 1 1959
            @ $76.50 $4972.50   *P.Co.of C. sold in savings a/c*
        $3500.00   same as above @ $57.00   1995.00
        $500.00   "   "   "   55.00   275.00   7242.50

McColl-Frontenac Oil;
        40 Shares $4000.00 6% preferred
            stock @ $60.50   2420.00

Woodland Dairy;
        390 shares 7% preferred stock @ $7.50   2925.00

Lord Nelson Hotel;
        $3000.00, 4% Bonds due 1947 @ $70.00   2100.00   *Sold*

Associated Telephones & Telegraph;
        $2000.00, 5½% Debentures due 1955
            @ $65.50   1310.00   *Sold*

International Hydro Electric;
        $3000.00, 6% Bonds, due 1944 @ $72.00   2160.00   *Sold*

Canadian Hydro Electric;
        20 shares 6% preferred stock @ $79.00   1580.00   *Sold*

Great Lakes Paper Co;
        $5000.00, 6% First Mortgage Bonds
            due 1950   @ $44.00   2200.00   *Sold*

Century Brewing Co.-
        75 shares common stock   @ $30.00 $2250.00   *75 shares sold*
        75   "   "   "   27.50 2062.50
                             4312.50

Purchased Med Hat Bonds   4000 ~
Sterling Royalties   2500 ~
Carlton   "   1250 ~
other Shares   1250 ~

                             $47624.14

23. Stocks and bonds held by Stewart Brothers as of the business year ending in 1934.

24 A & B. Taken from the Alberta brand registry, these show the ownership of the T-connected-T and HH3 brands. The HH3 brand can also be seen on page 4 of this book.

TT	LT	STEWART BROS LAND & LVSTK LTD BOX 100, PENHOLD, AB T CONNECTED T

24 A.

HH3	Stewart Supplies (Penhold)Ltd. Box 100, Penhold l. r.

24 B.

STEWART BROS.

N. STEWART   J. N. STEWART   T. STEWART

Penhold and Red Deer Districts

Coincidental with the Golden Jubilee of the City of Red Deer is the Golden Jubilee of the principals of this firm. Fifty years ago a strong belief in the future of the Western Plains, and especially the Red Deer and Penhold districts, coupled with the instinct of the pioneer, resulted in the Stewart family's migration to what is now the finest farming district in Alberta. After twenty years of homesteading and farming in the community, the firm of Stewart Brothers commenced in the farm machinery business in the Village of Penhold. Year by year, as the district has enlarged and developed, so also has the firm kept in tune with the times, expanding from the original implement firm to the hardware and lumber business, and continuing on into the hay and grain business, thus enabling them to give to the district the finest service on these lines of goods that is obtainable in the West. The firm has now established a branch in the farm machinery line in the City of Red Deer, in the firm belief that this district and its people will continue to show the spirit and sane judgment that has built the community to what it is today.

25. Stewart Brothers' greeting in the *Red Deer Advocate*, marking the City of Red Deer's fiftieth anniversary, in 1934. Jack, now a partner, is pictured between Norman and Tom.

BUSINESS YEAR	PENHOLD BUSINESS	PENHOLD FARM	RED DEER MACHINE	RED DEER LUMBER
1931	$771.56	$530.84(CPR) $64.91(McG)	-$634.68	
1932			$2744.96	
1933	-$9655.51		$353.25	
1934	-$175.45		$1251.29	
1935				
1936	$1047.42	$193.88	$1876.58	
1937	$1085.36	$1085.86	-$837.59	$1060.79
1938	$897.27	$1274.36	$1993.28	$3297.35
	OWNERS	**DRAWING**	**ACCOUNTS**	
	NORMAN	TOM	JACK	
1931	$125,471.87	$126,941.27		
1932	$123,738.97	$126.006.07		
1933	$115,281.54	$118,454.33		
1934				
1935				
1936	$141.214.38	$80,693.89	$20,113.47	
1937				
1938	$146,428.76	$83,356.14	$20,006.29	
1907		$1598.06	Salary was $35 per month	Account interest at 8%

26. 1931-1938 fiscal results, recreated by the author from information available.

27 A & B. This feature story ran in the November 27, 1935 issue of the *Red Deer Advocate* and announces the opening of the new Red Deer Implement office. The metal serving tray was given to guests at the opening of the new Red Deer Implement office

27 A.

27 B.

28 A-C. Various news clippings related to the new Stewart Brothers implement store.

Stewart Bros. Opening Draws Many Farmers

Five Hundred Interested Men Visit New Premises Monday — Illustrated Lectures Enjoyed

There was a splendid turnout of farmers on Monday for the formal opening of Stewart Bros. new building, and the program of lectures and demonstrations was a popular one. Dr. Ray E. Neidig, Agricultural Director of the Consolidated Mining and Smelting Co., gave an address on the purpose and use of fertilizers which contained a wealth of valuable information. Mr. Roy E. Smith, manager of the International Harvester Company's demonstration farm at Gull Lake, Sask., gave an excellent talk on farming, illustrated with talking pictures. The visitors were shown through the building, and the machinery on display was demonstrated for them. About five hundred people took advantage of Stewart Bros.' invitation.

28 A.

Stewart Bros. To Erect New Building

Within a couple of weeks Stewart Bros. will commence construction of a building for their lumber yard at Red Deer. The new building will be erected on the site purchased from the city at the corner of Gaetz Ave. and Third St. Southwest, and will have a frontage of 62 feet on Gaetz Avenue and a depth of 120 feet. There will be a driveway clear through the shed, with a showroom on the north side and offices on the south. A hundred-foot track shed will be built at the rear along the railway siding. South of the offices, scales will be installed and a work shed erected. H. D. MacKay will have charge of construction.

28 B.

BUY LOCAL LUMBER YARD

Stewart Bros. have taken over the Central Lumber Yard business, and are putting in a full line of lumber and building materials.

28 C.

208

Bird's-eye view of Stewart Brothers' holdings in Penhold, Alberta. (A) Implement store, including display room and repairs; (B) storage warehouse for twine; (C) service shop; (D) lumber warehouse; (E) home of Norman Stewart, Sr.; (F) garage for trucks and cars; (G) machine storage; and (H) granaries and storage.

Norman Stewart, Sr., (left) and Thomas Stewart, Penhold, Alberta, founded the firm of Stewart Brothers in 1902. They have been International Harvester dealers since that time, and now hold contracts in Penhold and Red Deer, Alberta.

The Stewart Brothers store in Red Deer, Alberta. A well-lighted showroom occupies almost one-third of the building, and presents a most attractive appearance to passers-by at all times.

Jack Stewart, manager of the Stewart Brothers' store in Red Deer, Alberta, being interviewed by our reporter, C. C. Brannan. Mr. Stewart is shown in his office where he can discuss business with prospects in private.

(Below) Seasonable machines are displayed in the Stewart Brothers' Red Deer Store. It is necessary to walk through the display to get to the repairs counter or offices.

Thirty-Eight Years Of "Doing What It Took To Get Started" Brings Success To Stewart Bros.

By C. C. BRANNAN

They "Got started, then kept on doing what it took to get started."

This formula advanced by Mr. C. W. Lockard, in the last issue of the International Harvester Dealer, very aptly describes the policies followed by Stewart Brothers in a long and successful career as McCormick-Deering dealers.

Away back in 1884 before the railway had reached that part of the country, Norman and Tom Stewart went out from eastern Ontario with their parents and settled on a homestead in the vicinity of Penhold, Alta. They were then very small boys, and since that time their activities have centered around Penhold and Red Deer, which is eight miles to the north.

Stewart Brothers started in business, under that name, in the village of Penhold in 1902. They were McCormick sub agents during 1902 and 1903, and signed their first Deering contract in 1904. Since that time their history has been one of continual development and expansion, until to-day, with their two agencies doing a combined volume of over $100,000 per year, they are foremost in the retail implement industry in the Province of Alberta.

Their's was no overnight development but a record of hard work, perseverance, good common horse sense and gradual expansion.

Their first store in Penhold was a frame building 25 x 40 feet. They built their present store in 1906. Since that time it has been renovated and modernized. It is now a very well laid out building, 32 x 86 feet which houses a hardware store, general office and repairs department. The illustration showing the bird's-eye view of Penhold gives some idea of the size of their operations in this village which might well be called "Stewartville."

Norman Stewart was the guiding hand in this carefully conducted program. He is the manager of the business, while Tom is chief of the outside operations which involve a very complete rebuilding and merchandising service.

In April, 1930, Stewart Brothers took over the McCormick-Deering contract in Red Deer, under the management of Jack N. Stewart, son of Norman Stewart. They gradually increased the volume of business at this point and in 1935 built their present Red Deer branch which is a model agency in every sense of the word. It is a handsome building of brick and steel, fully modern, measuring 50x105 feet. The showroom in front is 50x35 feet, and has a polished hardwood floor. The office, repairs department, tractor work shop, storage space on ground floor and basement, hydraulic operated freight elevator take up the remainder of the space. Large loading platform with railway trackage and truck loading space is also provided for.

Jack Stewart, the energetic manager of this branch, is 29 years old and has been brought up in the implement business. He has been, for the past two years, an alderman at the City of Red Deer, which is one of the most modern and progressive small cities of the west. It has a population of 3,000. The City Fathers pursue a rigid "pay as you go" policy with the result that they have no outstanding debts, have a credit balance in the bank and civic improvements of a very high calibre. It serves a mixed farming district which in

probably fifty years of settlement has never known a complete crop failure.

Another son, Norman, Jr., supervises the trucking operations of the combined agencies.

Stewart Brothers, in their two agencies, operate two D-2 trucks, one DS-30 and one D-35 besides barter trucks which are pressed into service in the harvest season. Their trucking operations include custom hauling besides taking care of the needs of the business which include delivery of new machines and return of trades and hauling of horses and lumber which are frequently taken in trade. Under young Norman Stewart's guidance the trucks are kept in first-class mechanical condition.

There are many angles to a big business such as this: No sale is too large or too small. One sale in 1939 included a TD-40 TracTracTor with bulgrader, Crawler Wagon and Tulsa Winch. On this sale alone, two carloads of lumber were taken in trade besides a large number of horses. Another sale for 1940 which was delivered in December, is the largest International truck ever sold in Canada—a Model DRD-426-F, retailing at approximately $13,000. On this sale they took sixty horses in trade besides a large quantity of lumber. They have an excellent outlet for these trades in retail lumber yards operating at both Penhold and Red Deer.

Trades where horses are concerned are made by Phil Tweeton, foreman of the Stewart Farm at Penhold, who is recognized as one of the most capable horse dealers in the west.

In the 38 years which they have been in business, Stewart Brothers have followed a consistent policy of systematic canvassing and farm demonstrations.

They employ four salesmen and under their policy of merchandising second-hand machinery, they never hesitate to take a trade of any kind at the right price. They employ a large rebuilding staff.

Their combined staff at Red Deer and Penhold consists of three in the office, four salesmen, five tractor mechanics, four general shop men who are employed in rebuilding binders and other used machines, two truck drivers, one horse buyer and farm foreman and three other farm employees.

They have built up an enviable reputation for merchandising trades. Every farmer for miles around knows that he can get a good buy in dependable used machines from Stewart Brothers. They have a shrewd policy of overhauling tractors and other machines in the slack season and at the beginning of harvest season they always have available probably 20 reconditioned binders ready to go to work in the field.

They enjoy the full confidence of the farmer trade in a section which is probably one of the most prosperous over a long period of any in the west. They have a reputation for fair dealing and up-to-the-minute sales and service.

In January of 1939 they conducted a joint power farming entertainment at Red Deer with an attendance of 486. It was the most enthusiastic meeting on the Calgary territory, and bore testimonial to the esteem in which Stewart Brothers are held.

29. This 1940 *International Harvester Dealer* article includes historical information and some great photos.

30 A & B. These photos of Kaye and Gwen, taken during the Second World War, are obviously staged and professionally done; I suspect it would have been an IHC initiative.

30 A. Kaye Stewart serving a customer at the parts counter in Red Deer.

30 B. Gwen Stewart promoting the features of an International Harvester cream separator.

31. Behind the custom-built dog house is my old workspace, including drafting board and file cabinet to the right of the stove pipe.

Ridgewood Residents Resent Hutterite Intrusion

Ridgewood community hall was packed to capacity on Thursday night when the residents of the district held a meeting in protest of the sale of land in their district for the establishment of a Hutterite colony.

The meeting was called to order by R. H. Edgar who had been appointed chairman. Secretary of the meeting was T. John Huckell of The Province. The meeting went through without interruption until midnight.

A long list of speakers protested emphatically that they did not want a Hutterite colony established in the district and brought forth many strong arguments as to why they did not want these people in their midst.

A motion by Mr. Moore was unanimously passed that a delegation of certain men be appointed to approach Mr. E. Stephenson whose land is in the process of being sold to the Hutterites and endeavor to have him change his mind and cancel the agreement of sale.

This delegation comprised of Messrs. Dave Ure, Oscar Lundgren, R. H. Edgar, B. Einarson, Gordon Johnson and Jim Morrisroe met with Mr. Stephenson on Saturday night and presented their case to him receiving a cordial welcome in his home and a patient hearing of their protests.

At Thursday's meeting the signature of practically everyone present was obtained to be attached to Mr. Moore's motion to indicate the unanimity of the feeling of the residents of the district in regard to the Hutterite colony.

Space will not permit resumes of the remarks of the speakers but all the following were anxious to do everything possible to find a solution to the Hutterite problem and deplored the fact that the finest country in the world should be troubled with peoples who do not live the Canadian way of life: R. H. Edgar, reeve of M.D. of Red Deer, Mr. Einarson; F. P. Galbraith, president Red Deer Board of Trade; Mel Cunningham, president of Alberta Board of Trade; J. K. Rimington, president Innisfail Board of Trade; Hershel Mover; Dave Ure, M.L.A.; F. D. Shaw, M.P., Harley Price; Max Wynn, Innisfail Legion president; Hugh McKay, Dr. Grant, V. Bjorkeland, Oscar Lundgren.

Mr. Hofer manager of the Hutterite colony was called upon to answer questions.

Mr. J. J. Letcher of Letcher and Daines the real estate firm who are handling the land transaction between the Hutterites and Mr. Stephenson was also called on to speak and answered questions asked him by a number of those present.

Fred Colborne of Calgary, M.L.A. for the air force also addressed the meeting having been asked by Hutterite Manager Hofer to come to Ridgewood.

EIGHT PERCENT WAR TAX MAY BE REMOVED

At the convention of the Union of Alberta Municipalities held in Lethbridge, October 30 and 31, one of the first announcements was that the 8% special war tax on consumer gas and electricity would be removed soon. J. J. Parr, secretary of the town of Vermilion, said his town had taken up the matter with the Dominion cabinet and definite assurance was given the tax would be removed at the next session. This tax had been the subject of several resolutions from various towns.

Hon. C. E. Gerhart, minister of municipal affairs said that taxes are not inflated in cities and towns like the cost of living. He said farmers were moving in greater numbers to the villages than to the large towns and cities.

Replying to the frequent request that the province carry 50% of the cost of education, he said that in some municipalities it was now paying 80%. He said that greater provincial financing of education might mean greater provincial control.

He warned that some town councils have been overspending their budgets and drawing on reserves. He considered it unfair to taxpayers to obtain money from reserves without authorization, and suggested that if this practice was not halted voluntarily, the government would step in.

The convention endorsed the policy of municipal taxation on government-owned property that is revenue producing.

There was definite opposition to daylight saving except on a national basis at the convention of Alberta Municipalities. Hon. C. E. Gerhart said the government was against daylight saving as carried on in a provincial sense. A good many opposed any form of daylight saving, but this was modified to provide for national action if necessary. The railways both in Canada and United States operate on standard time no matter what governments may do.

In the interest of high standards of cleanliness and courtesy it was carried that the government set up machinery to license restaurant employees and to examine cooks for proficiency before granting permission to engage in their trade.

KNEE HILL VALLEY HEREFORDS GO TO PEACE RIVER

Messrs. Frank Churchill and Bruce Dodd were in the Peace River country at the first of the week having trucked a consignment of cattle to their father-in-law Mr. Slette, which he had purchased from Mr. J Barclay of Knee Hill Valley.

32. This November 13, 1947 *Innisfail Province* article described the protest meeting against the Hutterite settlement, for which Norman's support was solicited, but not given

Penhold Celebrates Opening of Water and Sewer System

Congratulations were extended to the citizens of Penhold at a banquet held in the Memorial Hall on Wednesday evening last week by Hon. Dave Ure, minister of agriculture; Mayor Percy of Innisfail and Mayor Bunn of Red Deer for their progressive good citizenship in establishing a municipally owned water and sewer system in the village. Mayor W. O. Johnston presided at the banquet which was followed by a dance. Over 125 persons attended the banquet.

Penhold is thought to be the smallest community in Canada to have established its own water and sewer system. The population is around 160.

Total cost of Penhold's system is $15,000 and this has been financed by the issue of twenty year debentures. Digging on the system started in October 1947 and the water was turned on in thirty residences and business places on November 11th, 1948 and the sewer was connected up on December 7th last. Water is pumped from a ninety-six foot well into two, 300 gallon underground storage tanks.

———o———

33. This January 20, 1949 *Innisfail Province* article reports on Penhold's new water and sewer system — unusual for a community of just 160.

Arena Committee Presents Financial Statement

Following is the financial statement of the Innisfail Arena Fund as presented by the Innisfail District War Memorial Community Centre Society.

Statement of Receipts and Disbursements January 1st, 1951 to October 17th, 1952

Receipts

Individual subscriptions	14,017.21
Lions-Legion broomball	82.36
Legion carnival	75.00
Lions Dance Revue	62.62
Calf raffle	402.44
Ladies Auxiliary Canadian Legion	62.60
Loyal Orange Lodge, 1951	218.36
I.O.D.E. Drewie Lennox Chapter	28.20
Proceeds car raffle (Lions-Legion)	10,021.65
C. L. Olmstad, cement	14.50
Lions Club Carnival	401.00
Lions Club Swimming Pool, adjustment	59.46
Total	**$25,445.60**

Disbursements

Alberta marketing services, cement	562.00
Housez Ltd., photo arena	28.53
Alberta Lumber, roofing	2162.00
Lunches for workers	70.47
Organization expenses	53.70
C.P.R. Freight on lumber	1768.43
J. C. Calder, first aid kit	8.00
D. Walders, electrical supplies	1290.75
J.J. Letcher, fire insurance	163.26
Receiver General of Canada	23.22
Stewart Brothers, lumber	15520.90
Labor	2023.75
Fox Brothers, hardware	49.02
Innisfail Povince	96.40
Thompson Concrete	380.00
Daines Bros., bolts	29.45
Sundry: Excise, postage, etc.	27.10
Alberta Lumber, lathe	64.90
Bank charges	8.83
Calgary Power	18.00
Stanley Brock	8.65
Crane Limited	4.32
Bank Balance, Oct. 17/52	1083.92
Total	**$25,445.60**

The pledges made to the arena fund totalled $20,065 of which $14,017.21 (shown in statement) has already been paid in to the fund. The balance yet to be paid into the fund by those who had promised donations is $6048.79.

At a recent meeting of the committee it was planned to get the permanent ice area of the arena built into its permanent condition for the 1952-53 skating and hockey season.

The arena blueprints have received the official approval of the provincial government.

The 400 Club which has added to the arena fund to the extent of $10,021.65 is once more in operation after the holiday season lay off and a new Chevrolet will be awarded to the honorary president at a dance on Friday November 14th. The Legion and the Lions are in charge of 400 Club operations and membership tickets are now on sale at $10 each.

34. This October 13, 1952 clipping from the *Innisfail Province* outlines the expenditures toward the new Innisfail arena.

213

35. The Stewart Brothers threshing outfit in 1910 – Tom can be seen above the large wheel.

36 A. This is the kind of advertisement for Hume products that Graham would have seen, spurring the company to represent the Hume Pick-Up Reel, which was ideal for harvesting downed crops.

36 B. Graham Ford on the CPR station platform in Penhold in 1954, holding a handful of Hume Reel shipping forms.

37. General Ledger of the Capital Control Account, showing the yearly profits and distribution to the partners for the years 1945 to 1954.

38. Volunteers shingling the roof of the new Penhold Curling Club.

39. Stewart Brothers' new building supply store in Red Deer, pictured on an ashtray given to customers.

40. Charlie Parker and Norman Stewart (top hat), riding in Charlie's 1902 Oldsmobile in the Alberta 50th Jubilee parade in Red Deer.

41 A & B. Certificate of Incorporation of Stewart Supplies (Penhold)) Ltd., July 9, 1958, and the list of shareholders.

41 A.

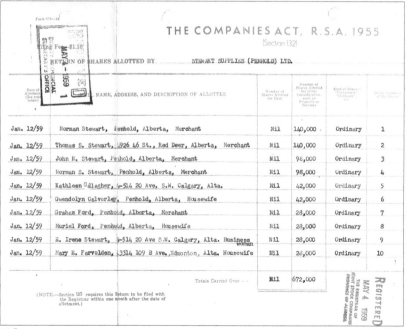

41 B.

42. The WRLA badge.

43 A-C. Pages from the 1909 *Lumberman's Actuary* that I found in an antique store.

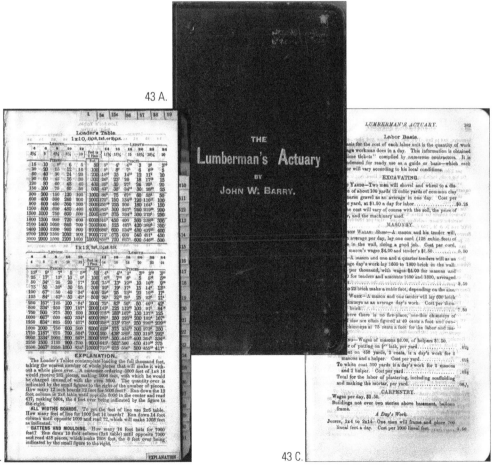

43 A.

43 B.

43 C.

44 A. Cover of the Inter-Provincial
Component Homes manual.

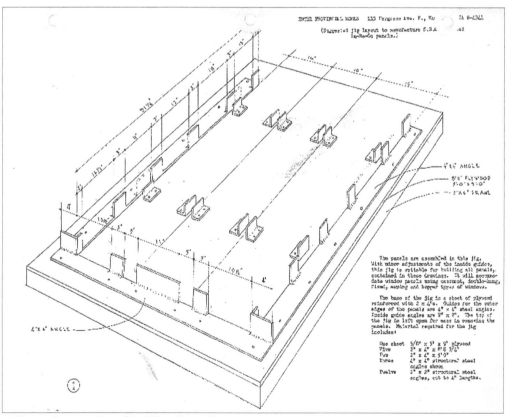

44 B. Inter-Provincial Home Plan 48″ wall panel jig.

District News___

Marjorie Smith receives her award from Wayne Gillette.

Marjorie Smith honored as Penhold's Citizen of the Year

Province correspondent and tireless community worker Marjorie Smith was honored for her contributions to the Penhold community last week, as the Lions club presented her with its first-ever Citizen of the Year award.

"I had no idea...it was a complete surprise," Mrs. Smith told the Province, noting that she thought she had been invited to the annual Charter Night due to her past contributions as auditor for the Lions' books.

Mrs. Smith joined the Province about three years ago this August, but had originally planned to make her stay as brief as possible. "It all started when I submitted a write-up on the 61st anniversary of the W.I., which led to this job," she noted.

She planned to stay only for a month, until another correspondent could be found—but no one else was located, and we're proud to have Mrs. Smith on staff with her lively and informative news items from Penhold.

Les and Marjorie established residency in Penhold in 1946, with Les taking over duties as agent for the Alberta Wheat Pool elevator. Following his death, Mrs. Smith went to work for Stewart Supplies for 18 years, from 1960 to 1978, when she retired at the age of 74 years.

A member of the Penhold Ladies Aid, and the Presbyterian Church Board, Mrs. Smith was honored for her diligent community work. She helped serve coffee and sandwiches to the volunteer workers, during construction of the curling rink in 1949, and has audited books for many other town clubs.

Mrs. Smith is also known in the community as a past provincial secretary of the Alberta Women's Institute, and can always be counted on for up-to-the-minute and concise reporting of W.I. activities.

Congratulations, Marjorie...it couldn't happen to a nicer person!

45. The Innisfail Province article about Mrs. Smith, Penhold's Citizen of the Year in 1960.

46 A-D. Front page of 1962 IHC dealer magazine and the full article on Stewart Supplies' 60th anniversary.

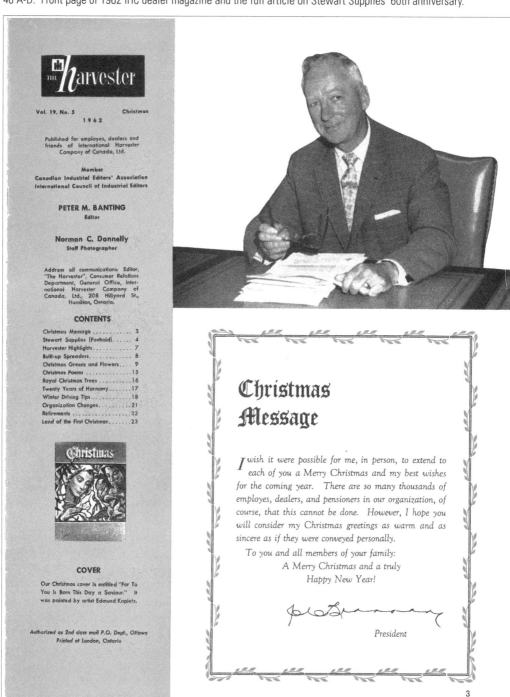

46 A.

AN ENVIABLE RECORD
60 YEARS OF CONTINUOUS SERVICE

THERE were less than fifty farmers in Alberta's Red Deer-Penhold area at the turn of the century. The only roads were trails which wound over the land, dodging the many little sloughs and heavier bluffs.

This was the scene in 1902 when brothers Tom and Norman Stewart quit their farm to become IH farm equipment dealers at the tiny hamlet of Penhold. With six hundred dollars borrowed from the bank, they started Stewart Bros. - - a business that has offered 60 years of continuous service to local farmers, and one that our Company is proud to have in its 1100 strong Canada-wide dealer organization.

Considering the fact that farmers were few, spread over a wide area, and had little or no money, it is surprising that the Stewarts would venture into the farm equipment business. But, like so many IH dealers, they had their eye to the future. They saw in their area wonderful pos-

sibilities for a mixed farming community. They knew that advanced farm machinery was fast becoming a necessity to economically grow grain and livestock. And the C.P.R. had just completed its Calgary-Edmonton line, opening the country to many new settlers.

The two brothers rented the farm they had homesteaded since 1884 and set up their business, counting on their farming experience and knowledge of machinery to help them become good farm equipment dealers.

The first years were difficult. But with the steadfast tenacity that is characteristic of IH dealers, the Stewarts kept the business solvent. They augmented their income from machinery sales by doing custom threshing throughout the area with a steam-powered thresher, while their youngest sister, Allie, rode eight miles a day on horseback to look after their office. Little by little the business began to grow.

Some early equipment sold by Stewart Bros. includes late 1920's McCormick - Deering combine, above, and tractor with angle lugs, right, used about 1919.

4

The Harvester

46 B.

223

Dealers in that day were called "Implement Agents," and agents they were. The Stewarts would hitch a driving team to a buggy or cutter and, armed only with a few implement catalogs and a price list, would canvass for sales.

"Canvassing in those days was pleasant," reminisces Norman Stewart. "We always took time for a good visit. We usually packed a gun and thought nothing of tying up the team for an hour if we ran across a flock of prairie chickens or partridges.

"There were neither cars, nor roads on which to run them. We often would remain out for two or three days at a time, working from some stopping place or staying overnight with a farmer. Even on these extended trips we were never more than 20 or 25 miles away from home. But when it took the better part of a day to get there, it paid to just stay there until the whole district had been covered."

Knowing the line was not difficult, because there were only a few kinds of machines to sell. For haying and harvest there were binders, mowers, and rakes. Tillage machines were: walking plows, an occasional sixteen-inch "sulky," and, very seldom, a two-bottom riding gang, none of which are made today. "We used to bring in sleighs and buggies by the carload," Mr. Stewart recalls.

Prices of these machines were as different from today's prices as are the machines themselves. "I remember buying a ten-foot McCormick dump rake for twenty-nine dollars, a year or so before we left the farm," says Norman Stewart.

"The cream separator was almost our bread and butter in those days. We sold hundreds of them. Everyone milked a few cows, and cream cheques were about the only form of cash we ever saw.

"Thus less than ten per cent of the machines were ever sold for cash. The usual settlement was a fall note for the full amount of the sale, in the case of small goods. Anything that sold for one hundred dollars or over was on a two or sometimes three-fall basis.

"Trade-ins were something we had never heard of. Nobody had enough machinery and if a chap did decide to dispose of, say, his walking plow for a riding gang, there was always a neighbor or several of them waiting to buy his old one.

"We often dealt in hay or grain, but this found a ready market, and we could soon turn it into money."

Christmas, 1962

It was my privilege to work with Stewart Brothers as their Zone Manager from 1938 to 1948. I learned at first hand about their business ability, and their reputation among farmers in the community for good service, fair dealing and integrity. I join with their countless friends in extending warmest congratulations on their 60th anniversary.

Norman Stewart knows that a demonstration is just as valuable today as 60 years ago when he canvassed in a buggy. Here he sells 150 spreader features to Jim Hamill, kneeling, and Wallace Douglas, second from left.

5

46 C.

224

Mr. Stewart is high in his praise of the Company, "whose co-operation could always be counted on. A good deal of sales help was always there for the asking, and right good salesmen the IH men were.

"At the end of the season, anything the agent had unsold was carried over, without questions and without Harvester charging any interest.

"Tractors began to take over as the main source of farm power after the end of World War I. The old Titan was the tractor that first gained popularity.

"About the mid 1920's the Titan was superseded by the McCormick-Deering 15/30. This new tractor, the forerunner of today's tractors, marked the first real breakthrough into complete tractor farming. It replaced horses in large numbers. Dealers everywhere were almost forced to trade in horses on many of their tractor deals. We were no exception. Luckily we had always kept a piece or two of farm land. At least we had a place to put our four-legged trade-ins. Many a time we had over a hundred head on hand.

"Today's tractor with its rubber tires, built-in hydraulic systems, power take-off, torque amplifier and large selection of speeds, is indeed a piece of precision engineering. As such it requires well trained and well equipped service, which we as dealers must provide.

"In the days of the old Titan, the farmer was a greenhorn indeed if he could not and did not pull off the head and grind the valves a couple of times a year. He also put in a set of rings from time to time, and a new connecting rod bearing whenever the engine hammered one out. Now, in all but a very few cases, those days are gone.

"Along with these older tractors we often sold International wood, and later 'all steel', threshers. Having spent a good many of our earlier years on and around threshing rigs, we liked to sell these machines. The International was always a smooth, easy-running thresher, and a good grain saver.

"The first combines came into our district in 1928. Most farmers believed that this was not 'combine country' and they caught on slowly. It would be almost impossible to farm without them now.

"Of all the machines we sold, none ever received the genuine affection which we had for the binder. To us it was a wonderful piece of engineering, and the tying mechanism, or knotter, was the perfect invention.

Stewart Supplies is a family business. Left to right are Tom Stewart, Graham Ford, Jack Stewart, Norman Stewart Sr., and Norman Stewart Jr.

"Even though threshing was the final operation, it always seemed that binding was the one that counted most. To see four good horses going down the field with an eight-foot binder behind them, the binder-whip sticking high in the air, and the discharge arms kicking out a bundle a couple of times a minute, gave one a feeling which could not be equalled by any other machine.

"Parts service was good on these machines. We took pride in being able to fill all parts orders, and Harvester certainly backed us up. Seldom did a farmer have to go home without at least a good second-hand piece if we happened to be out of what he wanted. They came for miles to get their repairs. It was a wonderful way of getting people into our store. While there, they also bought many other hardware items. Binder whips, nose nets, axle grease, machine oil, pots and pans, and even a new cook stove on occasion.

"It is hard to realize that those days are gone, that the binder is an obsolete machine. We still miss them as harvest time rolls around," reminisces Norman Stewart.

It was always the hope of Tom and Norman Stewart that their original partnership would eventually become a family corporation. When Norman's sons finished school, they joined the business: Jack, the eldest, in 1929, and Norman, Jr. in 1935. During World War II the boys served in the armed forces. To keep the business running, their sisters took over the management of Stewart Bros.' Red Deer office. Kathleen Stewart

became an excellent partswoman, and Gwen proved that she could sell any and all of the available machines, as well as handling office and bookkeeping work.

They did such a good job, in fact, that even today customers of Stewart Bros. express their appreciation of the service and help the girls provided during the difficult years of parts and implement shortages.

Today, Tom Stewart and his son-in-law, Graham Ford, and Norman Stewart and his two sons Jack and Norman operate the dealership. Other members of the Stewart family serve as partners.

In 1960 the business incorporated under the name Stewart Supplies (Penhold) Ltd., with a total of 10 shareholders.

For 60 years the Stewarts have operated their business, building it from a borrowed six hundred dollars in 1902, to a thriving organization in 1962 with a reputation for quality IH machines and quick, courteous personal service.

Speaking for himself and his brother Tom, Norman Stewart had this to say on the 60th anniversary of Stewart Supplies:

"Times have changed tremendously since we began. Farming methods, business procedure, and farm machines bear little resemblance to their predecessors of sixty years ago. But if we had it all to do again, I can think of nothing which would give us greater satisfaction than to serve the farmers of this good country in the way that we have been privileged to do these past sixty years."

6

The Harvester

47 A. The 30,000-bus. grain elevator on Stewart Supplies farm in Penhold

47 B. Svend Storm using a bale thrower to lob straw bales for bedding into the feed pen.

47 C. Dumping a load of silage into the bunker silo on the Stewart Supplies farm.

47 D. A view of the Stewart Supplies cattle feed lot in Penhold.

48 A & B. Portions of the business-winning eight-page flyer, this one showing an ad for an archrafter building.

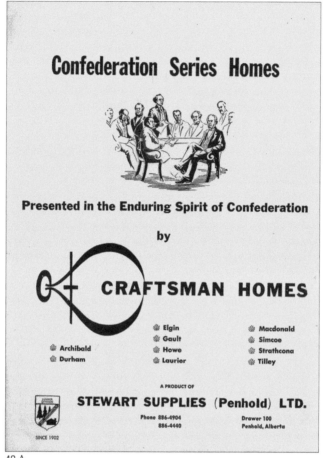

48 A.

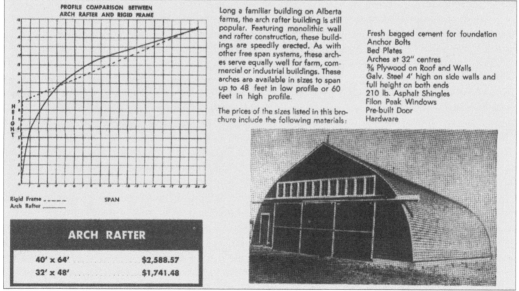

Long a familiar building on Alberta farms, the arch rafter building is still popular. Featuring monolithic wall and rafter construction, these buildings are speedily erected. As with other free span systems, these arches serve equally well for farm, commercial or industrial buildings. These arches are available in sizes to span up to 48 feet in low profile or 60 feet in high profile.

The prices of the sizes listed in this brochure include the following materials:

Fresh bagged cement for foundation
Anchor Bolts
Bed Plates
Arches at 32" centres
¾ Plywood on Roof and Walls
Galv. Steel 4' high on side walls and full height on both ends
210 lb. Asphalt Shingles
Filon Peak Windows
Pre-built Door
Hardware

48 B.

49. The Luisink brothers framing the archrafters for Stewart Supplies' new 48'x102' warehouse.

50. The 1968 machinery auction underway.

51. The Penhold Bonspiel wind-up dance in the new 48'x102' warehouse.

52 A-C. Construction of a 2500-bus. grain bin inside the new archrafter.

52 A. Ron Newton in the foreground.

52 B. Larry Miller, Ron Newton, and me. The fourth person behind   52 C.
us is unidentified.

53 A & B. Four-page flyer promoting prebuilt bins, feeders, shelters and trusses.

53 A.

53 B.

54 A & B. Construction plans for the 2500-bus. bins, drawn by Stewart.

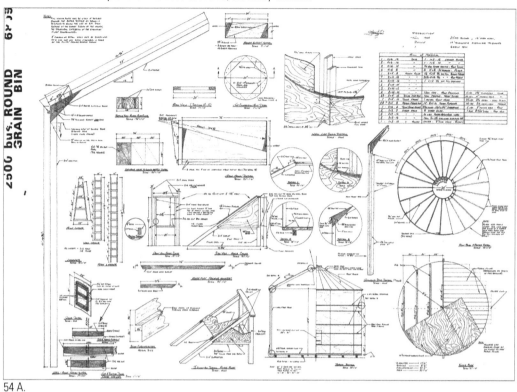

54 A.

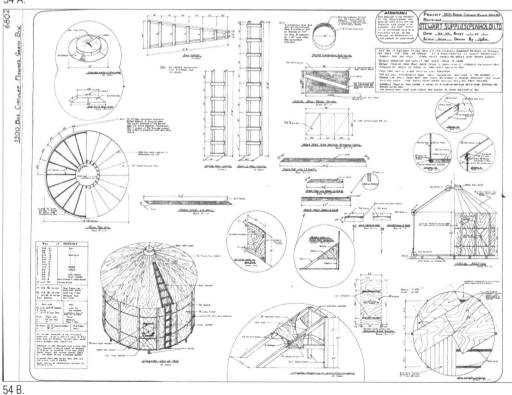

54 B.

55. 1970 sales flyer for plywood grain bins, featuring the Canadian Government tax rebate.

56. Casey den Boer working on an 8'x16' Cattle Feeder.

233

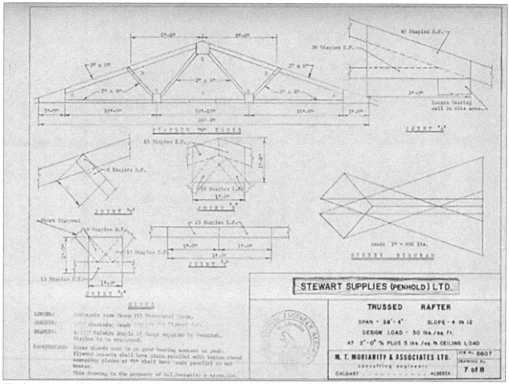

57. An example of the engineering for plywood gusset trusses.

58 A. Interior view of George Domoney's centre-gutter hog barn, showing raised centre walkway under heightened scissor-truss ceiling.

58 B. Exterior view of George Domoney's hog barn, with one of our V-bottom feed bins beside.

STEWART SUPPLIES (PENHOLD) LTD.

FARM OPERATING EQUIPMENT
LUMBER & BUILDERS SUPPLIES
FERTILIZER

Telephones
886-4440
886-4904

PENHOLD, ALBERTA

Dear Neighbor;

It is our understanding that the Lumber Yard located in Delburne has closed.

The loss of a Lumber Yard to a Community is never good. The special services and supplies offered by a yard cannot be duplicated by any other type of business. As a supplier who has served this district, may we remind you of the services we provide, be they concerned with new building, renovation, or the bits and pieces required for general repair work.

Our Building Supply Division carries an extensive line of Lumber, Plywood, Plasterboard, Hardboard, Cement, Posts, Doors, Windows, Mouldings, Insulation and associated Building Hardware & Tools.

We specialize in such yard pre-built items as Cattle Feeders, Fertilizer Bins, Feed Bins, Grain Bins, Roof Trusses and Arch Rafters. We also pre-cut buildings and construct such millwork items as stairs and pre-hung doors.

We offer a complete line of Package Homes under the Craftsman label and have contractors available to construct homes completely or in part. We also contract build Hog Barns, Cattle Barns, Cattle Sheds, Work Shops, Garages and Machine Sheds.

Our in yard drafting department is at your service for the design of custom homes, barns, sheds, elevators, truss rafters or other plan work. This service is offered at no extra charge to customers purchasing construction material from us.

Two trucks are at your service for the delivery of material. In truckload lots -- and loads may be pooled between neighbors -- no delivery charge is made except in the case of cash & carry items.

Neighbor; We have been in business for some 68 years -- since 1902, and we have no intention of pulling out now! Through the years, we have built a tradition of service and that is really what this letter is all about. We are here to serve you. Won't you let us try? - We are ready.

Yours truly,

Stewart Supplies (Penhold) Ltd.

"SERVING CENTRAL ALBERTA SINCE 1902"

59. The letter I wrote to residents of the Delburne and Elnora area.

60 A-C. The cover of our twenty-page *ADVENTURE '70 HOMES* flyer.

60 A.

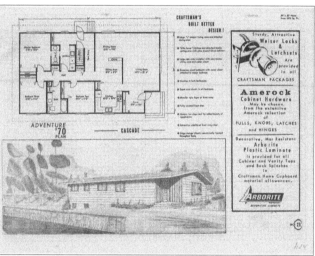

60 B.

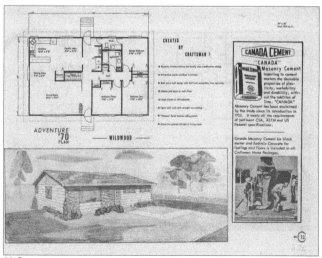

60 C.

61 A & B. Two articles from the *Red Deer Advocate* concerning the life and death of Tom Stewart.

The Advocate

GORDON J. GRIERSON
Publisher

J. E. BOWER
Editor

FRED TURNBULL
Honorary Chairman of the Board

F. P. GALBRAITH, Publisher and Editor, 1934-1970

Published at 4703 Ross Street, Red Deer, Alberta
by The Red Deer Advocate Limited

Second Class Mail Reg. No. 0200. Member of the Audit Bureau of Circulation

Saturday, November 10, 1973

And will a man's lifetime ever again span such monumental span in this region: ponder the time of Thomas Stevens Stewart, brought here as a three-year-old youngster in 1884 — a decade before even the railway was punched through Central Alberta?

The first summer they camped along the Edmonton-Calgary trail near today's Penhold. They lived in a sod-roofed log house at the Crossing that winter. They fled to Calgary the next spring when the second Riel Rebellion flared (south of town, you can still see marks on a hillside where they hid and buried some of their provisions . . .)

When they returned, his family began work improving the homestead — which ultimately became part of CFB Penhold. In his lifetime, "progress" saw the advent of the train and its near-obsolescence; the age of the horse on the Prairies and its virtual oblivion; and the era of the aircraft, which ultimately consumed the old homestead and which hadn't even been invented when the family came here. In later years, as part of Stewart Bros., of Penhold and Red Deer, machinery and lumber dealers, he had an influence on development for fifty miles or more in all directions. And that doesn't begin to touch the social change in that time.

Family man, community worker, businessman, a figure in history, he was being mourned today, dead a few weeks short of his 92nd birthday.

Funeral on Saturday for pioneer Stewart

Funeral services will be held Saturday for Thomas Stevens Stewart, the last surviving male pioneer whose family arrived in the Red Deer area in 1884.

Mr. Stewart died in Red Deer General Hospital Thursday. He would have been 92 on Nov. 25.

A native of Ontario, Mr. Stewart was born in London in 1881. His parents, Mr. and Mrs. John Stewart, came West in the spring of 1884. Through the summer, they camped beside the Calgary-Edmonton trail, pending completion of a home on a nearby homestead in the Penhold area.

Rainfall prevented construction of a home that year and in the winter, John Stewart moved his family into a sod-roofed log house at Red Deer Crossing. In 1885 the Stewarts and the family of Rev. Leonard Gaetz trekked to Calgary to seek safety during the Riel Rebellion.

They returned to the district when the rebellion was quelled and began improving their homestead on land now covered by CFB Penhold.

T. S. STEWART
. . . dies at 92

In 1902, in partnership with his brother Norman, Mr. Stewart went into business in Penhold. R. S. Harrison, who owned a small implement and lumber business at Penhold and Mr. Griffen, who had another small lumber yard there, offered to sell, With the aid of a $600 bank loan, both purchases were made and Stewart Bros. was established. The firm grew to become one of the best-known machinery agencies in Central Alberta.

Mr. Stewart married Laura Newland of Three Hills in 1910.

Though he "retired" from his business 21 years ago and moved to Red Deer, he kept active in it for several years, driving to Penhold for each day's work until he was 80. While living in Penhold, he served for several years on town council.

Mr. Stewart is survived by his wife Laura; a daughter, Mrs. Muriel Ford of Penhold, a grandson, Stewart Ford, a great-granddaughter, Maria, sister, Miss Mabel Stewart of Red Deer, and several nieces and nephews.

Funeral services will be held from Eventide Chapel, Red Deer, at 2 p.m. with Rev. Benson Jones officiating. Cremation will follow. Eventide Funeral Chapel is in charge of arrangements.

61 B.

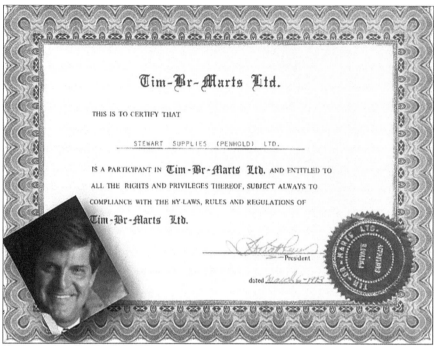

62. Stewart Supplies Tim-BR-MART buying group member certificate. The inset is a photo of Barrie Sali, the group's founder.

63 A-C. Preserved Wood Foundation (PWF) plans.

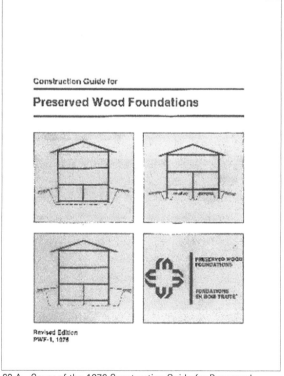

63 A. Cover of the 1976 Construction Guide for Preserved Wood Foundations.

238

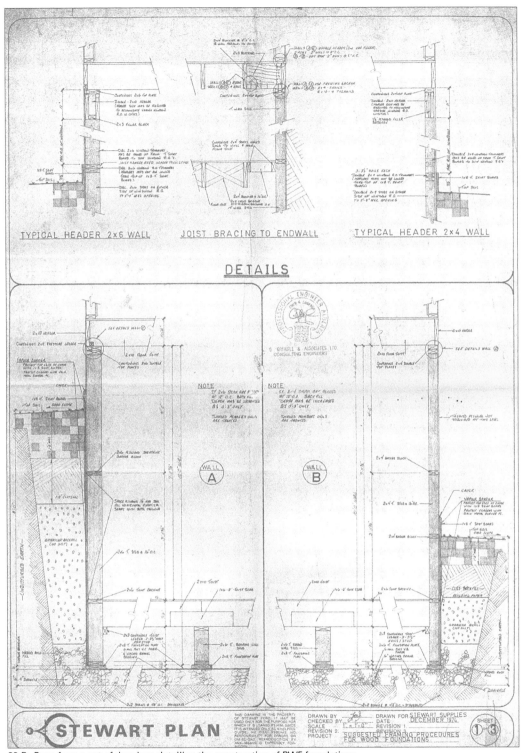

63 B. Page from a set of drawings detailing the construction of PWF foundations.

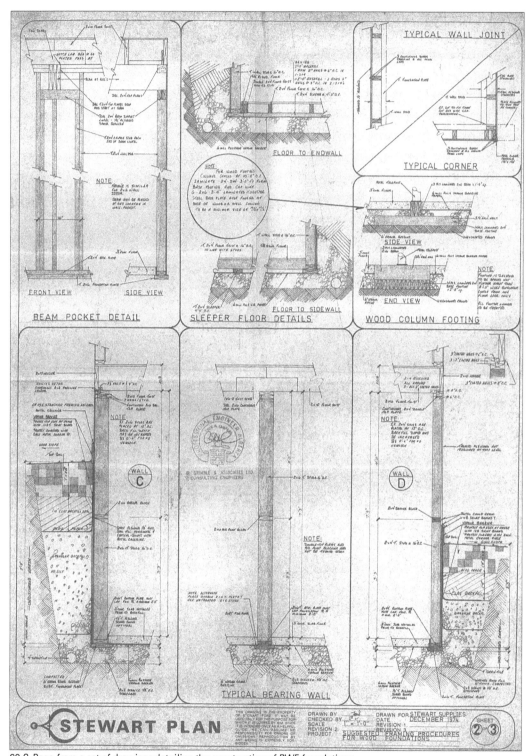

63 C. Page from a set of drawings detailing the construction of PWF foundations.

240

64. The PWF foundation for Alex Richards' caged laying house.

65. A post-pier PWF foundation for an archrafter shed.

241

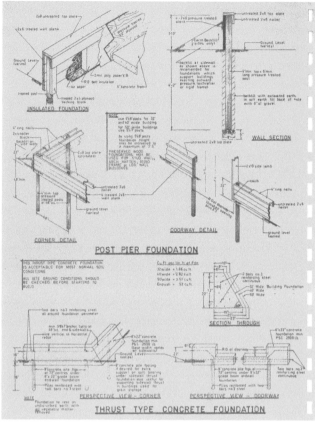

66. A plan for post-pier PWF and concrete foundations for archrafter sheds.

67 A. The thirteen-acre site of the UCM Properties development, in Penhold.

67 B. The Grenada fourplex used in the UCM Properties subdivision.

68 A sales poster created by MacMillan-Bloedel for its dealers.

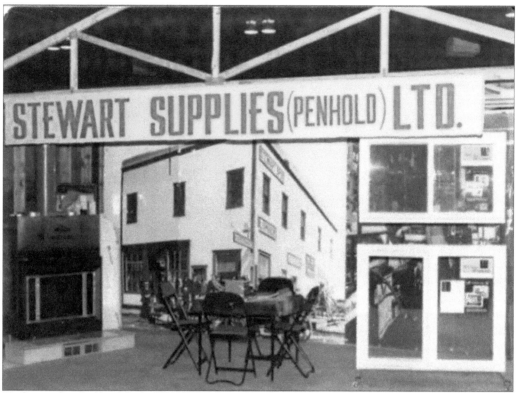
69. Stewart Supplies' booth in the 1981 HUDAC show with enlarged photos of the 1908 store as backdrop.

70. Bowen ("E") end-wall framing to first full-cross frame.

71. Our second fourplex, the Cascade. This line drawing became part of the company's plan book.

72. The new 50'x144' warehouse.

73. Skidding a ready-to-move (RTM) house out of the new warehouse.

74 A-C.   Front and back pages of the Grand Opening flyer for Stewart Supplies' new 50'x144' warehouse and truss plant; and a separate single-page flyer that accompanied the main flyer.

74 A.

74 B.

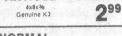

74 C.

UNRESERVED
AUCTION SALE
CASH — **CASH**

STEWART SUPPLIES
PENHOLD ALTA.
THE SALE WILL BE HELD ADJACENT TO PENHOLD TO THE SOUTH

HAVING RECEIVED INSTRUCTIONS WE WILL SELL BY PUBLIC AUCTION ON

FRI. OCTOBER 17
1975

SALE STARTS AT 10:00 A.M. SHARP — LUNCH WILL BE SERVED BY WILLOWDALE COMMUNITY CLUB

EXCELLENT Line Of POWER MACHINERY - MISCELLANEOUS

TRACTORS
Late Model 145 VERSATILE DIESEL 4 WHEEL DRIVE TRACTOR complete with cab, heater, dual hyds., Leon, dozer, 11' blade.
McCORMICK W 9 GAS TRACTOR.
FARMALL A TRACTOR.

HARVEST EQUIPMENT
IHC #914 COMBINE 12', pull type, belt pick-up and straw chopper (used 2 seasons).
#400 VERSATILE 18' SP SWATHER with cab.
IHC #230 14½' SP SWATHER with hay conditioner and pick up reel.
VERSATILE GRAIN AUGER 35', hydraulic motor drive with motor.
HYDRAULIC ORBIT MOTOR.
SMITH ROLLS BIN SWEEP with electric motor.

RIDING MOWER, CATTLE SUPPLIES AND OTHER ITEMS
YAZOO 60" RIDING MOWER.
New BEATTY Electric Automatic CATTLE WATERER.
Set of KEYSTONE DEHORNERS.
25 lb. PROPANE BOTTLE with torch.
MELRO-LYNN SEED TREATER.
SOIL SAMPLER with 12 volt electric motor.
3 - Sacks of MONSANTO GRANULAR AVADEX.
Set of 2½" Wide Tread BOB SLEIGHS with box.
2 - Set of BREECHING HARNESS.

SHOP & DIESEL EQUIPMENT, HEATERS
DIESEL TESTING EQUIPMENT, DIESEL PUMP.
POWER HACK SAW, WHEEL & BEARING PULLERS.
REZNOR OVERHEAD NATURAL GAS HEATER.
SPACE HEATER.
Heavy Duty DRILL PRESS up to 1" plus bits.
PORTABLE STEAM CLEANER, Kerosene fired.
PORTABLE AIR-O-MATIC AIR COMPRESSOR with tank and hose.
MILLER A/C ELECTRIC WELDER 225 amp.
ACETYLENE WELDER complete, cutting torch & tips.
2 - BATTERY CHARGERS.
SICKLE SERVICE UNIT for removing sections & riveting.
Heavy Duty SHOP GRINDER; Electric SHOP SANDER;
FORGE with blower; Electric VENTILATING FAN with 110 volt motor; Heavy LOGGING CHAIN approximately 30'; Quantity of CABLE with hooks & clamps.

TILLAGE EQUIPMENT & OTHER ITEMS
2 - IHC PRESS GRAIN DRILLS, 24x6 #100, fert. & grass seeder attachments, hydraulic lift, in new cond.
Set of MARKERS for 2 - 12' IHC grain drills.
2 - DRILL FILLERS 5" (grain or fertilizer) with hyd. motors, hose and control valve.
24' GRAHAM PLOW, heavy duty, 1" shanks.
16" SWEEPS, CHISEL POINTS, wing lift.
Hydraulic WING LIFT for Deep Tillage Cultivator.
New 8' DEEP FRAME GRAHAM PLOW, new tires.
IHC #500 14' Heavy DISC HARROW.
Set of New NOTCHED BLADES for IHC Disc Harrow.
45' EDWARDS ROD WEEDER, wing type.
45' MELROE Hydraulic HARROWEEDER with 9 - 5' sections of IHC Tine Tooth Harrows.
5 - 5' Sections Roll-up HARROWS & 25' Steel Drawbar.
14' LIFT HARROW.
7' ALLIED ROTOTILLER P.T.O. drive.
3' SIMPLICITY ROTOTILLER.
10' Brillion GRASS SEEDER, pneumatic transport wheels.
CALHOUN #450 FERTILIZER DISTRIBUTOR.

FUEL TANKS AND PUMPS
BOWSER ELECTRIC GAS PUMP.
300 Gallon GAS TANK with stand and hose.
Utility FUEL TANK 135 Gallon complete with pump.
Utility FUEL TANK 100 gallon complete with pump.
5 - Lubricating OIL TANKS with hand pumps.

LUMBER AND BUILDING SUPPLIES
Quantity of used Dimension LUMBER; 1" BOARDS; SHIPLAP; New WINDOWS & DOORS various sizes; HARDWARE SUPPLIES; Large Quantity of New IHC PARTS; MILLS WIRE WEEDER PARTS; FERTILIZER PARTS; HYDRAULIC HOSE; Made up HYDRAULIC HOSE; TRACTOR FILTERS; TRACTOR CLEVISES and DRAW PINS; New BALER CRANKS for IHC Balers; Various size ROLLER & LINK CHAIN V-BELTS & PULLEYS; New ROPE; FORKS; POST HOLE AUGERS; BROOMS; BELTING RIVETS; FISHING TACKLE; PLASTIC GARBAGE PAILS; KITCHENWARE; BOOSTER CABLES; STOVE PIPE; FLOOR WAX; GOPHER POISON; INSECTISIDES & WEED SPRAY; GLOVES & MITTS; A few USED PARTS BINS and Many Other Items.

HAYING EQUIPMENT
NEW HOLLAND #258 SIDE DELIVERY RAKE with rubber mounted teeth.
NEW HOLLAND #273 ENGINE DRIVE BALER.
HESTON STACK HAND #60.
BALE THROWER for IHC Baler.
Frost & Wood 5' HORSE MOWER.
3 - Hydraulic CYLINDERS 3½ x 8.

TRUCKS, LINDEN TRAILER, NEW HOISTS
DODGE TRUCK #700 with 16' Webb grain box and Stock Racks, Renn hoist.
INTERNATIONAL R180 TRUCK with 15' Cancade steel grain box and hoist.
MERCURY, 1963, ¾ TON TRUCK; 4 speed, and 10' Camper.
LINDEN 32' x 8½' Hydraulic Tilt Bed, GOOSENECK TRAILER with tandem dual wheels.
Quantity of new and used CAR & TRUCK TIRES.
Set of TRACTOR TIRES, RIMS and SPACERS.
1 - 10' x 20' TARPAULIN.
1 - 10' x 16' TARPAULIN.
4 - New MIDWEST HYDRAULIC HOISTS.

MIX MILL FEED MIXER
MIX MILL MODEL 3120 Automatic feed processing system with 5 hp electric motor, discharge auger in top cond. This mill was used in their grain elevator.

OFFICE EQUIPMENT AND SCALE
Old Style BURROUGHS CALCULATOR with steel stand.
SMITH CORONA CASH REGISTER.
REMINGTON TYPEWRITER.
Small TOLEDO SCALE, inspected in 1975.

PLEASE NOTE
STEWART SUPPLIES HAVE RENTED THEIR FARM THEREFORE THE REASON FOR THIS SALE, THEIR STORE HAS BEEN SOLD & THEY ARE SELLING THE BALANCE OF THEIR NEW PARTS & HARDWARE AS WELL.
PLEASE PLAN TO ATTEND AND BE ON TIME AS THERE ARE A LOT OF ITEMS TO SELL.
THEIR MACHINERY IS IN TOP SHAPE AND WELL TAKEN CARE OF AND YOU CAN BUY WITH CONFIDENCE FROM THESE RELIABLE PEOPLE. YOUR ATTENDANCE WILL BE APPRECIATED.

SIM'S & OGILVIE

KEITH SIM
LICENSE No. 54 - 010317
Bus. (403) 346-3160
Res. (403) 346-2743
RED DEER, ALBERTA

AUCTIONEERS AND SALES MANAGEMENT
Office Downstairs in AMA Building
P.O. Drawer 770
Red Deer, Alberta, Canada
Printed by Waskasoo Press Ltd.

GARFIELD OGILVIE
LICENSE No. 62 - 010373
Phone (403) 784-3604 CLIVE
★ TERMS CASH ★

75. 1975 auction bill listing the last of the machinery items.

76 A & B. Graham's 1975 calculations for obtaining the funds to purchase the shares of Jack Stewart and Gwen Calverley.

```
Assets evaluation re Stewart Supplies Ltd. as of Nov.30/75

Penhold property
                        Lot 7 Block 3          5000.00
                        Lot 8   "   3          5000.00
                        Lot 8   "   4          5000.00
                        Lot 9   "   4          5000.00
                                Post office
                        Lots 10-13 Service Stn 25000.00

                        Lots 20-34 Lumber Store
                                   shop etc   200,000.00

                        Lots 10-13 Blk 1        20,000.00

                        Lots 17-20  " 1         20,000.00

                        Lots C of T on 2A       50,000.00

                        Lots C of T on 2A
                        bought from Jannsen /75 25,000.00


Farm Land
                        Penhold tax roll 230
                        acres @800.00 per A    184,000.00

                        County of Red Deer
                        tax roll 835 acres
                        @ 600.00 per A         501,000.00

Red Deer Property

                        Thunderbird store      225,000.00
                        4½ ac block             30,000.00

Bank  Balance                                 100,000.00
Acc Rec                                        300,000.00
Term Deposits                                  257,500.00
Notes Rec                                       20,000.00
Investments                                     15,000.00
Mortgage                                         5,000.00
Inventory                                      175,000.00

                                                          2,222,500.00

Liabilities

Acc payable                   220,000.00
Shareholders loans            140,000.00                    360,000.00

Equity  224,000 shares                                    1,862,500.00

Value per shares     8.31

Less cost of with-
drawal from Company
50% taxes,capital     4.15
gains etc             4.16

Our offer to J.N.Stewart and Gwen Calverley is 4.00 cash for
their shares - 67,728 and 20,556 respectively for a total
of 88,284 @ 4.00 - /353,136.00
```

76 A.

249

Proposal re financing of purchase of 88,284 shares from J.N.Stewart and Gwen Calverley.

Borrow from bank 353,136.00

Security to bank — Income from Thunderbird and 45th street property 13,200.00 per annum

x Assign farm land lease that we have with C.Little 19,980.00

x The farm lease covers 555 acres, but there are an additional 200-300 acres at present in hay land, that we would think should be broken up and put into grain, which could generate a further 7200.00-10,800.00, which could be applied to the loan.

x Assign the interest on the term deposits now with the Royal Bank; 13,500.00

x At present there is 257,000.00 in term deposits at the Royal, but we have used a figure of 150,000.00, as some of this money might be required to pay of J.N.S. shareholder loan. 46,680.00

x The loan of 353,136.00 will be repaid with four notes all equal by the following shareholders:

Graham Ford
Muriel Ford

Stewart Ford
Eileen Ford

x In addition to the figure of 46,680.00, an additional 20,000.00 - 40,000.00 could be paid per annum, by the above four shareholders, from dividends derived from the profits of the business. These dividends might have to be kept lower than desired, due to taxes to these individuals.

x The titles to the two large Red Deer properties would be lodged with the Royal Bank. In the event of a sale, the proceeds would be deposited in term deposits and the interest from them, to be applied to the notes.

x We estimate that for tax purposes etc, these notes would be paid out in 7-10 years time. Personally we would like to do it sooner than that.

{ See Peter Powers re disposal of shares to Stewart. Should the portion of 88,000(?) be larger. Insurance

See Snow re term insurance & cap

76 B.

77 A & B. *Red Deer Advocate* articles about the Stewart Family donation to the Red Deer Museum building fund, and showing the table, chairs, and lectern donated by Stewart and Eileen.

$10,000 boost for the museum

The Red Deer and District Museum's $175,000 fund-raising campaign had scarcely started this week when the boost represented above strengthened hopes. If the $175,000 is raised here, it will be matched by the province. The gift: $10,000, in memory of Norman and Tom Stewart, long-time residents of Penhold, founders of Stewart Brothers machinery and lumber yards in Red Deer and Penhold. The gift was handed over to museum society president Gertrude Richards, RR3, left, by Gwen Calverley, Innisfail, centre, daughter of Norman Stewart; and by Muriel Ford, Penhold, on the right, daughter of Tom Stewart. In addition to the $175,000 sought in the fall canvass, the museum project is counting on $100,000 from the Chamber of Commerce Sweepstake Fund and $100,000 from the City of Red Deer.

Photo by Keith McNichol

77 A.

TABLE TALK — Museum board members try out the ultra posh new board room table that recently arrived from its manufacturers, the inmates of the Bowden institution. The 21-foot by five-foot-two-inch thick black walnut table was purchased, with other Stewart Room furnishings, with donations from both Stewart Supplies Ltd. of Penhold and from Stewart descendents, Eileen and Stewart Ford. Morris Flewwelling, museum curator, places the museum's new matching lecture on the table at which, clockwise from him are seated U Thobani, archivist Sylvia Bentley, Doris Northey, John Rich, Diana Anderson and Michael Dawe.

77 B.

78 A-C.   One of our picker-equipped trucks hoisting shingles onto a roof, and lifting a set of 60' Tim-BR-Frame trusses, plus a picker truck loaded with a rigid-frame building package and materials for three other job sites.

78 A.

78 B.

78 C.

79. An *AdViser* article about the Ducks Unlimited project on the business' Fleming Slough property, and the DU sign on the property.

At Penhold . .

Ducks, Geese Get New Home

Ducks Unlimited are involved in a massive wildlife habitat project at Penhold.

Site work is currently underway on ponding and nesting facilities on property owned by Stewart Supplies Ltd. on the western boundary of the town.

R.O.D. Construction of Strathmore are using a crane bucket to dig four miles of connecting trenches (between 26 and 30 feet wide and 3½ feet deep) and goose islands with their own moats. The trenches and moats will be filled by natural run-off.

It is the intention of Ducks Unlimited, that the slough, which has always been a popular spot for ducks, will in the future, attract geese.

Work at the site which started in mid-July is expected to be completed by the end of the month and the ponds and nesting sites could be ready for use by next summer.

The participating landowner in the County of Red Deer pilot project is the Ford family of Penhold.

Spokesman, Stewart Ford says he read about Ducks Unlimited's involvement in such projects and asked if their non-productive land qualified.

The Ford's are reimbursed for taxes by the Department of Environment for area taken out of production.

Mr. Ford says that the slough will be off-limits during nesting season and it's at the landowners discretion to open the area during hunting season. He added that the slough has always been off limits to hunters.

According to the R.O.D. Construction crane operator, there are several similar projects in the Hanna area.

Wildlife Project

This bucket crane is busy digging four miles of connecting trenches and 12 goose islands complete with moats at a farm near Penhold. Ducks Unlimited who are involved in the wildlife project on land owned by Stewart Supplies Ltd. hope to attract ducks and geese to the ponds and nesting area.

Processed Alfa

Alberta processed alfalfa prices are expected to range between $121 and $127 per tonne in the immediate future and could possibly increase later in the year to between $127 and $132 (ex spout Vancouver).

Bob Prather of Alberta Agriculture's market analysis branch says expected price increases could offset what could otherwise be a disappointing year for alfalfa producers in this province. He

points out that pr problems, rail rate (3 per tonne by Nove 1979) and continued cohesion in the indu all be key factors in

On the brighter ports to Japan are ex increase this year due in Alberta's processed products is experte time in other Pac countries as we Western Europe competitive position

THE PROPERTY OF

STEWART BROTHERS LAND & LIVESTOCK LTD.

SITE OF A

WETLAND CONSERVATION PROJECT

BUILT BY:

Ducks Unlimited Canada

about Metrication of our Industry

WRLA Director Stewart Ford (Stewart Supplies (Penhold) Ltd.) represents our Association on the Metric Commission's Sector 8.20 Sub-Committee and as the result of a Report received from him following the March meeting of that Committee; your Board of Directors held a special meeting in Calgary on May 12 for the purpose of establishing WRLA Policy regarding the introduction of "hard metric" in the lumber and building supply industry.

After prolonged and thorough examination, the Board adopted Stewart's report as WRLA Policy. His report was as follows:

1. *To commit our organization to metric conversion by M Day, November 1980.*

2. *To urge, from the dealer level, the panel industry to push their conversion by the carrot/stick approach of price and supply.*

3. *To call for the implementation of the New National Building Code which recognizes the hard metric panel support spacings, at the earliest possible date.*

4. *Urge a firm policy by our member yards to set our own house in order by the use of written and spoken metric at the point of sale.*

5. *To have our organization approach the Metric Commission and request a Consumer Aid Kit for our dealers and the Commission to make available to the public.*

6. *To use Metric terms in our advertising, Imperial terms only secondarily for a "phase-in" period.*

7. *That the public was ready and we should show positive leadership in getting on with the job.*

The Metric Commission has been advised of WRLA endorsation with emphasis on the fact that:

(a) *M Day will only achieve maximum impact if the National Building Code, C.M.H.C. Inspectors and hopefully, Provincial and Municipal requirements are, by that time, making the use of hard metric mandatory on new construction; and this is particularly true in the case of panel support spacing. Tradesmen will only buy and use metric tapes when the need arises.*

(b) *The need for a "Consumer Aid Kit" is self-evident and the WRLA will commit its members to assist in the distribution of such kits, at least to their customers.*

Regardless of the "pros and cons" of metrication, all Directors agreed that there is no merit in being half in and half out of metric. It was also agreed that once panel support spacing is 'hard' metric, the process of complete metrication will readily follow.

It was a pleasure for the WRLA to receive, from two entirely separate sources, commendation for appointing Stewart Ford as its representative on the Sector 8.20 sub-committee. Words such as "revitalized" and "extremely knowledgeable" were used. Thanks Stewart.

about WRLA Metric Seminars

Bill Darling is scheduled to conduct five three-day Seminars in Saskatoon, Edmonton, Calgary, Regina and Winnipeg during November. They will be heavy to hard metric if M Day is indeed, set for November 1980.

Watch for further announcements.

80. An article in the *WRLA Communicator* newsletter about my work with the Metric Commission.

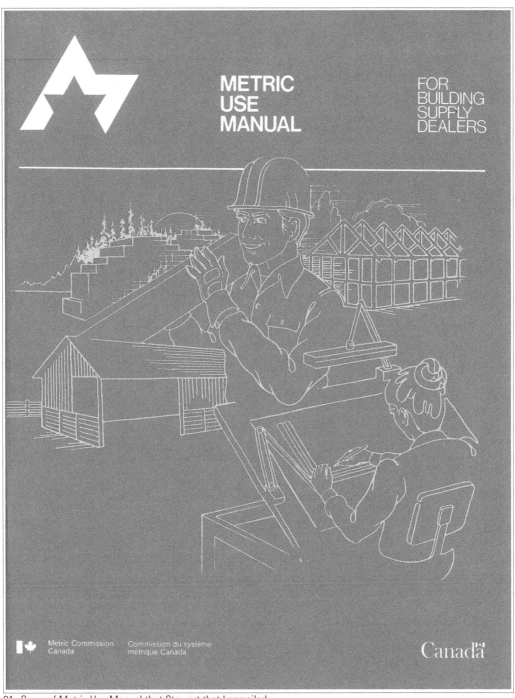

81. Cover of Metric Use Manual that Stewart that I compiled.

34

STRUCTURAL GRADE 2 & BETTER LUMBER

K.D. Spruce	2.44 m(8')	3.05 m(10')	3.66 m(12')	4.27 m(14')
2 x 4				
2 x 6				
2 x 8				
2 x 10				

-When describing a building, give the SI size rounded to the second decimal and the Imperial to the nearest inch.

eg.   7.32 m x 18.29 m (24' x 60') POLE CATTLE SHED
       133.80 m^2 (1440 sq. ft.)

12.1   TYPICAL ADVERTISEMENT SHOWING DUAL MEASUREMENTS

FIGURE 5

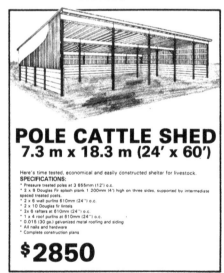

POLE CATTLE SHED
7.3 m x 18.3 m (24' x 60')

Here's time tested, economical and easily constructed shelter for livestock.
SPECIFICATIONS:
* Pressure treated poles at 3 655mm (12') o.c.
* 2 x 8 Douglas Fir splash plank 1 200mm (4') high on three sides, supported by intermediate spaced treated posts.
* 2 x 6 wall purlins 610mm (24'') o.c.
* 2 x 10 Douglas fir lintels
* 2x 6 rafters at 610mm (24'') o.c.
* 1 x 4 roof purlins at 610mm (24'') o.c.
* 0.015 (30 ga.) galvanized metal roofing and siding
* All nails and hardware
* Complete construction plans

$2850

POLE
MACHINE SHELTER
7.3 m x 18.3 m (24' x 60')

Simple in design and easy on the budget, this pole machine shed features 6 096mm (20') wide storage bays with a minimum ceiling height to 3 960mm (13'). Trussed beams and galvanized metal roofing and siding give strength and maintenance freedom.

SPECIFICATIONS:
* Pressure treated poles
* 2 x 6 wall purlins at 610mm (24'') o.c.
* Our own manufacture trussed beams for large clear spans over storage bays
* 2 x 6 rafters at 610mm (24'') o.c.
* 1 x 4 roof purlins at 610mm (24'') o.c.
* 0.015 (30 ga.) galvanized metal roofing and siding
* All nails and hardware
* Complete construction plans

$3450

82 A.

82 B.

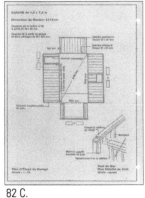

82 C.

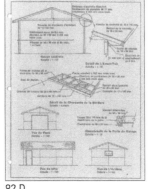

82 D.

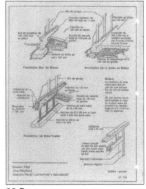

82 E.

83. An eighteen-suite apartment built by UCM Properties using Stewart Supplies' flat-floor and roof trusses.

From $600 loan Stewart Supplies has grown into million dollar venture

George Yackulic

Few Alberta businesses can match the enviable distinctions accumulated by Stewart Supplies (Penhold) Ltd. since a couple of sons from a pioneer homesteading family borrowed $600 in 1902 and sent their building supplies venture on to a fabulous history from its base in tiny Penhold.

The venture, now valued at considerably more than $3 million, has been owned and operated by members of the same tightly-knit family for 80 years — a rarity in a province that is only 77 years old.

The venture has developed such intense loyalty from its customers it now does business with third generations of many families and is widely known and respected across Central Alberta.

Despite being located in a small but progressive town that has grown to have a population of more than 1,500, Stewart Supplies has steadily expanded so that it requires a staff fluctuating between 12 and 20 employees who are busy with an inventory of stock valued at $500,000.

For many years its annual turnover of business has consistently ranged between $2 million and $3 million, and it is expected to be in that neighborhood this year despite the general slump in the building industry across Canada. The record business year for Stewart Supplies was posted in 1980.

The keys for success of the business always have been that Stewart Supplies has been a good corporate citizen and that it always has really cared about its customers. Even in the busy times of today, principals of the company have been known to visit building projects using their materials to assure that there is complete satisfaction.

The business, founded by brothers Norman and Tom Stewart, had to be completely re-organized between 1965 and 1976 as it ran out of male Stewarts. Since that reshuffling, it has been owned by the Ford family corporation, which consists of Graham

and Muriel Ford, she being a daughter of the late Tom Stewart; and Stewart and Eileen Ford, he being the only son of Graham Ford.

Stewart Ford, who was born in 1938, in Castor, where his father and mother were school teachers, is the president and general manager of Stewart Supplies and has full control of operating the business and is responsible for day-to-day operations.

His father Graham, who was born in 1913, in Castor, where he taught school for six years before moving to Penhold in 1939 to join Stewart Supplies, is the vice-president.

His wife Muriel is the company's secretary.

And Stewart Ford's wife Eileen, also a former school teacher, is the company's treasurer.

A fourth generation of the clan is beginning to creep into the business. The two children of Stewart and Eileen Ford — nine-year-old Maria and seven-year-old Tom — recently helped build a garden shed for Stewart Supplies and each drew a first cheque, for $5, from the company for the work.

The family venture consists of two divisions. Stewart Supplies operates as a business selling the complete lines of building materials and supplies. It also owns and operates a truss manufacturing plant.

A separate division, Stewart Brothers Land and Livestock Ltd., owns more than 900 acres of farm-

lands southwest of Penhold.

The history of the Stewart family in this area goes back almost a full century. Mr. and Mrs. John A. Stewart came here from Ontario in 1884.

The children included Norman, who was born in 1876, and Tom, who was born in 1881. Both died very much later in the Red Deer General Hospital, Norman in 1965 and Tom in 1973.

After growing up on the family farm, these brothers became interested in buying a building supplies business in Penhold that was being offered for sale in 1902. The owner of another such business there immediately offered to sell out to them as well. The brothers went to a banker and borrowed the $600 needed for the full purchase price of the two businesses, which they merged into their one venture.

That was the beginning of Stewart Supplies, and it was followed by decades of long and hard work, many risks, and the full co-operation of the founders' families to make the business grow and prosper. In its earliest years, the business paid monthly salaries of $20 to Norman and $15 to Tom for owning and operating the venture. But there were times when the business till could not afford $5 a month for each.

Both retained their financial interests and were active in the business right until they died. Meanwhile, they also had brought their children into the business, most of them being daughters, and had passed along financial holdings.

Norman's son Jack came into the business in 1935 to run a new Red Deer branch, which was started with a farm implement dealership and lumberyard in the downtown area. While he served overseas with the Canadian armed forces during the Second World War, girls in the family operated that branch. The Red Deer branch was closed in 1958 when Jack was needed at the company's main base in Penhold

and there were no members of the Stewart family to run the Red Deer operation.

Despite his advancing age, Norman Sr. continued to operate Stewart Supplies until he died in 1965 at the age of 91. He was succeeded as president by his son Jack, who headed the business until retiring in 1976.

Tom Stewart's daughter, meanwhile, had chosen teaching for her career and was doing that in Castor when she met Graham Ford, married him in 1936 and brought a much-needed male into the Stewart tribe. Mr. and Mrs. Ford, with their baby son Stewart, moved to Penhold in 1939 and Graham started working for Stewart Supplies as a truck flunkie. He was taken into the business as a partner in 1942 and became vice-president in 1965 on the death of Norman Sr.

The need for a corporate shuffle and re-organization became obvious as Stewart menfolk passed out of the picture in Stewart Supplies, and most of this was accomplished in the years 1965-76.

It was completed in 1976 when Graham and Stewart Ford and their wives bought out the last of the Stewart family interests outright, with the final stock purchases being from Jack Stewart and his sister Gwen. With the corporate finances of the successful business re-arranged and the stage reshuffled for another long and solid run, Graham Ford decided two years later to go into semi-retirement and leave running of the business to his son Stewart.

Stewart Ford has been with the business since completing high school in Red Deer in 1956 and during his rise to be the president and operating manager of Stewart Supplies he has done just about every job around the place. He also took a year and a half away from the business to work for Monarch Lumber to gain more experience. His wife, who married him in 1971, formerly taught school in Innisfail.

84. The *Red Deer Advocate* article by George Yackulic regarding Stewart Supplies' 80th anniversary.

85. Foundations and floor truss system for new Pine Hill Hutterite Colony residences.

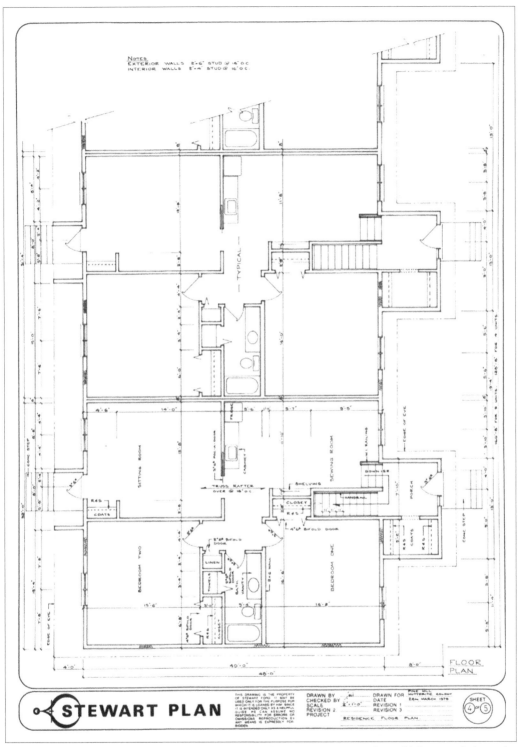

STEWART PLAN

DRAWN BY		DRAWN FOR	PINE HILL HUTTERITE COLONY
CHECKED BY		DATE	26th MARCH 1979
SCALE	¼"=1'-0"	REVISION 1	
REVISION 2		REVISION 3	
PROJECT		RESIDENCE FLOOR PLAN	

SHEET 4 OF 5

86. The floor plan I drew for the Pine Hill Colony residences. Our yard foreman, John Page, did the neat printing on the drawings.

259

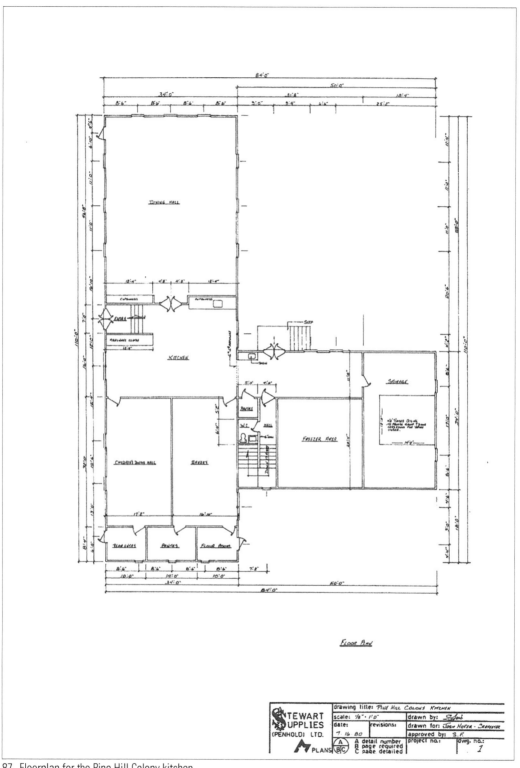

87. Floorplan for the Pine Hill Colony kitchen.

88. A view of the Pine Hill colony floor trusses. The original 1947 residences are seen in the background.

89 A & B. Elevation and floor plans of overflow residences at Pine Hill.

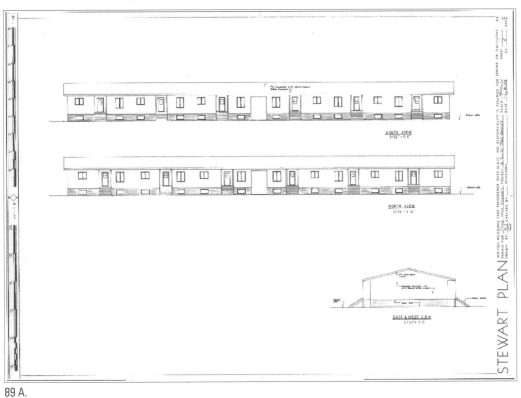

89 A.

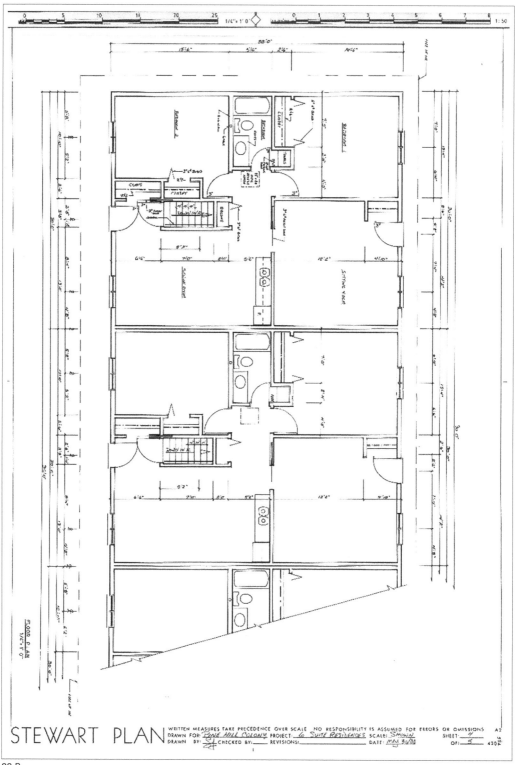

STEWART PLAN

WRITTEN MEASURES TAKE PRECEDENCE OVER SCALE. NO RESPONSIBILITY IS ASSUMED FOR ERRORS OR OMISSIONS   A2
DRAWN FOR: _Pine Hill Colony_ PROJECT: _6 Suite Residences_ SCALE: _Shown_   SHEET: _4_
DRAWN BY: _St_ CHECKED BY: ____ REVISIONS: ____   DATE: _May 30/86_   OF: _5_   420A

89 B.

$10,000 and that's not pumpkin seed!

By GREG MEACHEM
of The Advocate

CASTOR — It's not often, if ever, that a sane person would lay out a cool ten grand for a pumpkin, especially a full month before Hallowe'en.

But that's exactly what happened here when Graham Ford of Penhold purchased the large piece of fruit for $10,000 at a roast in recognition of long-time Castor sports enthusiast Allan Matthias.

The event was staged not only for the purpose of honoring Matthias, but as a fund-raiser for the new Castor curling rink, which should be in operation by fall of next year.

Ford's purchase was, in effect, a donation toward the cost of the $400,000, three-sheet rink.

"The bidding (on the pumpkin) started off at five dollars, then got to $50, then $500," said roast organizer Joe Willis. "When it got into the thousands, it was quite the deal. The fact it sold for $10,000 was a real surprise.

"Maybe we'll get the seeds and sell them," he joked.

Ford, who grew up in the Castor area, is no stranger to generosity. He's made substantial donations to the Westerner Association, Red Deer Library and Innisfail Curling Club in past years.

"The world has been good to me and I don't mind giving some of it back," said Ford. "Besides, you can't take it with you."

Ford, who left Castor in 1939 to farm in the Penhold area, jumped at the chance to help out his hometown.

"I helped build the original rink in Castor, so I thought it was only right I help out with the new one," he said. "And Allan and I grew up together, although he's a little older than I am."

The roast raised $14,000, according to Willis. Another $97,000 is needed before construction on the rink can start next May.

"It will take a lot of hard work, but we're confident we'll reach our goal," said Willis. "We plan on canvassing the town and doing anything else we can to raise money. Perhaps we'll hold a celebrity dinner and maybe even another roast."

If another roast if planned, it's hard to imagine organizers coming up with a local curling subject as colorful or successful as Matthias.

The 75-year old former owner of a car dealership and farm machinery outlet gave up curling just five years ago. His past achievements in the sport include reaching the final of the Alberta men's championships in 1965 and winning the Eaton's event of the Calgary Open bonspiel two years running.

He also won the Central Alberta men's curling championship in the early 60's and played baseball and hockey for 25 years.

"As a kid I grew up playing sports and I didn't want to give them up," he said. "I played everything as long as I could."

90 A. *Red Deer Advocate* article about my father's $10,000 pumpkin in support of the new Castor Curling Club.

90 B. *Innisfail Province* feature recognizing Graham's contribution to the Innisfail Curling Club.

91. My collection of memorabilia from the 1986 Junior Men's Curling Championship in Red Deer.

WRLA

YARDSTICK

ORGANIZED 1890

VOL 1 / NO 6 / NOVEMBER – DECEMBER 1988   PUBLISHED BY THE WESTERN RETAIL LUMBERMEN'S ASSOCIATION

Stewart Ford chosen "Mr. Lumberman 1988"

There was surprise, yet unanimous approval when President Dwayne Thomas announced that Stewart Ford of Stewart Supplies (Penhold) Ltd., Penhold, Alberta was the recipient of the annual "Mr. Lumberman Award" for 1988.

Stewart was born in Castor, Alberta, but his family moved to Penhold when he was just six months old.

He began his career in the building supply industry with the family firm at age 16, before moving to Monarch Lumber in Red Deer in 1957. He later moved to the store in Regina and then to Grande Prairie before returning to the family business in Penhold. He became

President in 1972.

In February 1979, Stewart sat as a Director of WRLA and later served as the WRLA representative on the Metric Commission. He chaired the committee that researched and prepared the Metric Use Manual.

During his time as a Director, Stewart was instrumental in the development and publication of the new WRLA Training Manual.

Stewart is married to the former Eileen Chizmazia and has two children, Maria and Tom, both of whom have shown an interest in the family business.

Congratulations Stewart — a well-deserved recognition!

Enthusiasm, High Spirits at Joint Convention

The 98th Annual WRLA Convention and the 49th Annual BSDA of B.C. Conference are now in the history books. For two days our respective members worked together, socialized and had the opportunity to exchange ideas and to discuss problems and everyone was the better for it.

Our opening "English Pub Night" with entertainment by the Michael Mitchell Band proved to be a popular icebreaker. What with "pints," fish and chips and the "roast beef of old England," together with the pub songs, members and wives from both sides of the Rockies joined in. A special presentation of Oilers' sweater No. IX to Gordon Roberts brought a round of applause from the audience.

Despite the absence of a representa-

See Photo Coverage On Page 8

Continued on page 3

CONTENTS

92. Receiving the Mr. Lumberman award in 1988.

A FAMILY BUSINESS PORTRAIT . . . Graham Ford, with wife Muriel, hands business over to his son Stewart Ford, with wife Eileen

Photo by CALVIN CALDWELL

Small business weathered storm

By ROSS HENDERSON
of The Advocate

As Small Business Week winds to a close, Central Alberta's small business community has a renewed sense of optimism about the future.

Stewart Supplies (Penhold) Ltd. may be the prototypical small business, privately held and handed down through three generations since the early 1900s.

Like most small or medium-sized businesses in the country, the 83-year-old company felt the brunt of the recession over the past several years. Now, there are signs of a comeback.

"We went through the recession with profit, loss, profit, loss," recalls company president Stewart Ford. "We are probably approaching profitability again."

The picture is looking a little brighter thanks to lower interest rates and increasing activity in the Central Alberta oil patch. Sales have increased by about 20 per cent, he says.

With 16 employees currently on its four-acre site — including a store, two warehouses and two rafter truss workshops — the business occupies a sizeable portion of the town.

Mr. Ford says a strong capital position allowed the business to weather the chill winds of the recession in good shape compared to other businesses.

"We're very fortunate. Unlike a lot of small business, we're not at the whim of our bankers," he says.

The recession also taught the importance of efficient management, he says.

Stewart Supplies is keeping a watchful eye on its inventory and keeping a tighter rein on its accounts receivable, for instance. It's also trying for more innovation in product development.

Meanwhile, the 47-year-old father of two says he enjoys being his own boss, which brings with it the obligation of two or three hours of evening work and weekend toil.

"The thrill I get out of it is being part of the creation of a building. It's a business that allows you a great deal of scope and creativity," he says.

Dalton McCambley, Central Alberta representative for the Canadian Organization of Small Business, confirms small businessmen are catching their breath again after the recession.

"Small business is now in the position where they can take more people on. In

the past few years, they've been forced to be very lean."

He bases some of that optimism on the fact there's been a "tremendous number" of small business startups in Red Deer in the past six months.

The new entrepreneurs are enticed by current lower interest rates, he says, but some also may have decided to go it alone after losing their jobs during the recession.

"The big thing is people feel there's an opportunity to go into small business," Mr. McCambley says. "It now makes sense to go into business for yourself."

The increased activity is also reflected in statistics provided by Brian Conrad, manager of the Federal Business Development Bank in Red Deer.

The bank's loan portfolio for the fiscal year beginning in April has jumped 20 per cent in dollar value compared with the same period a year ago, to total about $2 million in loan authorizations.

Those figures are derived from a 40-per-cent increase in the number of loans signed by the bank. Across Canada, the Crown corporation is expected to equal its best year recorded in 1980.

93. 1985 *Red Deer Advocate* article about the business' success. L to R: Graham, Muriel, me, and Eileen in the retail store.

94. The first of the company's ads after the GST came into effect.

267

95 A & B. The Moose Lodge in Red Deer, constructed by the Mike Richards/Apple Builders/Stewart Supplies team.

95 A.

95 B.

96 A & B. Rainbow Hutterite Colony residences and floorplans.

96 A. Completed residences.

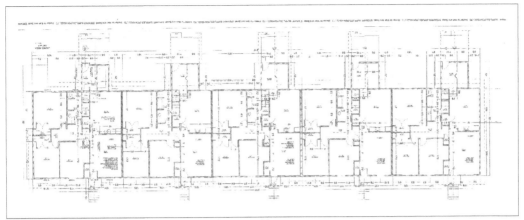

96 B. Floorplans for the new Rainbow Hutterite Colony residences.

97. The foundation walls of Rainbow Colony's Common Building.

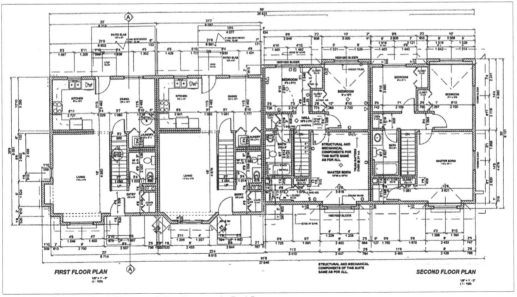

FIRST FLOOR PLAN

SECOND FLOOR PLAN

98. Seibel Construction's Kentwood development in Red Deer.

269

99. A tilt-door garage.

100. "C" section galvanized steel joints.

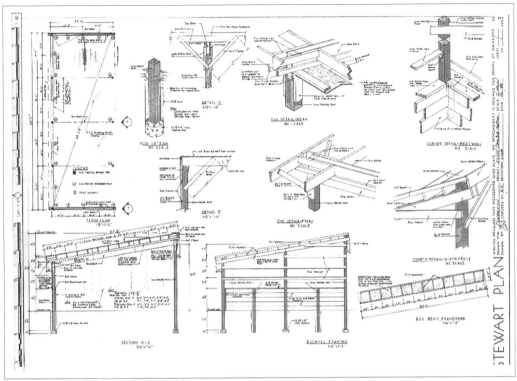

101. Design for a 24'x'64 cattle shed with no centre post.

102 A. Bill Lawrence (left) and Tom Ford (right), building a garden shed.

8x10 GARDEN BARN

Prebuilt - ready to go Gambrel roof garden barn features attractive and practical belled eves, 2x4 unitized construction, 3/8" wafer board ext. sheathing, 10 yr. asphalt shingles, 2x10 plank floor, 4x4 pressure threated skids and 48" wide door c/w locking hasp.

$489

1601-0810-GB

10x12 GARDEN SHED

Prebuilt - set to go. Our large straight wall garden shed rests on 4x4 treated skids. The 2x4 unitized construction is sheathed with 3/8" waferboard. The heavy duty floor is 2x10 plank and the roof is shingled with 10 yr. Domsan Asphalt shingles. Access is through a wide 48" door secured with a cocking hasp.

$539

1601-1012-GS

10x12 GARDEN SHED

Prebuilt and ready our Gambrel Roof Garden Barn sets on 4x4 pressure treated skids. Unitized joist-stud-rafter members are finished with 3/8" wall and roof sheathing with 2x10 planks forming the heavy-duty floor. Domtar 10 yr. asphalt shingles are featured on the roof and the door is a wide 48" with a locking hasp.

$569

1601-1012-GB

102 B. An example ad for garden sheds.

272

103. Our open-face machine shelter.

104. Exterior of Jack Hill's vehicle storage facility.

105. For the All Weather Windows 40th anniversary, Gord, Harry, and I re-created the original photo taken when I gave them their first order.

106. Eileen and me at the 1993 Labatt Brier.

STEWART
SUPPLIES
(PENHOLD) LTD.

LABATT BRIER
RED DEER 1994

PATRON

YEAR 2002

100th Anniversary
Commemorative Calendar

STEWART BROTHERS

STEWART SUPPLIES (PENHOLD) LTD.

107 A.

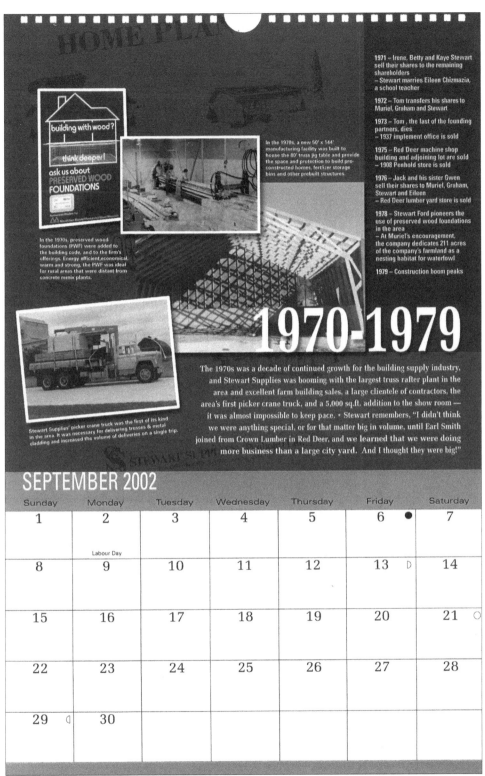

building with wood?

think deeper!

ask us about
PRESERVED WOOD
FOUNDATIONS

In the 1970s, preserved wood foundations (PWF) were added to the building code, and to the firm's offerings. Energy efficient, economical, warm and strong, the PWF was ideal for rural areas that were distant from concrete remix plants.

In the 1970s, a new 50' x 144' manufacturing facility was built to house the 80' truss jig table and provide the space and protection to build pre-constructed homes, fertilizer storage bins and other prebuilt structures.

1971 – Irene, Betty and Kaye Stewart sell their shares to the remaining shareholders
– Stewart marries Eileen Chizmazia, a school teacher

1972 – Tom transfers his shares to Muriel, Graham and Stewart

1973 – Tom , the last of the founding partners, dies
– 1937 implement office is sold

1975 – Red Deer machine shop building and adjoining lot are sold
– 1908 Penhold store is sold

1976 – Jack and his sister Gwen sell their shares to Muriel, Graham, Stewart and Eileen
– Red Deer lumber yard store is sold

1978 – Stewart Ford pioneers the use of preserved wood foundations in the area
– At Muriel's encouragement, the company dedicates 211 acres of the company's farmland as a nesting habitat for waterfowl

1979 – Construction boom peaks

1970-1979

Stewart Supplies' picker crane truck was the first of its kind in the area. It was necessary for delivering trusses & metal cladding and increased the volume of deliveries on a single trip.

The 1970s was a decade of continued growth for the building supply industry, and Stewart Supplies was booming with the largest truss rafter plant in the area and excellent farm building sales, a large clientele of contractors, the area's first picker crane truck, and a 5,000 sq.ft. addition to the show room — it was almost impossible to keep pace. * Stewart remembers, "I didn't think we were anything special, or for that matter big in volume, until Earl Smith joined from Crown Lumber in Red Deer, and we learned that we were doing more business than a large city yard. And I thought they were big!"

SEPTEMBER 2002

Sunday	Monday	Tuesday	Wednesday	Thursday	Friday	Saturday
1	2	3	4	5	6 ●	7
	Labour Day					
8	9	10	11	12	13 ☽	14
15	16	17	18	19	20	21 ○
22	23	24	25	26	27	28
29 ☾	30					

107 B.

retail**member**profile

From whaling to building supplies – Stewart Supplies celebrates centennial

The story of **Stewart Supplies (Penhold) Ltd.** begins in 1840 when **Calhoun Stewart**, a whaling captain from Dundee, Scotland brought his family to his new acreage in Godrich, Ontario.

Four years later, Calhoun's son, **John Hay Stewart**, moved his young family west to Fairlands, Alberta (some of his homestead is now part of the Red Deer Regional Airport). At the time, John Hay's family included 10-year-old **Norman** and 3-year-old **Tom**. A year after arriving in the west, young Norman was selling newspapers reporting on the Riel Rebellion. At first, the Stewart brothers farmed the homestead. A preview of their future success came in 1890, when a sample of Norman's wheat won a prize at the Chicago World's Fair.

In 1902 (three years before the Province of Alberta came into being), Norman and Tom purchased a lumber and implement business, along with a second lumberyard in Penhold, a tiny municipality in what is now central Alberta. Stewart Brothers was open for business! The operation did well and grew steadily, as did the area. In 1904, Penhold was incorporated as a village. In 1906, the Penhold Bridge was built over the Red Deer River with Stewart Brothers freighting materials to the site and weighing the steel for the new span. By 1907, the business's net worth had increased to $17,000. Commenting on these early days in a family history, Norman Stewart said:

"I often wonder how we managed in those years. It is a mystery that we didn't go under. We had no experience. More than that, we were very cautious and afraid to take a chance on anything. But our years on the farm stood us in good stead. We were well used to trading and bartering. It was the only way business was done back then. We've never really departed from it since."

In 1916, Stewart Brothers began selling Ford cars, John Deere plows, De Laval cream separators, B-H paints, and insurance. Tom recalled accompanying an older customer on a test drive in one of the newer model Ford cars. The customer came to a fork in the road and, being more familiar with a set of reins than a brake pedal, pulled back on the steering wheel and yelled, "WHOA." After pulling the Ford out of the poplars, the customer decided to leave the automobile to others.

In the 1920s, the operation sold International Harvester tractors, McCormick Deering farm machinery and Martin-Senour paint.

The next decade, which saw a devastating Depression sweep the land, was actually a period of growth for Stewart Brothers. Norman and Tom were not afraid to extend credit to a penniless farmer because they believed, "With a little help, he will prosper and pay back his debts." It has been stated that during these tough times, the highest credit rating in the implement business west of Winnipeg belonged to Stewart Bothers.

In 1931, the firm's net worth had increased to $276,716.98. In 1934, the brothers purchased a farm to enable barter in livestock, horses, grain and hay. A year later, the first Red Deer branch of the implement business opened its doors under the management of **Jack Stewart**, Norman's eldest son. In 1936, a lumber yard in Red Deer opened. In that same year, Tom's daughter **Muriel** wed **Graham Ford**.

A new implement office and repair shop were built in Red Deer the next year (1937). In 1938, Muriel and Graham had a son, **Stewart Ford**, and during the following year, Graham began working full-time at the store.

During World War II, 13 employees enlisted, including Norman's sons **Jack** and **Norman Jr**. Miraculously, all returned. During the war, Norman's daughters, **Kaye** and **Gwen**, ran the Red Deer operation. In 1942, the business reorganized and all members of Norman's and Tom's families became shareholders.

The 1950s saw an energetic 12-year-old **Stewart Ford** begin working part-time during the summer holidays. In 1951, the company became the western Canadian distributor for Hume pick-up reels (a machine that enabled downed crops to be harvested). A business roadblock occurred in 1954, when the Red Deer lumber yard burned to the ground. Undaunted, the family had a new yard built on the same site.

In 1958, the business was formed into a limited company under its current name – Stewart Supplies (Penhold) Ltd. – with the same partners becoming shareholders. Also in 1958, Stewart Ford became a full-time employee.

In 1959, **Jack Stewart** assumed management of the Penhold farm and the Red Deer implement office was closed. In that year, too, Stewart Supplies became the franchisee for Lu-Re-Co prefabricated homes.

108 A.

The '60s saw more changes as the decade began with Monarch Lumber leasing the Red Deer lumber yard (in 1964, they were bought by Revelstoke), a new machine shop being built in Red Deer, and the Red Deer implement office being leased to Sears. The International Harvester contract was terminated, ending what was the longest standing IH contract in North America. Stewart Ford left the family business for two years to work for Monarch Lumber, returning to the family fold in 1964. In 1965, founding brother Norman died. In Canada's centennial year, 1967, Stewart Ford opened the new retail office and showroom in Penhold.

More growth followed with the 1970s, including a 5,000 sq. ft. addition to the showroom. Preserved wood foundations were added to the firm's offerings. These foundations were ideal for rural areas far away from concrete mix plants. The last founding brother, Tom, died in 1973, and the company began consolidating, selling off some smaller shops and stores. Always wanting to give back to the community, 1978 saw Stewart Supplies donate 211 acres towards a nesting habitat for waterfowl. Discussing the decade, Stewart Ford said, "I didn't think we were anything special until **Earl Smith** joined from Crown Lumber in Red Deer, and we learned that we were doing more business than a big city yard!"

Rich in history, the business was not afraid of modern innovations. Thanks to Stewart's love of drafting, the company had been one of the only building supply outlets to offer home design services. And, in 1980, it was the first lumber yard in the area to computerize its customer sales and inventory processes. Still, the early part of the decade was tough on the industry as high interest rates led to the collapse of the construction boom. Thanks to a dedicated staff, inventory realignment and a loyal customer base, Stewart Supplies weathered the storm. In 1983, *Metric Manual*, a building industry aid, was assembled by Stewart Ford and published. In 1988, Stewart received a prestigious honour, being named WRLA's "Lumberman of the Year." That year, Stewart's son, **Tom Ford**, worked at the business during the summer months. His monthly salary of $730 was almost three times what his great grandfather Tom made in all of 1903!

A rare honour befell Stewart Supplies in 1993 when a company badge was granted from the Crown of Canada. This only happens to businesses that have a rich history and have become an integral part of Canadian society.

In 1996, with the passing of his parents Graham and Muriel Ford, Stewart and his wife Eileen became sole owners of Stewart Supplies (Penhold) Ltd., as well as Stewart Brothers Land and Livestock Ltd. In 2002, a century after the doors first opened, Stewart Supplies employs 10 people and provides the central Alberta region with construction supply needs. They also offer 'prebuilts' of smaller structures such as sheds and animal shelters. And Stewart Ford is still designing home plans.

Editor's note: To commemorate the store's 100 years in business, Stewart and Eileen, along with daughter Maria and son Tom, wrote and produced a beautiful souvenir calendar from which most of this information was gleaned. We thank the family for their assistance and wish them all the best during their year of celebration.

108 B.

279

By Jonah O'Neil

Stewart Supplies:
Shelter for Man and Beast

The Stewart Brothers 1908 store in 1921

"Joining the [Tim-BR-Mart] buying group did more to enhance our bottom line and level the competitive buying playing field with the large 'line yards' and 'boxes' than any other business decision I ever made."

"How do you describe a building supply company?" asks Stewart Ford. Stewart's business card features a blue and checkered chevron representing a sheltering roof held aloft by the man-beast, Centaur, surrounded by a garter bearing the motto "Shelter for Man and Beast". "Well," continues Stewart, "we were a shelter industry and of course we were involved with a lot of farm construction and homes; hence the slogan, which was made visual by Heraldry Canada in granting the badge to us."

History is what Stewart Supplies is all about. Two brothers – Stewart's grandfather and great uncle, who dealt in lumber and hardware – founded Stewart Brothers in 1902 in the town of Penhold, Alberta. In the 1930s, the company expanded into Red Deer as an International Harvester dealership and lumberyard. Stewart's father, Graham, came into the business full-time in July of 1939. Stewart started his career in 1950 at the age of 12, earning a dollar a day tailing a planer during the summer holidays on the Stewart family farm, which borders Penhold. He began working full-time for the family business at the age of 19, in 1957.

Stewart became the de facto draftsman for the company around that time. "My father had obtained a Lu.Re.Co (Lumber Research Company of America) franchise which comprised the plans for ten houses, advertising mats, instruc-

tions and the steel hardware for a 4' x 8' wall panel jig. We already had truss designs. Our first sale was a Veterans Land Act job in Penhold. We submitted the architect sealed plans to VLA and they rejected them! Thinking they were bad copies and difficult to read, I taped them on the large office window and traced them onto clean vellum paper and had them reproduced. Still not acceptable to the VLA! So I drafted them out on a small wood-framed linoleum drafting board of my father's, using a T square and a 30/60 triangle. Success! Fortunately, we had some excellent carpenters that we dealt with who straightened me out on a few things like stair headroom and door framing. The rest of my knowledge was built on observing the many professional plans which came in from customers and learning by example."

Up to 1968, the business was primarily a machine dealership with International Harvester with lumber and building supplies. In 1967, Stewart's father gave a year's notice that they would be ending the contract with International Harvester because he wanted to cut back. "And," says Stewart, "I had no love of machinery at all. At the time we were the longest established dealer for International Harvester on the North American continent. When International Harvester handed out 50-year pins, they handed out more of them at Stewart Supply than they did at any other dealership; my grandfather

was still alive, my great uncle was still alive, Jack Stewart was still there and my father was still there. So they all got ruby pins."

In 1954, the original partnership of Stewart Brothers was incorporated as Stewart Supplies (Penhold) Ltd. In the late 1960s, the Tom Stewart heirs which consisted of his daughter, Muriel, and her husband, Graham, and their son, Stewart, purchased the shares of the heirs of the other founding partner, Norman Stewart. With the death of Stewart's parents, Graham and Muriel, the company and its offshoots, Stewart Brothers Land & Livestock Ltd. and Stewart Brothers Holdings Ltd. came under the sole ownership of Stewart and his wife, Eileen.

Through the years, the company has faced some challenges. Stewart has the complete financial records of the business dating from 1902 to 1910, and for the 1930s. During the Great Depression, the business ran on promissory notes, which totaled around $200,000, half of which were "doubtful", meaning the note probably not be collected, and "okay", which meant there was a better chance of the bill being paid. "And it was just a shell game," says Stewart. "Someone would come in and be able to make a payment on their note; they might have been in 'doubtful' and they got switched over to 'okay'. And it just went back and forth. I asked my father how he ever got through it, and he said what you don't see is that, while the

108 C.

280

Some things don't change, states Stewart. "Basic selling is still the same, the necessity of product knowledge is still the same, and communicating with the customer so he understands what he is getting for his money is still the same. Those are standard truths that haven't changed from my grandfather's time to mine."

Second Word War was a horrible thing, it was also the salvation. The War brought prices up and it put money into peoples' pockets. In the late 1940s and '50s, a lot of the people who had problems making the payment on their promissory notes back in the '30s, came in and paid those old notes. This is the difference in character of the people we were dealing with."

In Stewart's generation, it was a period in the early 1980s that weren't any fun. "People were walking away from their houses, contractors were going belly-up, and we were left holding the bag."

Adds Stewart, "As a family firm, it's always been family, and I venture to say that one of the weaknesses was we never sought to, or could attract, outside people who would do the work while we managed it. We were always hands-on. And that came down to me, from my father, from my grandfather. So we just did what we could handle."

According to Stewart, the lumber and building materials industry has seen three technological and economic advances that have changed the industry. "The forklift changed the outer yard," says Stewart. "We got in flatcars of lumber instead of boxcars because that's what the forklift would handle. And of course we could load the truck much faster. And then that led into the trucks with pickers on the back. We were the first area lumberyard to have them, and for several years we were the only yard to have them. Our business was done at quite great distance, and now we could load five different loads on a truck, and head off to Rocky Mountain House and drop off all along the way – one delivery instead of five. Just the forklift was the key to the major change to how much material you could handle, and how you handled it; the picker truck was really the evolution of that."

"In the early 1970s independent building supply dealers, lead by the larger city yards, were grouping together under various banners to form buying groups. We were fortunate enough to be asked by Barrie Sali to join Tim-BR-Marts. Joining the buying group did more to enhance our bottom line and level the competitive buying playing field with the large 'line yards' and 'boxes' than any other business decision I ever made."

In the late 1970s and early 1980s, it was the computer that changed how business was done. In order to keep their price lists up to date, Stewart Supplies bought a $30,000 IBM with a 6 six inch screen "and the most beautiful keyboard I had ever typed on," says Stewart. In 1995, the company again spent $30,000, this time on a point-of-sale system. In 1995, they

bought a complete new system "and again it cost $30,000," says Stewart. "And every time it just does a whole bunch more stuff, faster, better, with more information. It was also in 1995 that I started to draft on computer."

But some things don't change, states Stewart. "Basic selling is still the same, the necessity of product knowledge is still the same, and communicating with the customer so he understands what he is getting for his money is still the same. Those are standard truths that haven't changed from my grandfather's time to mine."

When asked about some of the highlights of his career, Stewart replied, "We led the charge on preserved wood foundations. I got the WRLA Mr. Lumberman Award in 1988. Starting a family, which in a family business can either end your career or support it, and

the satisfaction of having worked with the three generations in the business."

The WRLA has played other roles in Stewart's career as well. He received his Retail Lumberman's Training Course pin in the 1950s, was a Director for a number of years, and was the WRLA delegate to the metric commission to the federal government in the 1980s.

On the first of June 2002, Stewart sold the equipment and inventory of Stewart Supplies (Penhold) Ltd. to Ed Stoi of Penhold Building Supplies Ltd. The business continues at the same location. Now semi-retired, Stewart manages his property holdings and continues to do some design work for his customers. Stewart and Eileen look forward to spending some time with their family, visiting Stewart's relations in Europe and touring the grandness of Canada. ○

The Stewart Brothers Penhold buildings in 1938

For their 100th anniversary in 2002, Stewart accepts a congratulatory plaque from the then-Executive Director Judy Huston

108 D.

109. Bulldozing the burned office building.

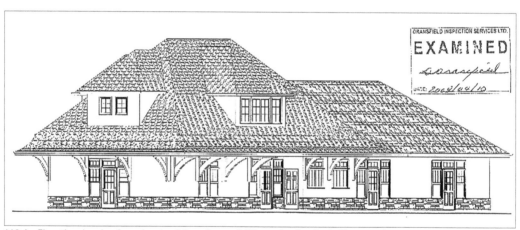

110 A. Elevation drawing from the plan I drew for my C.P.R.-station-inspired office building.

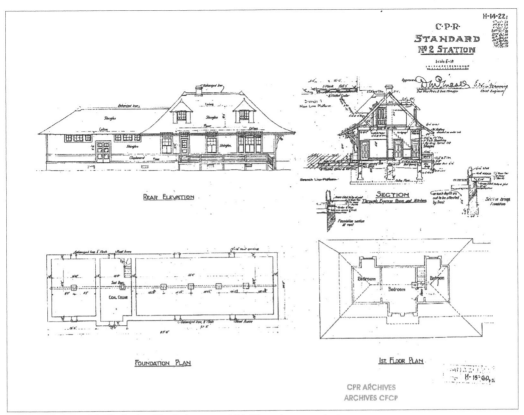

110 B. The original C.P.R. Station No. 2 plans, on which I based my own design.

CPSIA information can be obtained
at www.ICGtesting.com
Printed in the USA
LVHW070022110519
616484LV00004BC/15/P